DATE DUE

GOVERNMENT RISK-SHARING IN FOREIGN INVESTMENT

Government Risk-Sharing in Foreign Investment

MARINA VON NEUMANN WHITMAN

PRINCETON, NEW JERSEY

PRINCETON UNIVERSITY PRESS

1965

Copyright © 1965 by Princeton University Press
All Rights Reserved
L.C. Card: 65-14314
Printed in the United States of America
by Princeton University Press, Princeton, New Jersey

HG
4538
W417

Dp 1/1/65

B.1

TO THE MEMORY OF

JvN

PREFACE

This book grew out of a Ph.D. dissertation written for Columbia University during 1960 and 1961. In 1964 the study was completely revised and brought up to date as of the end of 1963.

The completion of this study has incurred more debts of gratitude than it is possible to enumerate. The greatest is to A. O. Hirschman, for his guidance and direction of both the conception and the execution of the original thesis. Peter Kenen, whose enlightening discussions helped more than once to cut through some particularly frustrating Gordian Knot, also has my deepest thanks.

The generosity of two foundations provided the financial support which freed me to pursue this investigation. A dissertation fellowship from the Earhart Foundation supported the initial stages of my work, and the Michigan Fellowship of the American Association of University Women enabled me to continue it. I am grateful, too, to the Department of Economics of the University of Pittsburgh for giving me some released time to complete the manuscript, as well as for making available the skilled and invaluable assistance of Lois Grodstein, who prepared the index, Betty Katz, who typed the final draft, and Betty Scanlon, who proofread and checked all the tables.

I am indebted for most of the basic data which form the core of this study to many staff members of various U.S. Government and international organizations. Were it not for their willingness to furnish, often at the expenditure of considerable time and effort, information otherwise unavailable, my work could never have progressed beyond the outline stage. Among those who became most deeply embroiled in my quest for data were: Thomas P. Doughty, Ellen C. Hughes, Leigh M. Miller, Laurence E. Potter, V. Lucile Sanders, and Charles B. Warden of the Investment Guaranty Program; Victor Chang, Y. L. Chang; Raymond E. Deely, and Lester Nurick of the World Bank;

vii

A. L. Beede and A. R. Perram of the International Finance Corporation; Arnold Weiss of the Inter-American Development Bank; Marjorie H. McHenry, Glenn E. McLaughlin, A. J. Redway, and R. Henry Rowntree of the Export-Import Bank; James B. Cash, Jr., Park D. Massey, Hamlin Robinson, George Rublee, Michael A. Speers, and George A. Wyeth, Jr., of the Development Loan Fund and its successor, the Agency for International Development; Samuel Pizer of the Department of Commerce, and Philip Schaffner of the Treasury Department. The affiliations here cited, and the titles by which many of these people are referred to in footnotes, refer to the positions they held at the time they furnished information to me; many of them have since moved on to more responsible positions in the same or different organizations. I am also grateful to the officers of a number of banking institutions, who remain anonymous at their own request, for their detailed and helpful replies to my queries about the views of the private financial community on the risk-sharing activities under discussion.

To the International Finance Section of Princeton University I am indebted for permission to use, chiefly in Chapter IV, large portions of my monograph, *The United States Investment Guaranty Program and Private Foreign Investment*, published by the Section in 1959.

Finally, my thanks go to my husband, to whose detailed and invaluable criticism this effort owes whatever clarity and grace of style it may possess. For the remaining imperfections in analysis and expression I am, of course, alone responsible.

Marina v.N. Whitman
Pittsburgh, October 1964

CONTENTS

TABLES

GOVERNMENT RISK-SHARING IN FOREIGN INVESTMENT

I · INTRODUCTION

A major concern of American foreign policy since the end of World War II has been to channel long-term capital, both public and private, to other nations of the free world sorely in need of funds for rehabilitation or development. In the early postwar years it was thought that government funds would have to serve only as a pump-primer, and that the international flow of private lending would soon revive and lift the burden from the taxpayers' shoulders. During the early 1950's these horizons receded, and it became more and more obvious that public money would have to stay at work for a long time if the United States and other countries of the advanced world were to make a major contribution to economic development. But the effort to build international bridges across which more and more private funds would move continued. Even when the United States developed severe balance of payments problems, toward the end of the 1950's, solutions were sought in terms of financing these international responsibilities rather than eliminating or drastically curtailing them.

Among the bridges constructed during the first eighteen years of the postwar era were a number of institutions through which public and private monies went abroad together. Through these risk-sharing institutions, the public body shares with the private investor a portion of the investment risk which the private investor might otherwise find prohibitive.

Six agencies, three under United States and three under international auspices, were engaged in risk-sharing activities with American private funds between 1945 and 1963. They are:

The Investment Guaranty Program (IGP)
The International Bank for Reconstruction and Development (IBRD or World Bank)
The International Finance Corporation (IFC)

The Inter-American Development Bank (IDB)
The Export-Import Bank of Washington (Eximbank)
The Development Loan Fund—Agency for International
Development (DLF—AID)

The first of these organizations is essentially an insurance
scheme, with public funds sharing the risk on a contingent
basis only. The three international institutions which fol-
low all possess some form of guaranty powers, but they
are primarily lending or investing institutions, engaged in
the direct commitment and disbursal of public monies to
projects, some or all of which are also financed in part
by private funds originating in the United States. Finally,
the Eximbank and the DLF—AID are hybrids, utilizing
both joint public-private lending and various types of
guaranties to mobilize private capital in the United States
for long-term investment abroad.

Only two of these six organizations—the Investment
Guaranty Program and the International Finance Corporation—are concerned solely with the international movement
of private capital. The other four have disbursed many
billions of dollars of purely public funds for rehabilitation
and development, and this lending function often over-
shadows their risk-sharing activity. Partly for this reason,
such organizations operated for many years, and new ones
were created, without its ever becoming clear how well
they were functioning as international bridges for private
capital. How do the policies and activities of these organizations relate to the stimulation of private capital outflows
from the United States? How successful have they been
in harnessing private American funds, first for the rehabilitation of Europe, and later to meet the expanding capital
needs of the less-developed areas? What role has the joint
public-private investment arising out of these risk-sharing
activities played in implementing the foreign policy objectives of the United States in the years since World War II?
And, finally, just how much private money from the United

States has been lent or invested abroad in conjunction with the activities of these risk-sharing institutions? These questions are the focus of this investigation of the international risk-sharing activities of six public lending and insurance agencies between 1946 and 1963.

It turns out that, in the 1946-1963 period, an estimated $6.7 billion of private American capital—about one-eighth of the long-term private capital from the United States invested abroad during those years—went into long-term foreign lending or investment through the medium of one of the six agencies. As Table 1 shows, the lion's share of this "agency-related" investment—more than $5.1 of the $6.7 billion—is accounted for by the two oldest of the six institutions, the Export-Import Bank and the World Bank.

TABLE 1

U.S. Private Capital Invested Abroad in Conjunction with the Risk-Sharing Agencies, 1946-1963

(in millions of U.S. dollars)

Agency	Amount[a]
Investment Guaranty Program	766.3
International Bank for Reconstruction and Development	2,440.5
International Finance Corporation	119.0
Inter-American Development Bank	119.0
Export-Import Bank of Washington	2,680.9
Development Loan Fund—Agency for International Development	545.5
	6,671.2

[a] Estimates.
Sources: See Table 24.

The figures for private capital used in this discussion include only long-term funds: loans or investments of at least a year's duration. This distinction eliminates most of the large short-term capital flows which generally take place under stimuli quite different from those relevant to long-term investment decisions, and focuses on those capital movements that are likely to have a lasting effect on the economy of the receiving country. At the same time, the figures used here are measures of the "gross finance" provided to other countries by individuals and corporations in the United States. That is, the annual data on long-term private capital movements have been cumulated over the 1945-1963 period, without any netting out of refundings or repayments. In part, this is simply because much of the data on agency-related private investment were available only in gross form; in part, it reflects the assumption that long-term money which has been both lent and repaid had some definite effect on the borrowing economy during the interim, and should therefore be counted in assessing the magnitude of the contribution made by such funds to economic development.

Although my statistics necessarily include funds going to all destinations, I am primarily concerned with developmental investment in the less-advanced areas of the world. No other type of capital outflow is so important to the foreign policy objectives and national interest of the United States, and therefore no other type is so clearly eligible for public encouragement. Indeed, this stress on developmental capital is characteristic of the six institutions themselves. True, those that existed during the immediate postwar years concentrated then on European rehabilitation, but by 1963 four of the agencies were engaged exclusively, and a fifth primarily, in the mobilization of funds (both public and private) for use in the less-developed regions. Only the Export-Import Bank, whose original purpose was the facilitation of United States exports, was still devoting a significant part of its loan activities to transactions among advanced countries.

The ultimate question is, of course, what contribution has American private capital channeled through the risk-sharing agencies made to economic development abroad, and what contribution can it be expected to make? Dollar figures alone cannot provide a complete answer. A given sum of money invested in one way may make an important contribution to the recipient country's economy, whereas the same amount, invested in a different project or a different place, may make no contribution at all or even be harmful. This is particularly true because the term "underdeveloped" covers such widely differing levels of economic advancement. An investment which would be highly productive in a relatively advanced country like Brazil or India might be premature and therefore wasted in one of the less-advanced African nations. The present investigation does not make such distinctions, which would require a case-by-case or country-by-country approach; this study is only the first step in a comprehensive evaluation of the role played in economic development by the risk-sharing institutions.

Of course, the risk-sharing institutions and the techniques they use do not stand still. The three-year period ending with 1963 saw the opening of a new multi-national lending institution engaged in risk-sharing operations, the Inter-American Development Bank; the absorption of many of the formerly scattered U.S. programs into the newly formed Agency for International Development; and the creation of the Foreign Credit Insurance Corporation, a syndicate of private insurance companies which joins with the Export-Import Bank to provide both political and credit-risk protection for long-term financing of American exports. We can be sure that some changes in policies and administration will continue to be made with nearly every session of Congress in the case of the American organizations or meeting of the Board of Governors in the case of the international institutions. At the same time, it seems likely that the basic techniques described here for attracting private capital into foreign economic development will be used for some time to come, and that we can get a good idea of what to expect from the risk-sharing mechanism by looking at its impact during the nearly two decades which elapsed between the close of World War II and the end of 1963.

II · PRIVATE CAPITAL MOVEMENTS
AND THE NATIONAL INTEREST

The risk-sharing institutions under discussion were created in response to the particular exigencies facing the world of the mid-twentieth century, and are in many ways something new under the sun. But every important creditor nation in modern Western history has at some time or other interfered with the international flow of private capital, either by restriction or by encouragement. And each of them, from mercantilist Holland in the sixteenth century to laissez-faire Britain in the nineteenth, sought a balance between the same opposing forces the United States faces today: The desire to encourage foreign lending for political and economic advantage, and the instinct to discourage it, both to avoid foreign entanglements and to conserve capital for domestic needs.

If governments have often been of two minds as to whether they should encourage or discourage foreign lending by their citizens, the makers of economic theory have been equally confused. The economic justification for such governmental interference is that the free-market mechanism, left to itself, does not always lead to the most desirable allocation of capital among the nations of the world. But does this mechanism, predicated on the principle that capital will go where it can get the highest return until returns are everywhere the same, lead to the export of too much domestic capital, or too little? Should the government, therefore, limit such exports or stimulate them?

WORLD WELFARE VERSUS THE NATIONAL INTEREST

If it is the welfare of the world as a whole that they are interested in, it seems clear that governments should in many cases encourage foreign investment. There are a number of reasons why private foreign investment is likely to be smaller than the optimum international allocation of capital would require. In addition to ignorance or sheer inertia, excessively high estimates of the risk involved in foreign investment will often prevent a proper comparison of domestic and foreign investment opportunities. From Adam Smith, David Ricardo, and John Stuart Mill onward, economists have recognized that fear of the unfamiliar will often lead an investor to keep his money at home even when he could earn more on it abroad.[1]

Some of the obstacles to socially desirable capital flows are only fancied, but some of them are very real. There are many ways in which governmental action can create a difference between the return which a given investment earns, in terms of social benefit, and the return the investor receives. This divergence between the social and the private marginal productivity of capital can be in the form of increased risks, reduced profits, or both. Higher taxes, broader social legislation, and greater direct restrictions on profits than exist in the investor's home country or in other foreign countries represent the types of political action which may prevent the inflow of foreign private funds from being as great as the criterion of optimum world allocation would require. "In fact," J. E. Meade points out, "differences in social philosophy in different countries . . . may well be one of the most potent forces at work in the modern world causing free movements of factors between nations to lead to uneconomic results."[2]

There are a number of reasons, then, why a potential investor may be inclined to keep his money at home even though it could be used more efficiently abroad. But do modern investors actually display this reluctance to venture beyond their own national boundaries? There are many indications that they do. The lack in the United States of a

[1] Adam Smith, *Wealth of Nations*, IV, 2; David Ricardo, *Principles of Political Economy and Taxation*, VII; John Stuart Mill, *Principles of Political Economy*, III, 17. Quoted in: Carl Iverson, *Aspects of the Theory of International Capital Movements*, London, 1935, pp. 95-98.
[2] J. E. Meade, *Trade and Welfare*, London, 1955, p. 417.

broad, well-organized, and active market for foreign securities suggests that individual investors are quite hesitant about such ventures, although by the early 1960's a revival of a New York market for the long-term securities of a few privileged countries was clearly under way.[3]

American corporate investors have given much more explicit evidence of the non-price rationing which they practice against foreign investments. "In practically every company we interviewed," a Department of Commerce survey reported, "United States investment has a priority over foreign investment . . . individual propositions were not compared directly with opportunities for investment in the United States . . . rather United States investment opportunities were taken up first, and if any funds remained, they might be available for foreign investment."[4] If this behavior is indeed characteristic of many American corporate investors, who are the major potential source for foreign investment funds, then the free-market mechanism alone cannot be expected to bring about the most efficient world allocation of capital resources.[5]

The encouragement of capital exports may, in many cases, help to increase income and output in the world as a whole. But it is with national governments, not a world

[3] See: Paul Heffernan, "Long-Term Debt Terra Incognita," *The New York Times*, May 7, 1961, Section III, p. 1. He concludes: "The debt securities of these historic exporters of investment capital [Great Britain and West Germany] are timely signs of the post-war stirring of an international long-term market. . . ."

[4] E. R. Barlow and I. T. Wender, *Foreign Investment and Taxation*, Englewood Cliffs, N.J., 1955, pp. 166-167. This book, whose authors took part in the analysis of the Commerce Department's 1952 *Survey of Factors Limiting Investment Abroad*, is based on the results obtained from the questionnaire data from this survey.

[5] There are specific institutional arrangements, of course, which may create a presumption in the opposite direction. For example, the European Common Market, because of its inevitable trade-diverting aspects, has doubtless brought about capital inflows into the area to take advantage of an enlarged market behind tariff walls. In such a situation, investments promising private profits for this reason only are probably not productive from the social point of view.

government, that measures for such stimulation generally originate, and even the increasingly important international lending agencies are largely supported and partly controlled by the major capital-exporting nations, particularly the United States. And the question of international capital flows may look quite different from the point of view of national, rather than world, economic welfare.

When world efficiency is the criterion, individual estimates of the risks entailed in foreign investment are generally too high; yet from the point of view of the home country's economic interest, these same estimates may sometimes be too low. There are certain risks—those of confiscation, repudiation, or profit-restricting legislation, for example—which the private investor may correctly assess as being equally great at home and abroad, yet from the national viewpoint, the foreign and domestic risks would not be equal at all. If the investment is made at home, the nation will retain its benefits even if they are lost to the investor, but if it is made abroad, the lender and his country suffer the loss together.[6] This distinction may exist even in some cases of ordinary business failure; the stockholders in a railroad may lose everything through bankruptcy, yet the road and equipment will remain and may turn out to be a valuable national asset. Similarly, taxes imposed at home on domestic income and profits are retained by the nation, but those imposed by foreign nations on investments abroad and the income from them are lost.[7] This distinction holds, in fact, for any redistribution of income away from capital. If labor manages to capture a larger share of the earnings of a domestic enterprise, for example, the investor's loss is the worker's gain, but if the investment is on foreign soil, such a redistribution represents a loss of income to the nation.

[6] J. M. Keynes, "Foreign Investment and the National Advantage," *The Nation and the Athenaeum*, xxxv (Aug. 9, 1924), 584-587.
[7] J. Carter Murphy, "International Investment and the National Interest," *Southern Economic Journal*, LXX (July 1960), 11-17.

In any country which is growing and changing there are sure to be external economies from the investment process —benefits stemming from structural changes in the organization of an industry or of the whole economy which a private investor cannot consider in calculating the expected return on his investment, since no single investment can achieve them. Who should reap the benefits of these gains? If it is world income we are interested in maximizing, there is a strong case to be made for encouraging the export of capital from advanced nations to less-developed ones, on the grounds that the opportunities for creating external economies are much greater in underdeveloped areas.[8] Existing interest rate differentials, according to this argument, are generally not great enough to be a true measure of the need for capital in a less-developed country, since they reflect also the lack of cooperating factors— trained labor, entrepreneurial talent, and "social overhead" investment—necessary to make private capital productive and profitable. If the investment process begins, the creation of these cooperating factors will be spurred and later investors will reap the benefits of external economies created by their predecessors.

If a government is interested primarily in the economic welfare of its own nation rather than of the whole world, however, it may want to limit the export of capital rather than encourage it. For the external benefits of the investment process will be reaped by the nation in the case of domestic investment, but most probably by the recipient country in the case of foreign investment.

A government's policy toward the export of capital by its citizens may also be influenced by what foreign investment is likely to do to the nation's terms of trade. Will the value of the imports which the country can get in return

[8] This argument is presented in abstract, rigorous form in: J. E. Meade, Chap. XXVI. A looser and more topical discussion of it is given by Thomas Balogh, "Some Theoretical Problems of Post-War Foreign Investment Policy," *Oxford Economic Papers*, No. 7 (March 1945), 93-110.

for a unit amount of its own exports grow or decline? The terms-of-trade advantages resulting from most profitable foreign investments are clear: expanded markets for the lending nation's products and better or cheaper sources of raw materials and foodstuffs. But will the fall in import prices be enough to offset the drop in export prices which so often accompanies a transfer of capital resources abroad? The answer depends very heavily on whether the foreign production stimulated by capital exports is complementary or competitive with the major industries of the lending nation.[9] Great Britain during her heyday of foreign investment was a small industrial island with a rapidly expanding population and a growing demand for food and raw materials. Her trade with the primary-producing nations in which she invested most heavily therefore was complementary, and the terms of trade moved steadily in her favor. But the United States today is an important primary producer as well as manufacturer herself and has no such rapidly growing demand for foodstuffs; imports stimulated by her foreign investments are more likely to be competitive with her own production. Whereas the terms of trade seem to have moved in favor of the suppliers of capital in the nineteenth century, there is much more doubt about the outcome in the twentieth.[10]

[9] Iverson, p. 163.

[10] Actually, a large number of economic factors in third countries as well as in the investor and investee countries are involved in the determination of how the terms of trade shift as a result of investment in any particular case. For a detailed discussion, see: Charles R. Whittlesey, "Foreign Investment and the Terms of Trade," *Quarterly Journal of Economics*, XLVI (May 1932), 444-464, and T. Balogh and P. P. Streeten "Domestic versus Foreign Investment," *Bulletin of the Oxford University Institute of Statistics*, XXII (Aug. 1960), 217-220. In challenging the view that the terms of trade must necessarily move against primary producing countries, Theodore Morgan also stresses ". . . the importance of *not* generalizing on the experience of other countries or regions, from the experience of one." "Long-Run Terms of Trade Between Agriculture and Manufactures," *Economic Development and Cultural Change*, VIII (Oct. 1959), 16.

There is no question that, all other things being equal, foreign investment imposes a burden on a country's trade balance, requiring an export surplus large enough to finance the outflow of capital. In a world of flexible prices and wages or flexible exchange rates, adjustment to this new situation is likely to be made by means of a shift in the capital-exporting nation's terms of trade; in a world where prices and wages are quite rigid, at least in the downward direction, and exchange rates fixed, the process of transferring capital abroad is likely instead to put pressure on the lending nation's balance of payments. And, although balance of payments considerations have little if any direct relevance from the cosmopolitan viewpoint, they may be extremely important when seen through the eyes of a particular nation. More specifically, for the United States of the late 1950's and early 1960's, balance of payments difficulties became a major factor in all decisions relating to foreign economic policies.

In the real world, where all other things are never equal, we do not know but can only guess at the net effect of foreign investment on the balance of payments of the United States during the postwar years. If direct flows of funds alone are considered, long-term private foreign investment has not itself contributed to the balance of payments deficit; during this period, the interest, amortization, profits, and dividends returned to this country have generally exceeded the outflow of new funds.[11] But when we

[11] Income on U.S. private foreign investment as a whole has exceeded the net outflow of new funds in all but six years of the postwar period, and by more than $3 billion over the period as a whole. During recent years, there has been a tendency in the opposite direction; net capital outflow exceeded income in five of the seven years of the 1957-1963 period, and by $1.7 billion over that period as a whole. However, the years in which net capital outflow exceeded income were also years in which there was an unusually large outflow of *short-term* private funds. This pattern, combined with the fact that the yield on short-term claims is known to be far below that on long-term investments, suggests that the balance between outflows and inflows of funds for *long-*

try also to take into account the effects of foreign investment on the exports and imports of the United States, no
clear-cut answer emerges. Some evidence for 1957—the
only year for which any such data are available—suggests
that the imports into the United States of goods produced
by U.S. controlled direct investment enterprises abroad
have somewhat exceeded exports directly to these same
enterprises, thus increasing the balance of payments pressure. But these direct effects are not the most important
ones. To what extent do the products of U.S. controlled
enterprises abroad compete with American exports in
foreign markets, and to what extent do these enterprises
simply permit the United States to retain, in the form of
dividends, interest, and other income, a share in foreign
markets that would otherwise have been entirely lost to
foreign competition? How much of the increase in income
in foreign countries resulting from American investments
will come home in the form of increased demand for U.S.
goods? And what effects does foreign portfolio investment have on American exports and imports? Without
answers to these questions, there can be no definite conclusions about the long-run relationship between foreign
investment and the U.S. balance of payments. Nonetheless, in the short run, investment outflow could be considerably curtailed without affecting the return flow from
existing investments anywhere near as much. And a substantial surplus on the private foreign investment account,

---

term private foreign investments has remained favorable to the
United States even during the more recent period. Income on
direct investments, the major component of long-term private
foreign investment, has exceeded the outflow of new funds in
every postwar year except 1957, and by more than $14 billion
over the period as a whole. The excess of income over outflow
in direct investment was greater during 1961-1963 than at any
other time since World War II. See: U.S. Department of Commerce, *Balance of Payments, Statistical Supplement* (revised edn.),
Washington, 1963, pp. 3-4 and *Survey of Current Business* (Aug.
1964), 10-11.

however temporary, might help to reduce the immediate pressure on the balance of payments.

In sum, there seems to be good reason for stimulating the export of capital from advanced nations in the interest of world betterment. But the effect of foreign investment on the economic welfare of the lending nation itself is far less clear, and the particular problems of the United States in the mid-twentieth century might well have led its government to check rather than encourage the export of capital to other nations. That the government followed a policy of encouragement rather than restraint suggests that it was operating on some broader criterion than the immediate maximization of national income.

POLITICAL CONSIDERATIONS TIP THE SCALES

When the political interests of the United States are brought into the picture, the reasons for government encouragement of foreign investment become clear. International business investment has long been recognized as a useful tool of diplomacy, and the problems and objectives of the United States in the postwar era have enhanced its importance as an adjunct of foreign policy.

Ever since the end of World War II, the American export of capital has taken place within the framework of struggle with Soviet Communism, first in the rebuilding of the war-devastated economies of Europe, then in the fulfillment of the rising economic aspirations of the people in the less-developed areas of the world. The urgency of development for the 84 per cent of the world's population which lives in low-income countries is a major concern of both sides in the East-West struggle, and it is obvious that the vast capital requirements of an industrialization program must be met from one of two sources: internal savings or foreign funds. When we contemplate the prospect of mobilizing sufficient savings from populations existing on incomes which are a mere fraction of those in advanced nations, it is hard to deny the allegation that the alternative to development with Western capital is development "driven through by totalitarian means, with forced saving and iron discipline at home and Communist aid and guidance from abroad."[12]

Because the struggle for world power is focused on questions of material welfare, the economic gains accruing to capital-receiving countries from foreign investment can yield enormous political advantage for the lending country. When such assistance is given to countries with strategic locations or resources, it may in the long run help reduce American military aid and domestic defense expenditures. And wherever international capital movements contribute to the political stability of the recipients and increase the possibility of their development under Western rather than Communist aegis, they perform a function which, although it cannot be measured directly in economic terms, is vital to the national interest. Thus the internationalist framework within which the benefits of international capital movements have always been argued is today linked with the national interests of the United States by the exigencies of world competition between rival economic systems.

This does not mean, of course, that there should be no limits on efforts to increase capital exports to less-developed areas. There can be unproductive investments in less-developed countries no less than in advanced ones, and it is even possible that by pumping too much money into an economy from the outside one might eventually destroy internal initiative and actually retard advancement.

[12] H. V. R. Iengar, "India's Approach: Shades of Grey," in: International Industrial Development Conference, *Private Investment*, San Francisco, 1957, p. 139. Communist-bloc commitments of economic aid (mostly in the form of long-term credits) to less-developed countries between 1955 and 1963 were estimated at about $4.9 billion. Actual expenditures on these commitments totaled about $1.6 billion. U.S. Congress, House, Committee on Foreign Affairs, *Foreign Assistance Act of 1964, Hearings*, 88th Cong., 2nd Sess., 1964, Part I, p. 73.

But the fusion between the national and the world view-point does imply that the national benefits from foreign investment may often exceed the private returns, and suggests the desirability of political measures to increase capital exports above the level they would reach under private incentives alone.

We cannot know the extent of government stimulation of private capital exports necessary to compensate exactly for the deficiencies of the private-market mechanism. But, in view of the present political interests of the United States, overstimulation is probably preferable to under-stimulation. One of the observations resulting from this study is that such overstimulation may well be the price the U.S. Government must pay for domestic support of its foreign aid program. Such support is crucial to the conduct of our foreign policy, and its importance provides an additional basis for public encouragement of private capital exports.

THE EXPORT OF PRIVATE CAPITAL: THE
GOVERNMENT'S VIEWS

During the half century since the United States began its transition from debtor to creditor nation, the government's views on foreign investment have varied widely. The official position has ranged from William Jennings Bryan's comment as Secretary of State that "when you go abroad you have to take your chances" to President Coolidge's dictum that "the person and property of a citizen are a part of the general domain of a nation, even when abroad."[13] The "battleship diplomacy" era, ushered in by President Taft's words: "Our foreign policy may well be made to include active intervention to secure for our merchandise and for our capitalists opportunities for capital investment which shall incur to the benefit of both

[13] Quoted in James W. Angell, *Financial Foreign Policy of the United States*, New York, 1933, p. 73.

countries concerned,"[14] was terminated by the international financial collapse of the 1930's. There followed a period during which the government could do little but look on as foreign investors licked their wounds and proclaimed "never again."

During the closing years of World War II, when it had become apparent that much of the burden of world rehabilitation and reconstruction would fall on the United States, the question of capital exports again became central to American foreign policy. Officials recognized that in the chaotic conditions of the immediate postwar era international capital flows would have to be on a government-to-government basis. But they were concerned with the best means of achieving an early restoration of the flow of private funds. As early as 1944, Dean Acheson, then Assistant Secretary of State, pointed out the complementary nature of public and private foreign lending and urged that official encouragement of private investment abroad be incorporated into the United States' postwar economic policy.[15] During the same hearings, the Deputy Administrator of the Foreign Economic Administration stressed the need for some form of government guaranty, without subsidy, to facilitate private lending abroad. His feeling was that "I am afraid it will be some time before you can expect a large volume of private lending without any guaranty."[16]

The resumption of private capital flows was again a central issue at the 1945 Bretton Woods Conference of the Allied Nations, as it considered the problems of worldwide economic reconstruction and development in the postwar era. High hopes were voiced that the two international lending institutions established at the Conference,

[14] Quoted in: Eugene Staley, *War and the Private Investor*, New York, 1935, p. 148.

[15] U.S. Congress, House, Special Committee on Post-War Economic Policy and Planning, *Postwar Economic Policy and Planning, Hearings*, 78th Cong., 2nd Sess., 1945, pp. 1081-1082.

[16] *Ibid.*, p. 783.

the International Monetary Fund and the International Bank for Reconstruction and Development, would hasten the recovery of private foreign lending. These organizations were expected to encourage the international movement of private funds in two ways: indirectly, by creating the conditions of economic stability necessary to induce private lending and, in the case of the Bank, directly, by serving as an intermediary through which private funds could be mobilized for foreign lending and investment ventures which they would not dare to enter into directly.

"The time and extent of private capital investment abroad, either directly or through the IBRD, will determine to a considerable extent the ability of the Government to withdraw from the field of large-scale foreign lending without sacrificing the basic objectives of its foreign policy."[17] With these words, an early report of the National Advisory Council on International Monetary and Financial Problems (NAC) voiced a hope which has been an important part of the rationale for political stimulation of private foreign investment ever since. The NAC, composed of cabinet-rank members of the Executive Branch,[18] was established under the Bretton Woods Agreement Act of 1945 "to coordinate the policies and operations of the representatives of the United States on the International Monetary Fund and the International Bank for Reconstruction and Development, the Export-Import Bank of Washington and all other agencies of the Government to the extent that they make or participate in the making of foreign loans or engage in foreign financial exchange or

[17] U.S. National Advisory Council on International Monetary and Financial Problems, *Report of Activities, Feb. 28, 1946 to Mar. 31, 1947*, Washington, 1947, p. 23.

[18] Although the composition of the NAC has varied slightly from time to time, it has always included the Secretaries of the Treasury, State, and Commerce Departments, the Chairman of the Board of Governors of the Federal Reserve System, and, usually, the Chairman of the Board of Directors of the Export-Import Bank.

monetary transactions."[19] It also advises and assists the President on policy matters in this area, and its semiannual reports are generally regarded as reflecting current Administration policy.

This insistence that private initiative should be urged to take over the emergency activities of governments as soon as possible was a recurrent theme of official statements on the foreign economic policy of the United States during the early postwar years. It permeated the 1948 Report of the Herter Committee on Foreign Aid[20] and, in the same year, became one of the NAC's chief criteria for deciding between grants and loans as the appropriate instrument of government foreign aid in specific cases: "We should take care not to insist that these countries contract additional dollar debts which will absorb so much of their dollar earnings as to operate to the disadvantage of future trade and private investment."[21]

The urgent desire to get foreign lending and investment back into private hands as soon as possible had a number of deep-rooted sources. Perhaps the most obvious is the traditional American predilection for private enterprise, and the resulting concentration of managerial and technological skills in private hands. For this reason, private foreign investment is generally held to carry with it greater "fringe benefits" than public lending, in the form of technical know-how, entrepreneurial judgment, and the whole ethical-cultural complex of ground rules which are essential to the development of an economy on a private enterprise or even a mixed private-public basis. The opponents of this view insist that developing countries can obtain the same advantages, without foreign private owner-

[19] *Bretton Woods Agreement Act*, 59 *Stat.* 512, 22 U.S.C. sec. 286 (1945).

[20] U.S. Congress, House, Select Committee on Foreign Aid, *Final Report on Foreign Aid*, 80th Cong., 2nd Sess., 1948.

[21] U.S. National Advisory Council, *Report of Activities for the period Oct. 1, 1947 to Mar. 31, 1948*, Washington, 1948, pp. 19-20.

ship and the accompanying debt-service burden, through technical assistance programs or management contracts with foreign firms. But during the late 1940's and 1950's the preference for private lending garnered support from a growing conviction of the importance of transmitting the capitalist outlook to the increasingly powerful underdeveloped nations along with the wherewithal for material betterment.

Private capital movements also enjoy the reputation of being free of the political strings inevitably attached to government-to-government transactions. In Gunnar Myrdal's words: "Without the fixed idea that credit is business, that profitability is important, and that there is a market where economic demand and supply for capital meet, international finance spills over into the indeterminate ocean of power politics, where the crackpots and the demagogues swim with great pleasure."[22] The international lending agencies were designed to sever this tie between economic assistance and political domination, and may offer a viable alternative to the courses weighed by Myrdal. But it is not likely that the sovereign nations of the world will ever give such agencies, whatever their merits, control over sufficient funds to do anywhere near the whole job of external development lending.

But the most fundamental basis for the American's preference for private investment is the simple desire to conserve public funds. Behind every denunciation of public grants of capital as a bureaucratic waste of scarce resources and a drain on the taxpayer's pocket lies the legislator's horror of increased taxes or government deficits, and the government administrator's experience with time-consuming, crippling dependence upon annual Congressional appropriations. The more the foreign lending burden is shifted to private hands, the less will be the strain on an always inadequate national budget—this is the com-

[22] Gunnar Myrdal, *An International Economy*, New York, 1956, p. 112.

mon thread of hope running through nearly every official pronouncement on the international economic responsibilities of the United States.

With the switch in emphasis from Europe to the less-developed areas and from reconstruction to development, heralded by President Truman's 1949 announcement of his "bold, new plan," the Point Four Program, the Government reiterated its desire to turn over as much of the field of foreign lending and investment as possible to private enterprise. The President's original enunciation of the Point Four Program said that "We should foster capital investment in areas needing development,"[23] and the stimulation of private investment became announced policy with the statements of Secretary of State Dean Acheson: "We put primary emphasis on the need for stimulating an expansion of foreign investment,"[24] and of Secretary of the Treasury John Snyder: "It is the policy of this Government that foreign investment for desirable purposes should be undertaken through private channels insofar as possible."[25]

As the international economic responsibilities of the United States were transferred from the European to the world stage, the complementary nature of public and private investment and the crucial role such intermediary lending institutions as the Eximbank and the World Bank were likely to play in the restoration of private capital flows became more and more obvious. A State Department official summed up the prevailing official view when he said that "We believe there remains a role for Government financial assistance (both grants and loans) to foreign areas, but we believe that private U.S. investment must play a larger role than it has in the recent past . . . in-

[23] *The New York Times*, Jan. 21, 1949, p. 4.
[24] *Ibid.*, March 31, 1950, p. 1.
[25] U.S. Congress, House, Committee on Banking and Currency, *Export-Import Bank Loan Guaranty Authority*, *Hearings*, 81st Cong., 1st Sess., 1949, p. 2.

vestment in basic sectors of foreign countries by these organizations [Eximbank and IBRD] will itself help foster the conditions under which [private] capital can do its best job."[26] This viewpoint was reiterated in the two major reports to the President on foreign economic policy made during the years immediately following the announcement of the Point Four Program and its legislative implementation in the Act for International Development. The first of these, the Gray Report,[27] placed greater emphasis on the need for public investment as a necessary prerequisite for private than did the Report of the International Development Advisory Board[28] a year later, but both stressed the need to widen the scope for private funds in international economic development.

Despite the apparent emphasis of all these statements, in comparing the actions of the Truman administration with the public utterances of its members, one cannot avoid the impression that at least part of the enthusiasm for private capital outflows was in the nature of lip service, paid by members of an executive branch anxious to minimize Congressional resistance to its export of public funds for development. The private view of government officials seems to have been that, under existing conditions, public capital was the dominant member of the complementary relationship and would remain so for some time to come.

The voice of private enterprise grew stronger with the advent of the first Eisenhower administration. The tone was set by the President's first State of the Union message, in January 1953, in which he said that the foreign economic policy of the United States should include "doing whatever the government properly can do to encourage the

[26] Wilfred Malenbaum, "America's Role in Economic Development Abroad," *Department of State Bulletin*, xx (March 27, 1949), 371-376.

[27] Gordon Gray, *Report to the President on Foreign Economic Policies*, Washington, 1950.

[28] U.S. International Development Advisory Board, *Partners in Progress*, Washington, 1951.

flow of American investment capital abroad."[29] In his message to Congress the following year, President Eisenhower presented as the Government's foreign economic program the conclusions of the Randall Report, which suggested as objectives the curtailment of aid, the encouragement of private investment, the facilitation of currency convertibility, and the expansion of trade. It recommended that the Government assist underdeveloped countries to obtain American funds without resort to grants except where U.S. security is importantly involved. It emphasized the inadequacy of the United States' public-loan resources for the total investment needs of developing countries, and stressed the need for reliance on private investment. The stern tone of this Report suggested a new hardening of views on foreign aid: "At present, as the need for economic aid for postwar recovery disappears, demands are increasing for general economic aid unconnected with recovery from war or preparation for defense. Underdeveloped areas are claiming a right to economic aid from the United States. . . . We recognize no such right."[30]

RECEDING HORIZONS

The second Eisenhower administration maintained the stand that private investment is the preferable vehicle for economic development. But, at the same time, a new note was heard in discussions, hearings, and reports, an acknowledgment of receding horizons for the restoration of private capital flows to their prewar dominance and a recognition that, more often than not, public investment was a prerequisite for private capital flows rather than a competitive substitute for them.

A retrenchment of the private-enterprise enthusiasts was inevitable in the face of the obstacles blocking private de-

[29] *The New York Times,* Feb. 3, 1953, p. 4.
[30] U.S. Commission on Foreign Economic Policy, *Report to the President and to the Congress,* Washington, 1954, p. 9.

velopment in many less-developed nations. Generalization from the European case had led to an exaggerated view of the substitutability of private for public capital in development investment under modern political conditions. With the assistance of Marshall Plan and other U.S. Government funds, the major countries of Europe had rapidly recovered to the point where they again offered security and profit to private investors, and private funds from investors in the United States had begun to flow in. But this pattern of increased private investment following close on the heels of public lending and taking over the latter's task has not been duplicated in other parts of the world. Economic development is a far more complex and slow-moving task than reconstruction, and private funds will not meet directly the basic "infrastructure" needs of underdeveloped countries—schools, roads, and other facilities from which it is difficult to capture monetary returns. They might do so indirectly, through loans to governments, but this would require a revival of international portfolio lending on a scale that seems unlikely, particularly where backward countries are concerned. And until these essential facilities are provided, private funds are not likely to substitute on a large scale for the most urgent tasks of public lending abroad. Large private business investments may, in fact, increase rather than decrease the demand for public funds, by making shortages of basic facilities in the host countries more apparent and their provision more urgent.

A further obstacle to development under private auspices is the hostility to such investment which runs high in many of the countries whose development is most important to the United States. Even those statesmen in less-developed areas who favor the encouragement of private investment often fear that a public statement to this effect might spell political death. Many leaders in these countries, denying the non-political nature of private investment, cite experiences with European colonialism and American dollar diplomacy as proof that foreign business investment and political domination often go hand in hand. But the underlying basis of their hostility is probably the lack of a commonly accepted set of criteria between borrower and lender. Among investors, as American businessmen are quick to point out, the profit motive is paramount, and this fact must be clearly understood by potential host countries if private funds are to be made available to them. To backward countries with a desire for rapid self-betterment, the derivation of local benefits from the development of their own resources and the expansion of opportunities for their own people are most important. Fears and misunderstandings arising from these differing viewpoints often lead to behavior which one party or the other regards as hostile to its own interests.

The recognition of these problems, and of the complementary relationship between public and private lending, had never entirely disappeared from postwar discussions of international development. This understanding was, in fact, chiefly responsible for the entry of the Eximbank into the field of development loans and for United States support of the IBRD as an institution to perform a similar function under international auspices. But in the mid-1950's, a number of political events increased the sense of urgency for development assistance. One was the growth (beginning in 1954) of a Soviet program of long-term credits and technical assistance to less-developed countries outside the Soviet bloc. Another was the anti-Americanism (or, more properly, anti-United States-ism) evident in Vice President Richard Nixon's reception during his ill-fated tour of South America. And, finally, the emergence of several newly independent and impatient African states, with many more colonies and territories on the brink of political self-determination, suggested that the political price might be high if the United States relied on private funds to do the job of development assistance alone.

The two sides of the U.S. Government's views on development investment were reflected in the creation, almost simultaneously, of two new agencies for such investment. One was the International Finance Corporation, first suggested in a 1951 report to the President and finally given U.S. approval late in 1956. It came into being shortly thereafter as an IBRD affiliate "to further economic development in its less-developed member countries by investing, without government guarantee, in productive private enterprises in association with private investors who can provide competent management."[31] The IFC was created as a catalyst for private foreign investment rather than as a substitute for it, and reflected strongly the conviction that private funds, if properly stimulated, could and should take over the task of foreign investment for development.

The second agency, the Development Loan Fund, was created by new legislation and a $300 million appropriation under the Mutual Security Act of 1957. It was also designed to aid economic development by loans for sound projects that were unable to obtain financing elsewhere. Here, however, the emphasis was on public investment in its own right, with the mobilization of private funds added only as a minor and somewhat rhetorical afterthought. Although the legislation expressed the hope that DLF loans would ultimately help improve the climate for private investment, its major emphasis reflected the increasing recognition that, in the foreseeable future, public loans would also be required if U.S. policy objectives with respect to development were to be implemented.

The two major reports on foreign economic policy made to the President during 1957 also reflected the mental confusion and readjustment concerning the role of private foreign investment which characterized political thought

[31] "U.S. Agencies and International Organizations Which Foster Private American Investment Abroad," 71 *Harvard Law Review* (April 1958), 1108.

and action during those years. Both reports maintained unchanged the preference for private investment as the ultimate vehicle of capital transfers for economic development, but in both a recognition of practical limitations, of receding horizons, is also apparent. The Fairless Report stated unequivocally its position that "Foreign investment of private capital is far more desirable than investment by the Government."[32] It took what may be termed the "purist" view of the situation, that the major burden for creating a climate favorable to foreign investment rests with the receiving governments rather than with the United States, and that "foreign areas can get the most from economic cooperation with us if they accept us for what we are: that is, a nation in which the reservoir of industrial ability, skills, and capital resides, not in government, but in private hands."[33] Yet, side by side with this apparently unyielding statement, is the suggestion that our Government should explore the large area between purely private and purely public projects, arranging to employ public and private funds jointly through the utilization of government guaranties, government loans to private investors with loss-sharing provisions, and joint investments. The Report also favored the continuation of loans by public lending agencies to aid productive development and thus lay the groundwork for private investment.

The Johnston Report, issued at approximately the same time as the Fairless, was less schizophrenic in its assessment of the present situation. It recognized that it would be some time before foreign private capital could be expected to play a major role in Asian and African development, and suggested that the basis for a large increase in private investment should be built through the coordinated use of public loan funds for social overhead investment. Yet the ultimate objective remained the same; the hopeful con-

[32] U.S. President's Citizen's Advisors on the Mutual Security Program, *Report to the President*, Washington, 1957, p. 8.
[33] *Ibid.*, p. 9.

clusion was that "as the less-developed countries achieve greater economic development and greater trust in the United States, opportunities for foreign private investment will grow, and then private investment can, should and will take the burden of development away from the government."[34]

During the closing years of the 1950's, this dual attitude toward foreign private investment persisted. On the one hand, continuing stress was laid on the catalytic effect of private funds invested in underdeveloped areas. Under-Secretary of State Douglas Dillon stressed that "Each [American investment abroad] tends to be a focal point of capital accumulation for further useful investment in the country and, more important, each investment tends to stimulate complementary and/or supplementary investments on the part of local capital."[35] At the same time, Administration support for the International Development Association (an affiliate of the World Bank) and for such regional institutions as the Inter-American Development Bank and an Arab-world development bank[36] indicated an increased appreciation of the need for large amounts of public capital for development. For all these institutions were predicated on the use of public funds, including substantial amounts of United States money, to make more or less "soft" loans to less-developed nations. In the past, similar propositions, from the United Nations Economic Development Association proposal of 1948 to the Special U.N. Fund for Economic Development plan originated in

[34] U.S. International Development Advisory Board, *A New Emphasis on Economic Development Abroad*, Washington, 1957, p. 13.

[35] U.S. Congress, House, Ways and Means Committee, *Private Foreign Investment, Hearings*, 85th Cong., 2nd Sess., 1959, p. 9.

[36] Political difficulties have prevented the creation of an Arab-world development bank. But the Inter-American Development Bank, described in Chapter VII, has had an increasingly important role in the financing of Latin American economic development since it opened for business in 1960.

1953, had perished on the rocks of opposition by the U.S. Congress, which had felt that development by such means would hinder rather than encourage allegiance to a free enterprise system.

THE NEED FOR GEOGRAPHICAL SELECTIVITY

Increased support for international public lending institutions was one indication of the U.S. Government's more cautious views on what should be expected from international flows of private capital; its emphasis, beginning in 1959, on geographical selectivity in the application of investment incentives was another.[37] This insistence on selectivity arose from the feeling that encouragement of American investment in areas other than the underdeveloped countries was a luxury our balance of payments no longer allowed.[38]

Actually, the reports of the NAC had begun to reflect a concern with the status of the United States' balance of payments as far back as 1953. At a time when the question of the dollar shortage and its alleviation still dominated official thinking, the NAC pointed out that U.S. imports were rising a good deal faster than her exports, reducing the surplus on current account which had to cover the nation's large capital exports. But it was not until 1959 that this concern began to impinge seriously on the Government's enthusiasm for promoting private investment abroad. Of the two reports to the President that year con-

[37] The central point of a long speech by Senator Aiken of Vermont, which is to be found in the Senate Congressional Record, cv (Aug. 25, 1959), 16888-16893, is the necessity for selectivity in the application of tax and guaranty incentives for foreign investment. Under-Secretary Dillon had the same point in mind when he stated, a few weeks earlier, that investment incentives were no longer necessary in Canada and Western Europe, but vital in underdeveloped areas. "Administrative Views on Legislation to Promote United States Private Investments Abroad," *U.S. Department of State Bulletin*, XLI (July 27, 1959), 128.

[38] Richard N. Gardner, "Strategy for the Dollar," *Foreign Affairs*, XXXVIII, 440.

cerning foreign investment and development, the Straus Report (Department of State) concluded that across-the-board tax reductions should be granted only to business enterprises operating in less-developed countries, and the Boeschenstein Report (Department of Commerce) suggested that the same selective principle should govern the granting of government loans and guaranties to private enterprise. This last suggestion was quickly implemented; as of January 1, 1960, the Investment Guaranty Program was limited by law to investments in the less-developed areas of the world.

The major legislative proposals concerning foreign investment advanced during the early 1960's were guided by this same principle. The Kennedy administration's largely unsuccessful attempt of 1961 to eliminate the right of foreign subsidiaries of U.S. companies to defer the payment of American taxes on their profits until such profits are remitted back to the United States in the form of dividends was limited to foreign subsidiaries in developed countries only. Similarly, the proposal for an interest-equalization tax on new foreign security issues marketed in the United States, proposed by the President in 1963 and passed by Congress in the summer of 1964, specifically exempted the issues of less-developed countries, corporations operating primarily in such countries, and the international lending institutions. And finally, the 1964 proposal for a 30 per cent tax credit on certain classes of new direct investment in less-developed countries is solidly grounded in the principle of geographical discrimination in the encouragement of foreign investment.

The principle of geographical selectivity in investment stimulation reflects both the United States' balance of payments problems and its policy objectives concerning foreign economic development. Even if the balance of payments were the only concern, the discouragement of all foreign investment would be a measure of doubtful efficacy. Although a drop in the outflow of private funds would improve the balance on capital account in the short run, such maneuvering would be self-defeating over the long term. For a drop in the rate of foreign investment would soon begin to affect the return flow from such investment, and the effect would increase progressively with time. Furthermore, the relationship between foreign investment outflow and income cannot be considered in isolation from the other items in the balance of payments. The Department of Commerce's 1960 study of *U.S. Business Investment in Foreign Countries* pointed out that "A major result of assembling these data on the overall effects on balance of payments of direct foreign investments is to point up the inadequacy of conclusions about these effects based solely on considerations of the relationship between net capital outflows and income receipts."[39] We know in a general way, for example, that a drop in American exports of capital would almost certainly cause a drop in the exports of United States goods, many of which are financed by this same capital, but we have no idea how large this drop would be. As was pointed out earlier, there are numerous and complex relationships between foreign investment and other components of the balance of payments about which we have little systematic information. All we can say is that the net effect of foreign investment on the balance of payments varies greatly from case to case, and that it is probably impossible ". . . to decide whether the discouragement of foreign investment as a whole would help the balance of payments . . . in the long run."[40]

There is evidence, however, ". . . that investment in advanced countries is, on balance, more likely to worsen the balance of payments than investment in underdeveloped

[39] U.S. Department of Commerce, Office of Business Economics, *U.S. Business Investments in Foreign Countries*, Washington, 1960, p. 67.

[40] Mac Dougall, Sir Donald, *The Dollar Problem: A Reappraisal* (Princeton Essays in International Finance #35), Princeton, 1960, p. 61.

countries."[41] In the early postwar years, any increase in the dollar receipts of the rest of the world tended to increase United States exports promptly. But by the late 1950's, the increase in dollar payments and reductions of shortages of goods in other high-income countries had created a situation wherein dollar receipts were often used to buy goods from countries other than the United States, to purchase gold, or to build up dollar balances.[42] By 1960, a leading American expert was convinced that "The resources put at the disposal of the low-income countries help to increase their investment. The resources put at the disposal of Europe merely serve to increase the surplus of that area. They are thus not being used for any purpose, except to add to Europe's reserves at the expense of our own monetary reserves."[43]

Policy considerations reinforce the case for geographical selectivity. By the end of the 1950's, it was generally felt that investments in industrially advanced nations were no longer subject to extraordinary risks and therefore neither required nor deserved extraordinary incentives as compensation. And, whereas it was no longer evident that the foreign investment of American private capital in amounts larger than would take place under the free operation of the private enterprise system would contribute to the economic growth of the advanced nations of the free world as a whole, there was considerable evidence that government-induced capital flows would spur the progress of less-developed countries. The so-called fringe benefits of direct

[41] *Ibid.*, p. 62.

[42] Edward M. Bernstein, *International Effects of U.S. Economic Policy* (Study Paper No. 16 for the Joint Economic Committee, 86th Cong., 2nd Sess.), Washington, 1960, pp. 74-75. Opposing views on the effect of private foreign investment on the U.S. balance of payments are succinctly stated in Bela Balassa (ed.), *Changing Patterns in Foreign Trade and Payments*, New York, 1964. The affirmative side is argued by Elliott Haynes, "Are Overseas Investments a Drain?," the negative by Benjamin Graham, "The Case Against Foreign Investment."

[43] Bernstein, p. 90.

foreign investment, for example, such as the introduction of entrepreneurial and managerial skills and the development of a trained labor force, are a far more important contribution to economic development in the less-developed than in the advanced countries, which either possess these factors already or are in a position to purchase them commercially.

Not only are less-developed countries more likely than advanced ones to benefit from government-induced inflows of capital from the United States, but the economic progress of such countries is of particular importance to the political objectives of the United States, as evidenced by the fact that nearly all our foreign-aid funds are directed toward this group. For the political situation in Europe had by the late 1950's become relatively stabilized, and the ground of the battle for men's minds with world Communism had shifted to the less-developed areas of the world. And, finally, private foreign investment may help to stimulate the development of an indigenous private sector in less-developed countries, but it is not likely to have this effect in economically advanced nations. Most of these countries have already worked out their own patterns of division between the public and private sectors, patterns which are not likely to be altered by the influence of increased private investment from the United States.

PRIVATE INVESTMENT AND DEVELOPMENT PLANNING

The emphasis on geographical selectivity in investment stimulation is only one aspect of a broader shift in governmental thinking, from general support of private capital flows for their own sake to more discriminating efforts to encourage these flows in such a way as to maximize their contribution to the over-all objective of economic development. This subtle shift in viewpoint, which permeated the Administration's proposals for foreign assistance legislation in 1961 and was heavily emphasized in subsequent proposals as well, is a natural outgrowth of the "receding horizons" outlook of the late 1950's, with its recognition that flows of public and private capital to less-developed countries are likely to be complementary rather than competitive. One of the bluntest statements of this viewpoint was made in a Summary Presentation by the Department of State in 1961, which declared that "Where such unusual conditions are present, we should not delude ourselves or countries receiving our assistance that 'private enterprise is doing the job'; we are merely creating the best combination we can devise of private and public resources to accomplish a task in the public interest."[44]

But this statement did more than reiterate the idea of complementarity. When, in the sentence preceding the one just quoted, it emphasized that "The justification for unusually large Government financial participation in a private venture abroad is *not* to exhibit U.S. business abroad, but rather is to accomplish a given task as effectively as we can,"[45] it was voicing the novel view that private foreign investment is to be encouraged not as an end but as a means, the end being assistance to economic development. This viewpoint was echoed during hearings on the Foreign Assistance Act of 1962 by the spokesman for AID, when he declared as the agency's policy that ". . . actions aimed at providing incentives or protection to U.S. private enterprise shall be for the objective of enlisting private American business in the public purpose of assisting economic growth in less-developed countries."[46]

Underlying the shift in the Government's perspective on private foreign investment was a new emphasis on coordinated planning in economic assistance, reflected in the 1962 statement of the Executive Branch that "AID's plans

[44] U.S. Department of State, *An Act for International Development: A Summary Presentation*, Washington, 1961, p. 109.

[45] *Ibid.*, p. 109.

[46] Statement of Frank M. Coffin, Deputy Administrator, AID, in: U.S. Congress, House, Committee on Foreign Affairs, *Foreign Assistance Act of 1962, Hearings*, 87th Cong., 2nd Sess., 1962, Part II, p. 354.

are on an overall country basis, and its programmers look at both public and private sectors of the economy."[47] Although the development of predominantly private enterprise economies in the less-developed countries remained the ultimate goal of American assistance, it was increasingly felt that comprehensive planning was essential during the transitional period if American foreign aid funds were to be put to most efficient use. The objective, therefore, was to encourage private foreign investment to fit into the over-all development plan for a given country, ". . . to provide incentives, protection and—where needed—direct financing, for American private enterprise to do that portion of the job which it can perform best."[48]

Perhaps surprisingly, this more discriminating and more qualified concept of the basis for government encouragement of American private enterprise abroad carried with it a greater rather than a reduced emphasis on the need for new and more effective means of stimulating private participation. For one thing, it stressed the desirability of certain non-traditional forms of foreign investment, such as joint ventures involving local as well as American capital and management, which are especially likely to require government stimulation to get under way. For another, it recognized that the contribution of American private enterprise to economic development need not be confined to the investment of capital, and it therefore led to the development of several programs, such as the increased use in the foreign aid program of technical and management contracts with American firms and the crea-

[47] U.S. Congress, Senate, Committee on Foreign Relations, *Foreign Assistance Act of 1962, Hearings*, 87th Cong., 2nd Sess., 1962, p. 556.

[48] Statement by Frank M. Coffin, Chairman, Program Development Group of the President's Task Force on Foreign Economic Assistance, and Managing Director, Development Loan Fund, in: U.S. Congress, House, Committee on Foreign Affairs, *The International Development and Security Act, Hearings*, 87th Cong., 1st Sess., 1961, Part iii, p. 903.

tion of the Executive Service Corps, which enable American business to provide technical and managerial skills even where conditions are not suitable for actual investment. Such programs are outside the scope of this particular discussion, but they can make an important indirect contribution to the stimulation of private capital flows by helping to create an atmosphere conducive to such investment.

In 1963, as in 1945, the ultimate restoration of private capital's dominant role in international lending and investment remained a major goal of American foreign economic policy. But, during the intervening years, the economic and political obstacles abroad to the immediate achievement of this objective had become increasingly clear. At the same time, the development of balance of payments problems at home had made indiscriminate unilateral efforts to encourage the outflow of private funds more difficult and expensive. For both these reasons, the United States Government had by 1963 substituted critical scrutiny for blanket approval in the political instruments used to encourage the export of private capital.

III · PUBLIC STIMULATION OF PRIVATE FUNDS: THE INSTRUMENTS

There are three types of action a modern government can take to facilitate and encourage foreign investment. One centers on the placement of capital and includes finding and publicizing investment opportunities abroad, removing obstacles to profitable investment, and influencing potential investors to utilize their funds in specific areas or specific types of loans or investments. The second encompasses all the measures a government can take to protect its citizens' capital *after* foreign investment has taken place. And finally, a government can enter directly into the international capital market through the use of state loans, investments, or guaranties.

During the battleship diplomacy period, the United States Government aggressively encouraged the export of private capital to particular areas in support of specific foreign policy objectives, such as the support of the "open-door" policy in China and the Monroe doctrine in Latin America, or the restoration of economic and political stability in Europe after World War I. Official pressure was exerted both on potential lenders at home and on potential recipient countries abroad. Secretary of State Knox had enunciated the right of the State Department to control foreign investment in 1912 and, although the private and informal nature of dealings between governments and bankers makes it hard to tell how much pressure was exerted, the State Department did on a number of occasions "invite American bankers to consider the possibility of making loans to foreign governments."[1] Among the foreign loans which the Government encouraged in

[1] Jacob Viner, "Political Aspects of International Finance," *Journal of Business,* I (April and July 1928), 344. The State Department at different times also vigorously solicited loans to Nicaragua, Guatemala, and China.

this manner were one to Liberia and one to Honduras in 1912.

During the 1920's, the President himself joined in the Government's efforts to stimulate private participation in loans for postwar European reconstruction. In 1924 President Coolidge specifically urged the participation of American private capital in the Dawes Plan Loan to Germany, and the Treasury Department gave "formal approval" to the proposed League of Nations Loan to Austria in 1928. During the widespread recriminations which followed default and losses on many of these loans, it became clear that the American public had generally misunderstood the meaning of "government support" of these issues. There were severe doubts concerning the ethical propriety of official encouragement without government guaranty, when the Government's action led the investing public to make unduly low estimates of the risks entailed in a loan without in any way altering the actual risks incurred.

Pressure on foreign governments during this period most often took the form of diplomatic concession seeking for American capital. The efforts of the State Department to have American bankers included in a consortium of lenders to China during the 1908-1918 decade is an example of this sort of activity. The State Department also intervened to assure American participation in a number of Near and Far Eastern oil concessions during the years 1908-1923. Treaties negotiated with a number of Caribbean countries during roughly the same period secured a variety of special rights and privileges for American investors.

In protecting the existing foreign investments of its citizens, the United States Government took even more direct action. Even after it had specifically renounced the use of force for the collection of international debts in the 1909 Hague Convention, the U.S. Government occasionally went as far as military intervention in protecting American investments. It took such action in Mexico in 1916 and in Nicaragua and Shanghai in 1924. More frequently, the Government's intervention took the form of "dollar diplomacy," the forcible supervision of the finances of the debtor country in order to ensure the re- payment of debts. Such behavior appears to have had considerable effect in inducing capital exports to selected "spheres of influence." In discussing its effectiveness with respect to the Caribbean, James Angell remarks that the substantial increase in American investment there was "not primarily the consequence of the government's direct solicitation to American capitalists, but rather of its pro- vision of those conditions of security which are necessary to make large investments abroad even a possibility."[2]

Although these aggressive methods of investment pro- tection seemed to achieve their immediate objective, their political legacy is dubious. They led, among other things, to the association of the United States with an inflexible policy of anti-revolutionism in Latin America—a reputa- tion which was still giving trouble in the 1960's. In any case, with the wholesale defaults of the 1930's and the institution of the "good neighbor" policy in U.S. relations with Latin American nations, the use of military interven- tion and overt dollar diplomacy ceased. In fact, by the late 1930's, President Roosevelt and Secretary of State Cordell Hull suggested that friction and hostility might be avoided if some U.S. private investments in public utilities and basic resources were to be withdrawn from such countries as Mexico and Venezuela.[3]

The State Department did intervene to prevent discrim- ination against American holders of defaulted bonds in Germany (1933) and Brazil (1934). It also participated in the arrangement of settlements for expropriated American properties in such countries as Mexico, Bolivia, the Soviet

[2] James W. Angell, *Financial Foreign Policy of the United States*, New York, 1933, p. 98.
[3] Bryce Wood, *The Making of the Good Neighbor Policy*, New York, 1961, pp. 34ff.

Union, and Fascist Italy. But its protective efforts were limited to official protest or diplomatic representation, and it failed, in most cases, to recoup more than a small part of its nationals' losses. Success generally depended on the bargaining strength inherent in the status of the balance of payments between the nations involved and, since the United States was a net creditor on current account, she was in a poor bargaining position.[4]

The U.S. Government also sponsored the formation, in 1933, of the Foreign Bondholders' Protective Council, a private corporation which protects the interests of its members in negotiating adjustments on defaulted bond issues. Its efforts met with at least partial success in most cases, and in June 1958 it announced that Bolivia, the last Latin American country to remain in default from the 1930's, had completed adjustment arrangements and resumed debt servicing. But it was unable to prevent substantial losses in the process of readjustment, and it was not designed to deal at all with the problems of proprietary (direct) investors.

POSTWAR METHODS OF INVESTMENT STIMULATION

In the years which followed World War II, efforts of the United States Government to stimulate the flow of private funds abroad faced two obstacles: the bad memories of investors who had been severely stung in the international financial collapse of the 1930's, and the drastically altered political conditions of the postwar world, to which both the Government and the private citizens of the nation had to adapt. To meet these challenges, a variety of mechanisms for the placement and protection of American capital abroad were evolved during the years between 1945 and 1963.

Since ignorance of conditions in other countries is a major reason for investors' hesitation to invest funds

[4] Cleona Lewis, *America's Stake in International Investments*, Washington, 1938, pp. 418-419.

abroad, one of the tools utilized by the U.S. Government to spur the placement of capital abroad is the dissemination of information about investment conditions and opportunities in foreign countries. Diplomatic and consular officials, U.S. aid and technical missions, and other members of the State Department all transmit investment information to the Commerce Department, which distributes it through a variety of business and financial media. These include the Department's own publications: *Foreign Commerce Weekly, Investment Opportunities Abroad,* and a number of country-by-country study series, *Investment In . . . , Establishing a Business In . . . ,* and *Basic Data on the Economy of. . . .* American diplomatic and consular officials are expected to provide information, advice, and assistance on specific business problems, and the Commerce Department carries on business-consulting activities and arranges contacts between U.S. firms and foreign governments and corporations.

With the initiation of the Investment Incentive Program in the International Cooperation Administration's Office of Private Enterprise in 1959, the unearthing of private investment opportunities was placed specifically within the context of the United States' broad effort to assist the economic development of less-developed areas. One of the functions of this new program was to take the initiative in identifying and working up foreign investment opportunities to the point where they are ready to attract private financing. These activities were carried over with the Office of Private Enterprise into AID, and in 1962 it was decided to focus particularly intensive efforts on bringing investment opportunities and potential U.S. investors together through pilot or prototype programs in four key countries: Colombia, Nigeria, Pakistan, and Thailand. The sponsorship of investment feasibility studies of particular industries in particular countries, conducted by outside "expert" consultants, was carried over from ICA into AID and, in addition, AID was given legislative authority to help finance pre-investment surveys undertaken by potential investors themselves.

Although the United States' behavior in the postwar era suggests that this country no longer considers it politic to force other countries to create internal conditions that will be attractive to foreign investors, the spread of a favorable foreign investment climate remains an important aim of our government. "A serious and explicit purpose of our foreign policy," said President Eisenhower in his 1953 State of the Union message, "is the encouragement of a hospitable climate for investment in foreign nations."[5] This encouragement includes propaganda on both diplomatic and popular levels, constantly reminding underdeveloped areas of the advantages to be gleaned from foreign investment, and a readiness to give advice and assistance to countries desiring to improve their investment climates. In 1959, the Foreign Investment Incentive Program gave formal organization to the heretofore scattered and uncoordinated activities in this area. Under this program, the ICA Office for Private Enterprise was charged with helping the less-developed countries to improve the legal, administrative, and social climate for private investment and to develop the business and financial institutions necessary for the expansion of the private sector.[6] The Office of Development Finance and Private Enterprise carries on these same functions in AID, along with a particular emphasis on the sponsorship of development banks and other industrial development institutions to serve as focal points for the growth of an indigenous private sector in developing countries.

In the protection of existing investments, the use of force has also given way to persuasion, propaganda, and bargaining. But the weakness of such methods, already appar-

[5] *The New York Times*, Feb. 3, 1953, p. 14.

[6] ICA, Office of the Deputy Director for Private Enterprise, "Private Enterprise and the Mutual Security Program," Washington, 1960 (Mimeo.) pp. 5-7.

ent in prewar days, has been intensified by the wholesale and specifically anti-capitalist nature of most expropriation in the postwar world. In dealing with such countries as Hungary, Yugoslavia, and Cuba, the strength of the United States Government's position depends largely upon the existence of frozen assets in this country which can be seized, with somewhat doubtful legality, for the payment of claims or at least used as a weapon in bargaining. Since the ideological struggle in which the world is presently engaged generally makes it unwise for the United States to employ military force in such cases and often renders the offending nations either immune or impassive to economic sanctions, the ex-post protection our government can offer to investors who face losses abroad is slight indeed.

THE TREATY APPROACH AND ITS DIFFICULTIES

Faced with this situation, the United States Government has since World War II concentrated on the ex-ante or preventive aspects in its search for new methods of governmental protection for private foreign investments. It has placed considerable emphasis on the negotiation of both multilateral and bilateral treaties dealing with the treatment of such investment. Potentially the most important of the multilateral treaties was the Charter of the International Trade Organization, which was signed by 53 countries at the 1948 Havana Conference. But, after two years of discussion, the United States Senate failed to ratify it, chiefly because of concern over the exceedingly vague protection given foreign capital and the considerable rights of control conceded to capital-receiving countries.

Another such effort at multilateral agreement, the agreement signed by 20 American nations at Bogotá in 1948, provided a number of apparently satisfactory assurances regarding the treatment of foreign investments and the convertibility of earnings and capital. But these commitments were essentially nullified, from the investors' viewpoint, by reservations subordinating them to "the conventional laws of each country" and making foreign investments "subject to the jurisdiction of the national courts."[7] The resulting document was regarded as vague and dangerous by American businessmen and as unacceptable by many Latin Americans because it made too many concessions to foreign investors. There could be little hope that a treaty so received would do much to stimulate the flow of private capital abroad. A number of draft investment charters or codes have since been proposed,[8] but none has gotten past the suggestion stage, "chiefly, it would appear, because the relevant rules of international law are still too much in dispute to permit broad agreement on a really meaningful definition of the investor's rights and obligations."[9]

After these setbacks, the United States concentrated on the less demanding bilateral approach. In the first fifteen years of the postwar era, modernized Treaties of Friendship, Commerce, and Navigation, containing an investment clause, were negotiated with 11 underdeveloped countries; by 1963, 8 of these had been ratified by both signatories.[10] The investment clause generally covered such topics as the right of United States capital to enter freely into business, national or non-discriminatory (most-favored-nation) treatment for established investors, free-

[7] Seymour J. Rubin, *Private Foreign Investment: Legal and Economic Realities*, Baltimore, 1956, p. 82.

[8] These proposals are described in detail in: A. A. Fatouros, *Government Guaranties to Foreign Investors*, New York, 1962, pp. 69-92.

[9] United Nations, Economic and Social Council, *The Promotion of the International Flow of Private Capital* (E/3325, Feb. 26, 1960), New York, 1960, p. 8.

[10] The eight are: Ethiopia, Greece, Iran, Israel, Korea, Muscat and Oman, Nicaragua, Pakistan. The treaties with Colombia, Haiti, and Uruguay, although signed ten or more years ago, have not been ratified by both parties and hence have never entered in force.

dom from restrictions regarding ownership and management, assurances of convertibility of earnings and capital, and provision for prompt and adequate compensation in the event of expropriation.

The problem in extending this bilateral approach is essentially the same as in the multilateral case. A treaty must be based on prior consensus; it can only record, not create, the existence of a favorable investment climate. And in many areas, this consensus between capital-exporting and capital-importing nations simply does not exist. On the question of expropriation, for example, the views of American investors and capital-importing nations are poles apart. The right of a sovereign nation to expropriate is universally recognized, but the United States insists that this right ". . . is coupled with and contingent upon the obligation to make adequate, effective and prompt compensation."[11] Does this mean compensation in dollars, or will payment in local currencies do? Should the amount and type of compensation be determined by a national body or by international arbitration? There are no commonly accepted answers to these questions because there is no international standard of what constitutes adequate and effective compensation.

Treaty provisions regarding currency convertibility also raise the question of how much control over her internal affairs a country can be expected to sign away. Nearly all such documents permit the suspension of convertibility under certain conditions and even the provisions of the Uruguayan Treaty, the one most favorable to investors, are sufficiently vague and open to abuse as to make investors uneasy. Yet an underdeveloped country cannot be expected to give absolute exchange priority to foreign investors.

The so-called Calvo clause in the constitutions of many Latin American nations makes the negotiation of treaties with them a particular problem. This clause states, in

[11] Rubin, pp. 9-10.

effect, that a foreign investor's government may not interfere in his behalf in matters affecting his relationship with the host government. American investors are loath to forswear the protection of their own government in the event of hostile action by a foreign sovereign power. And the United States Government itself refuses to recognize the Calvo doctrine even when the investor has specifically agreed to it. The Government feels that "it, as a government, has an interest in the foreign investment that its national cannot give or contract away."[12]

The common denominator of all these specific difficulties with the treaty approach is the investor's conviction that a government bent on harassment and persecution of foreign investment can always get around any specific safeguards written into a treaty. Without a common outlook and a sense on both sides of the mutual benefits of private investment there is no way to determine at what point legitimate regulation leaves off and expropriation begins. In recent years investors have often come to fear creeping expropriation in the guise of taxation or regulation more than the outright variety. The draft international codes for foreign investment drawn up by the National Association of Manufacturers and the International Chamber of Commerce indicate that the American businessman wants far greater freedom and far more safeguards than the less-developed countries consider proper, and than their governments could promise without losing popular support. Among the more controversial requirements are freedom from regulations regarding ownership by or employment of nationals of the host country, and the subordination of the host country's constitutional laws to some international standard of fair treatment.

Finally, the protection afforded by treaties is limited by the fact that "risks of confiscation or seizure cannot be fully eliminated through treaties so long as the possibility exists of a change in government in the foreign

[12] *Ibid.*, p. 62.

country through revolution or war."[13] Obviously this problem has existed as long as treaties themselves, but the political instability of many underdeveloped areas increases its importance, particularly since the government which succeeds to power may well be one which does not recognize the rights of property owners at all and which may help consolidate its position by the very act of repudiating such treaties.

PROPOSALS FOR TAX INCENTIVES

In the absence of effective means of protecting private capital already committed abroad, the traditional forms of government action to encourage new foreign investment—chiefly persuasion, propaganda, and the provision of information—are not likely to have much effect by themselves. In recognition of this fact, both the government and the business community have proposed a variety of more radical stimulants for foreign investment. Of the incentives proposed, some form of tax relief for foreign investors has been more often suggested, and more hotly disputed, than any other.

A host of technical changes, most of them relating to the treatment of credit for foreign taxes paid, were proposed during the 1950's to make American tax laws more favorable to foreign investors.[14] But the really major changes suggested, aside from the complete elimination of United States taxation on all income from foreign sources, were of two types. The first would have permitted foreign branches and domestic subsidiaries of U.S. corporations to defer American taxation of their income until it is remitted to the parent corporation for dividend distribution, as foreign subsidiaries were already permit-

[13] U.S. Department of State, *Point Four*, Washington, 1950, p. 73.

[14] The history and current provisions of U.S. tax policy relating to foreign investment are described in: Peggy Brewer Richman, *Taxation of Foreign Investment*, Baltimore, 1963, pp. 37-56.

ted to do under existing laws.[15] The second would have
granted to all foreign corporate income an across-the-
board reduction in the domestic tax rate of 52 per cent,
such as has long been enjoyed by enterprises operating in
South America under the Western Hemisphere Trade
Corporation Act of 1942 and in China (today Taiwan)
under the China Trade Act of 1922.[16]

A number of powerful business organizations and government advisory groups have argued that such favorable
tax legislation would be the most effective way to increase
foreign investment quickly and substantially.[17] Such a tax
reduction or elimination, they feel, would not only have
a tremendous psychological incentive effect, but would
also permit returns to increase to a point where they
would outweigh the extra risks of foreign investment, and
would eliminate the competitive disadvantage American
companies suffer when competing abroad against other
foreign corporations paying no taxes in their home countries. The United States, they say, is in a minority among
industrialized nations in taxing the earnings from foreign
investments.

Opponents of such tax measures point out that they
would be quite frankly a subsidy, violating the principle of
tax equity, which holds that taxes must be equal on all
earnings, regardless of geographic origin. In addition,
many people fear a substantial loss of Treasury revenue
from across-the-board tax measures. Finally, there is the

[15] Such deferral provisions were the main object of the Treas-
ury-sponsored Simpson Bill, introduced in 1952, and were among
the several important tax-incentive provisions of the Boggs Bill,
on which extensive hearings were conducted in 1959. Neither of
these bills was enacted into law.

[16] The Boggs Bill also provided for worldwide extension of the
14 per cent (average) tax reduction enjoyed by Western Hemisphere Trade Corporations.

[17] For some of these arguments, see: U.S. Council of International Chamber of Commerce, *Intelligent International Investment*, New York, 1949; International Development Advisory
Board, *Partners in Progress*, Washington, 1951; National Foreign
Trade Convention, *Reports*, New York, 1950-1962.

possibility that "if such income is not taxed, the effect may be to cause U.S. investment resources to move abroad in a manner inconsistent with the optimum international allocation of resources and detrimental to the economic interests of the U.S."[18]

It is possible, of course, that the political advantages of foreign investment might be powerful enough to override these ethical and economic considerations in the name of the national interest. The United States has seen fit to violate the principle of tax equity for the sake of specific foreign policy objectives a number of times in the past (as in the cases of China and Latin America). It is possible that the revenue loss might be offset by reductions in foreign aid, defense expenditures, or other less obvious gains. And if there are social gains from foreign investment not taken into account in private decisions, the effect of such a subsidy might be to correct rather than to distort the worldwide pattern of resource allocation.

In any case, it is certain that such political advantages could result only from selective rather than over-all tax incentives, which "would merely continue and expand the current pattern of United States private capital movement overseas,"[19] with its emphasis on developed countries and on the extractive industries in less-developed areas. And in fact, with the development since about 1959 of increasingly serious concern about the United States' balance of payments, most recent proposals for tax concessions have been based on the principle of geographical selectivity. This principle of selectivity is reflected in the

[18] Oliver Oldman, "United States Tax Laws and Treaties Affecting Private Foreign Investment," *Federal Bar Journal*, XIX (Oct. 1959), 344. For the more common arguments against general tax measures, see: Norman Buchanan and Howard Ellis, *Approaches to Economic Development*, New York, 1955; E. R. Barlow and I. T. Wender, *Foreign Investment and Taxation*; U.S. President's Materials Policy Commission, *Resources for Freedom*, Washington, 1952.

[19] Statement by Stanley H. Ruttenberg, U.S. Congress, House, Committee on Ways and Means, *Foreign Investment Incentive Act, Hearings*, 86th Cong., 1st Sess., 1959, p. 512.

various attempts which have been made to negotiate tax-sparing treaties, which would permit companies operating abroad to claim U.S. tax credit for taxes forgiven by the host country in order to attract foreign investment, with less-developed countries which are particularly anxious to encourage such investment.[20] It is reflected, negatively, in the exemption of less-developed countries from all recent suggestions for curbing the outflow of investment capital, such as the largely unsuccessful attempt to eliminate tax-deferral for the reinvested earnings of foreign subsidiaries in 1962,[21] and the Interest Equalization Tax enacted in mid-1964, which effectively increases the interest cost to foreign sellers of bonds in the U.S. market by 1 percentage point.[22]

Finally, the selectivity principle underlies the Administration's 1963-1964 proposal for a 30 per cent tax credit on new investment; this credit would be restricted not only to new investments in less-developed countries, but to certain specified types of industries "most closely related to economic development and involving the greatest risks."[23] This latest proposal represents an attempt to take into account several of the many types of selectivity which are relevant to the national interest, and to disprove the view of a leading expert on international tax

[20] Such treaties have been negotiated with India, Pakistan, Israel, and the United Arab Republic, but as of 1963, none had been fully ratified. See Richman, p. 55.

[21] In the final legislation, tax deferral was eliminated only for certain types of foreign "tax-haven" operation.

[22] The securities of international lending institutions like the World Bank and the Inter-American Development Bank are also exempt from the Interest Equalization Tax.

[23] U.S. Congress, House, Committee on Foreign Affairs, *Foreign Assistance Act of 1964, Hearings,* 88th Cong., 2nd Sess., 1964, Part I, p. 46. The qualified industries are listed as: "Manufacturing, retailing, processing or marketing of agricultural products, ownership and operation of hotels, fishing, certain service industries, and under limited conditions, wholesaling and construction. Among the excluded industries are: extraction of minerals, refining, shipping, banking, communications, and insurance."

law, ". . . I have not heard of any administratively tolerable or technically workable tax reduction or exemption device that would not reward the useless along with the useful, the old along with the new, . . . the riskless along with the risky."[24] But in this attempt the principle of tax equity is thrown to the winds, as the U.S. Government puts itself in the position of passing on the merits of particular investments, with an enormous advantage accruing to those investors in the favored category.

In evaluating tax incentives as a stimulus to private investments in developing areas, perhaps the most important question of all is raised by evidence that general tax measures might have considerably less effect than their supporters claim. Two major surveys of business views on foreign investment, one prepared for the government in 1951 and the other in 1959, both report that, while a majority of businessmen interviewed said they favored major changes in the tax laws, only a relatively small minority cited U.S. tax laws as a deterrent to foreign investment or indicated that the alterations they suggested would make any difference in their own investment plans.[25] The chief interviewers for another such study, prepared for the Commerce Department in 1953-1954, came to a much stronger negative conclusion ". . . the role of U.S. taxation in investment decisions has been minor in the past and changes in U.S. taxes alone cannot be expected to have a significant effect upon the attitudes of the executives responsible for investment decisions."[26] The main difference between investors and non-investors,

[24] Kingman Brewster, Statement before the Second International Investment Law Conference of the American Society of International Law, Washington, 1958, p. 2.

[25] See: National Industrial Conference Board, *Obstacles to Direct Foreign Investment*, New York, 1951, p. 22, and U.S. Department of Commerce, *Reportorial Review: Responses to Business Questionnaire Regarding Private Investment Abroad*, Washington, 1959, p. 1.

[26] E. R. Barlow and I. T. Wender, *U.S. Tax Incentives to Direct Private Foreign Investment*, Cambridge, Mass., 1954, p. 2.

they say, is psychological, and "as long as non-investors have no idea of the rate of return they can obtain on a foreign investment, any improvement in this unknown rate of return cannot affect their decision to invest overseas."[27]

GOVERNMENT ENTRY INTO PRIVATE CAPITAL MARKETS

The biggest step a government can take to stimulate the export of private capital is to enter into and alter the capital market itself, by giving guaranties or loans to its own investors and thus sharing their risks or increasing their profit opportunities. Although there are important differences between government guaranties of private loans and direct participation by the government, with its own funds, in such loans, the two mechanisms are alike in several of their effects on private foreign investment.

Even when government guaranties or loans are made on terms which do not entail any subsidy to the private investor, they perform an important function in spreading or "pooling" the risks of foreign investment. By offering guaranties at a premium which covers the actuarial risk involved, or by making participation arrangements which ensure that the public portion of the investment will share future profits equally with risks, the government can have an important effect in stimulating the flow of private funds. For a government is singularly well equipped to perform the risk-pooling function. Because of its size and the funds at its command, it can spread the risks over a vast number of individual investors, and is also in a much better position than any private institution to "sit-out" adverse circumstances. Thus, by offering on a commercial basis services which no private commercial institution is equipped to offer—insurance against the political risks of foreign investment, for example[28]—the gov-

[27] *Ibid.*, p. 5.
[28] In some instances such insurance is offered by private firms, as in the case of the Hermes Company in Germany, but only

ernment can effectively encourage private capital flows to foreign areas.

Actually, government funds more often participate with private capital on a fixed-interest basis at relatively low rates in comparison with the risks entailed. And guaranty premiums are usually determined by some arbitrary notion of "fairness" rather than on an actuarial basis. Under these conditions, the government may be granting a subsidy to private investors by not merely spreading but actually sharing itself in some part of the risk which would otherwise be borne entirely by private enterprise.

Government participation can also encourage foreign investment by increasing the investor's confidence and even reducing the investment risks which are political in origin. Government or international intermediary institutions can not only increase the potential investor's knowledge of and interest in foreign opportunities, but also provide, by their participation, confidence that the investment in question must be sound and is not likely to suffer from arbitrary treatment at the hands of the host government. Apparently "United States venture capital invested abroad desires as much United States government protection [in the form of participation] as it is feasible to obtain against potentially detrimental acts of the foreign government."[29] Both reasoning and experience suggest that foreign governments might hesitate more to take arbitrary action against enterprises in which public institutions participated than against purely private ventures. There are several bases for such hesitation: fear of reprisals by the government thus injured, concern over adverse effects on the

---

when government reinsurance facilities are available—and always utilized. In the case of the insurance offered American exporters by the Foreign Credit Insurance Association, the Export-Import Bank assumes the political portion of the risk.

[29] William B. Dale and Richard N. Bale, *Private U.S. Venture Capital for Investment in Newly Developing Economies*, Menlo Park, 1958, p. 22.

host country's international credit rating, and the fact that in many cases nationalistic hostility may be less toward such investments than toward purely private ones.

The risk-spreading, risk-sharing, and risk-reducing effects represent the most important characteristics which all forms of government participation have in common. There are also important differences, however, between the effects of state participation in private investment through guaranties and through loans. For one thing, the two forms of participation operate on risk in somewhat different senses. State guaranties affect "risk" as it is usually defined, by pooling, sharing, or reducing the probability of loss attached to a given investment. Government loan participations may also reduce this pure probability but, whether they do or not, they will always reduce the amount of money to which this risk probability applies: the minimum amount which the private investor must provide in order to take advantage of a given investment opportunity. The sum of money involved is not generally regarded as one of the elements in figuring risk, but in the context of foreign investment, it makes sense to regard both types of government activity as "risk-sharing" in their incentive effect.

STATE GUARANTIES: THEIR EVOLUTION AND SCOPE

Although the concept of public guaranties is not new, the scope and function of such plans have changed considerably during the past century. Most of the earlier schemes were guaranties in the strict sense, that is, they represented a blanket undertaking on the part of the guarantor to answer for another's liability. Government assurances in the post-World War II era are also generally referred to as guaranties, and will be here, but most of them are more accurately described as insurance schemes, providing protection only against certain specified risks. Unlike blanket guaranties, these insurance programs are applicable not only to loans but to equity investments or any other form of financial participation.[30]

In the 19th century it was generally the capital-importing governments alone which acted as guarantors, assuring the payment of dividends at a certain rate despite failure or default. Generally no fees were charged for such guaranties; some of the plans required that an enterprise earning more than the guarantied rate of profit should apply the excess to compensating the government for sums paid under the guaranty in less profitable years, but this provision was nearly always honored in the breach.[31] In consequence, these guaranty schemes almost always amounted to large state subsidies, and were generally regarded simply as an alternative to the issuance by a state of its own bonds to obtain funds for reloaning to favored banks or enterprises.

The most impressive instance of this variety of guaranty was the guarantied-bond boom on the London capital market which lasted for more than half a century. This boom undoubtedly had its origins in the tremendous profitability of one of the first ventures so financed, the Erie Canal. Railroad investment was a favorite object of such issues, and numerous lines in India and the eastern United States were "built by private corporations insured against loss by public bounty,"[32] as the promise of "a sure 5 per cent"[33] brought out a flood of middle-class savings.

[30] Ralph W. Golby, Address before the Second International Investment Law Conference of the American Society of International Law, Washington, 1958 (Mimeo.). The U.S. Government has recently reintroduced the concept of the comprehensive repayment guaranty on a limited basis in the extended-risk and Latin American housing guaranty programs of AID. Such guaranties have so far been made available for loan investments only, and even in these cases only the principal, and not the interest, is covered by the guaranty. See pp. 290-294.

[31] J. H. Williams, *Argentine Trade under Inconvertible Paper Money*, Cambridge, Mass., 1920, p. 89.

[32] L. H. Jenks, *The Migration of British Capital to 1875*, New York, 1927, p. 74.

[33] The terms under which the bulk of British investment in

As British investment abroad increased steadily, other countries caught the fever, and by the '60's and '70's Canada, France, Russia, Austria, Hungary, and Turkey were all using the guaranty system to attract foreign capital into railway development. Both private bankruptcy and public repudiation were common; in several states in the United States and, later, in Argentina, the burden of government guaranties proved the largest single cause of government default,[34] while in India the taxpayer paid heavily for British capital invested in his country. The existence of guaranties undoubtedly encouraged extravagance and wasteful duplication, and foreign funds were not always administered with the prudence domestic investors might have demanded. But the railroads were built, built sooner and probably better than they would have been otherwise, and in this sense the system must be regarded as successful.

The motives behind the guaranties just described, issued by the borrowing countries, were chiefly economic. Such backing for the obligations of a country's own colonies for similar reasons have been common, but otherwise guaranties by the lending government have been relatively rare, and their origins almost invariably political. A total of 12 loans to a number of European countries, most of them jointly guarantied by a combination of larger European powers, represent a complete roster of such transactions prior to World War II.[35] The outcome

India, the largest single unit of international investment during the 19th century, was made, were set by the two guarantied-interest railway contracts signed in 1849. They provided for a 5 per cent interest guaranty by the East India Company, the semi-public body which administered India for the Crown, of all capital deposited with it by the railways, net receipts were limited to 10 per cent annually, and at the end of 99 years the railways would become the property of the government without compensation except for the machinery, plant, and rolling stock. David Thorner, *Investment in Empire*, Philadelphia, 1950, pp. 168-179.

[34] Williams, pp. 116-127.

[35] Cleona Lewis, *America's Stake in International Investments*, Washington, 1938, pp. 232-237.

of these loans, only 3 of which were ever paid in full by the debtors, indicates strongly that economic soundness and productivity were not the chief criteria followed by the guarantors.

The nearest predecessors of the present guaranty operations, both chronologically and in terms of similarity, were the export-credit guaranty schemes adopted by a number of European countries during the 1920's.[36] The British Government experimented with a series of complicated programs, each of which guarantied a certain portion of the exporter's investment in a given transaction. In return for this guaranty, the rights of the exporter were turned over to the government, which was empowered to take steps to recover the debt in event of default. The British plans and their numerous imitators invariably lost money because, in the opinion of most analysts, they were insuring not political but ordinary business risks. But the final straw came in 1931, when the economic crisis and ensuing exchange controls forced the default of solvent debtors, and the British Government was forced to revert to the private insurance principle of paying only upon proof of the debtor's bankruptcy, not simply in cases of non-payment at maturity.

As a result of the lessons learned from these experiences, as well as of an altered view of the proper relationship between government and private enterprise, the government guaranty schemes developed between 1945 and 1963 are generally more limited in scope. But, although they are essentially insurance schemes, their functions are clearly distinguished from those of commercial insurance.

One important difference between public and commercial insurance in this context is the type of risk with which each is properly concerned. Commercial insurance is designed to deal with measurable risks whose probabilities

[36] The interwar credit schemes are described and their performance analyzed in E. M. Shenkman, *Insurance Against Credit Risk*, London, 1935, pp. 177-339.

can be known in advance, either *a priori* or on the basis of accumulated experience. It is not equipped to handle risks which cannot be quantitatively measured either by the calculation of probabilities (because these risks are often cumulative and therefore lack the independent causes which the law of large numbers demands) or by actuarial tables (because past experience adequate as a basis for such tables is lacking). Yet it is these immeasurable risks which stand in the way of capital flows; measurable risks, insofar as the capital market compensates for them by higher rates of return, are not a serious obstacle.[37] But the political risks faced by foreign investment in the mid-twentieth century are of the incalculable variety, and with them government guaranties alone can cope.

Private and public insurance schemes are distinguished in purpose as well as in coverage. A private insurance company does not attempt to reduce the risks it covers; its objective is simply to estimate them accurately and, on the basis of these estimates, establish a premium which will provide for the necessary payments to policyholders plus operating costs and profits. A government acting as guarantor generally also charges fees and uses them to set up a reserve fund for payments, but it generally has no actuarial basis for assuming that such reserves will be adequate, and considers the reduction of the risks themselves by its very participation in them as part of its objective. For the state's role, at least where political risks are concerned, may be as much preventive as compensatory: "The primary economic function of the State guarantee lies in diminishing the probability of the loss itself."[38]

Obviously, a state guaranty can perform a preventive function only as long as it limits its coverage to risks which are controllable by the action of other govern-

[37] Ragnar Nurkse, *Internationale Kapitalbewegungen*, Vienna, 1935, pp. 24-27.
[38] Shenkman, p. 169.

ments; this, indeed, would seem to be a sensible definition of "political" risks. To be most effective in preventing losses, guaranties should ideally be bilateral. Only when the borrowing as well as the lending government becomes a party to the agreement does the agent whose activities determine the incidence of loss stake its international credit standing on the avoidance of such loss. Unilateral guaranties can be effective, but they are far more likely to turn out to be subsidies in the long run and to be granted only when the guarantor government has an interest in the continuation or expansion of specific foreign investments strong enough to outweigh the increased likelihood of having to pay out under guaranty contracts. The risk to the guarantor is lessened if the host government has the opportunity to approve, or at least to veto, the projects of guaranty applicants; some degree of bilateralism is implied by the act of approval, or even failure to veto.

THE MINGLING OF PUBLIC AND PRIVATE FUNDS

Unlike state guaranties, public loans to private enterprise for foreign investment (and their even more common variant, private participation in government-initiated loans or investments) are essentially new under the sun. Except in the sense that tax deferral represents a hidden form of public "loan" to private enterprise, such joint ventures had taken place in only a few isolated instances until 1945. The idea of institutions established for the specific purpose of mingling public and private money in foreign investment was hammered out in the conferences of Allied economists planning for the economic problems of the postwar world while World War II was still in progress. Between 1945 and 1963, three international institutions—the World Bank, the International Finance Corporation, and the Inter-American Development Bank—and two agencies of the United States Government—the Export-Import Bank and the Development Loan Fund—Agency for International Development—undertook such joint ven-

tures in an effort to stimulate the flow of private funds
abroad.

When a government uses its own funds to participate
with private investment it is in a sense going one step
beyond the issuance of guaranties, since its liability is now
direct rather than contingent. In addition to the effects
on risk which they share in common with state guaranties,
government loans have certain unique effects of their
own. They can, for example, stimulate private investment
not only by reducing risk but also by increasing potential
profits through the so-called "leverage effect." The "leverage" exerted by government funds comes about because,
as the earnings rate on the total capital investment rises
above the rate of interest on loan capital provided from
outside the firm's own funds, the rate of return on the
equity portion of the investment rises progressively faster
than where no loan capital is involved.[39] In cases where
the ratio of loan to equity capital is high, the leverage
factor could easily be more important to the equity investor than the over-all rate of return—provided initially
that the latter was higher than the interest rate paid on
debt capital.

The effect of the leverage principle on the private investor's risk is more complicated. As far as income is
concerned, the risk of loss is increased rather than reduced, since the "break-even" over-all rate of return is
clearly higher when fixed-interest loan funds, from whatever source, are involved in a capitalization than when
they are not. But in another sense, when "risk" is regarded
as including not only the probability of loss but also the
size of the capital investment to which that probability is
attached, the availability of public funds can serve to
reduce the private investor's risk by providing from the

[39] The leverage effect is thoroughly discussed by Dale and Bale,
pp. 15-16, who also indicate graphically the exact effect various
proportions of outside loan capital have on increasing profits (or
losses) as the over-all rate of return rises above (or falls below)
the rate of interest paid on loan funds.

outside some portion of the funds which he would otherwise have had to put up himself in order to undertake a given foreign venture. The risk thus reduced is not income risk but capital risk,[40] the danger that the private funds invested in the enterprise may be lost through some misadventure. It is precisely this type of risk, as opposed to ordinary business risks which are more likely to result in loss of income, with which potential foreign investors are most concerned and which constitutes the "peculiar" risks of investment abroad.

Opportunities to play the leverage game with low-interest public funds can often serve as a powerful incentive to foreign investment, but the public agencies are generally uneasy about this form of assistance, apparently feeling that it is a more blatant form of subsidy than the sharing or reduction of risk probabilities. Since opportunities for leverage can arise only when public funds are invested in conjunction with private *equity* capital, the question generally does not arise in the case of the World Bank or the Inter-American Development Bank, and the International Finance Corporation's profit-sharing schemes also tend to limit such possibilities. The United States agencies have paid lip service to the avoidance of such profit possibilities by establishing maximum limits on the ratio of public to private capital in any given enterprise. But these limits have not always been observed in practice, and the history of the Eximbank affords several impressive examples of the operation of the leverage effect.

The availability of public loan funds helps reduce the obstacles to private investments not only in the general ways just described, but also in one quite specific and important fashion. Because of the high risks of depreciation or inconvertibility of foreign exchange in many areas, direct investors frequently insist on acquiring a substantial part of their loans funds locally, hesitating to risk their

[40] The author is indebted to Professor Peter Kenen for this distinction.

own dollars or to incur fixed dollar obligations. But in most underdeveloped countries, where well-organized capital markets and mature credit institutions are generally lacking, funds for long-term investment in productive enterprises are in extremely short supply and are available, if at all, only at prohibitively high rates of interest. This shortage of funds available to the foreign investor is often aggravated by the host government's objection to a firm's borrowing the bulk of its funds locally, on the grounds that it is unfair for an enterprise, particularly when it has the name of a well-known parent organization to trade on, to earn high returns on a small dollar equity investment.

Since most of the large direct investors abroad regard retained earnings and local borrowings as the major source of funds for expansion,[41] the lack of such funds may often prevent investment even in cases where dollar financing would be obtainable at reasonable interest rates. In such cases public loans in the currency of the host country may ameliorate a risk which is very often a bottleneck to investment, and thus release a flow of private equity funds larger than the sums actually expended by the lending agency.

Finally, public lending institutions can, and increasingly do, encourage private investment abroad by taking the initiative in seeking out potentially promising investment opportunities, developing them to a point where they might appear attractive to potential investors, and establishing effective lines of contact through which to make them known to those in control of funds that might be available for such ventures. In this capacity the public

[41] A survey of 115 large U.S. corporations with extensive foreign operations revealed that retained earnings and local borrowing were the primary sources of financing for foreign capital expenditures. Jack N. Behrman, "Promoting Free World Economic Development Through Direct Investment," *American Economic Review*, L (May 1960), 271-273.

institutions are not acting directly upon either risks or profit prospects, but merely unearthing situations in which both these factors might be attractive to potential investors if only they knew about them. This is merely a modern instance of the traditional capital-placement device of keeping the business community informed about foreign opportunities, but performed within a new institutional framework singularly well-adapted to the task by virtue of its contacts with and knowledge of both the borrowing and the lending parties to the international transactions.

The most obvious advantage of autonomous public lending or guarantying institutions which enter into the private capital market is their potential effectiveness in conditions too unfavorable to permit the more conventional forms of government encouragement of private capital to operate successfully. Numerous observers of postwar economic conditions have demanded the creation of "new instruments and new forms, in the legal and institutional sense, for the international transfer of capital funds" and the restoration of the long-term capital market.[42] The specialized financing institutions we are discussing are probably the best potential means of providing a crucial link between the expanding capital markets of the industrialized world and the expanding capital needs of the less-developed areas. At the same time these institutions, unlike pure government lending, are in a position to "protect the old decorum of handling credits as business."[43] They can judge loan applications on the basis of probable productivity rather than on political grounds or according to some criterion of need appropriate to grant but not to loan assistance.

By participating in the capital market through such agencies a government can be as selective as it wishes. It can examine applications for its participation on a case-

[42] Gunnar Myrdal, *An International Economy*, New York, 1956, p. 114.
[43] *Ibid.*, p. 115.

by-case basis, applying as many different criteria as it pleases to determine whether or not the national interest would be served by a given investment. If, on the other hand, the government has no desire to keep such close control over the destination of its loans and guaranties, it can delegate the responsibility of selection to specialized institutions, public or private, to any desired degree. The general institutional framework within which such participation assistance takes place is a highly flexible one.

The growth of public lending and guarantying institutions, along with the proliferation of other forms of governmental encouragement of international capital flows, is rapidly forcing us to develop new definitions of private foreign investment. Is investment *private* merely because private funds are utilized, or must the owner of these funds also share some of the risk involved? And, if so, how much of the risk? Instead of a neat juxtaposition of private *versus* public investment, we are faced with a seemingly unbroken continuum: moving from private investment without any government assistance at all, through the use of government information services, tax relief, limited guaranties (insurance), joint public-private lending, and total repayment guaranties to loans made entirely from public funds.

There is no question that this blurring of distinctions destroys the pure price criterion of the productivity of capital movements without creating another unambiguous standard to take its place, and makes impossible any clear-cut answer to the question of whether political action is under or overcompensating for the deficiencies of the market mechanism where foreign investment is concerned. It is for these reasons that economists sometimes object to the use of "artificial" public stimuli which interfere with the private capital market, arguing that the most a government can properly do is try to reduce market imperfections by disseminating information on foreign investment conditions and opportunities, and then simply hope for a change in the attitude of private investors.[44]

To this viewpoint and its policy implications there are two major objections. The first is that to maintain, in the face of current world conditions, that one can refrain from political stimulation of capital exports and thereby preserve the operation of the free-market mechanism is simply naive. The fact is that governments today are so enmeshed in every aspect of economic life that there is no longer any such thing as an economic decision free of their influence. The actions of foreign governments dominate the prospects of foreign investment, while governmental actions and institutions at home affect, no less crucially and in countless different ways, the profitability of the domestic uses of capital to which the prospective investor must compare the opportunities abroad. In an economic environment dominated in any case by political considerations and restrictions, the pure market standard being sacrificed through government incentives is one which did not exist to begin with.

The other economic argument against the doctrine of non-interference is that, although there seems little chance that the uneconomic restraints on capital lending will soon vanish or even lessen appreciably if the international capital market is left to itself, there is some hope that the governmental incentives applied to overcome them might ultimately be self-liquidating. For if, through experience with foreign investment stimulated by governmental incentives, lenders developed a more accurate picture of the opportunities and risks involved and borrowing countries felt the benefits of such investment sufficiently to modify hostile actions and attitudes toward it and to reap rewards in the form of economic expansion, the present imperfections of the private market-mechanism would be

[44] This point of view is taken by Walter P. Egle in "American Foreign Lending and the International Dollar Shortage," *Weltwirtschaftliches Archiv*, Band 81, Heft 2 (1958), 220-238.

substantially reduced. There are a number of uncertainties involved, of course, and not even the elimination of every one of them could make external economies internal or subsume political considerations under the private profit calculus. But the importance of both external economies and political considerations where investment in less-developed areas is concerned is due in large measure to the growing discrepancy between their economic status and that of the more advanced countries. In the narrowing of this gap lies the greatest hope for the development of conditions which will make possible the unrationed flow of private funds from one country to another free of either political inducements or political restrictions. Until that time comes, the growing area between purely public and purely private capital exports will remain a crucial one. And the risk-sharing institutions, whose functions and effectiveness this book tries to assess, occupy a large piece of this middle ground.

IV · THE INVESTMENT GUARANTY PROGRAM[1]

THE EARLY YEARS

Although a number of U.S. Government and international agencies have similar and often overlapping authorizations to insure funds invested abroad by American citizens or corporations, the only sustained instance of this form of encouragement in the postwar era has been the Investment Guaranty Program which, by 1963, had maintained operational continuity under the aegis of five successive foreign-aid agencies. This Program came into being in 1948 as part of the Economic Cooperation Act "to promote world peace and the general welfare, national interest and foreign policy of the United States. . . ."[2] Emphasizing from the first the role private enterprise should play in the reconstruction of Europe, Congress provided that the ECA Administrator might facilitate the use of private trade channels in a number of ways, which could include making: ". . . guaranties to any person of investments in connection with projects approved by the Administrator and the participating country concerned as furthering the purposes of this title (including guaranties of enterprises producing or distributing informational media)."[3]

The provisions of the guaranty legislation, as they finally emerged from Conference, represented the first of a long series of compromises between House enthusiasm for the Program and Senate opposition to it. They empowered the Administrator to issue guaranties of convertibility of income or compensation for sale up to the amount of the

[1] A somewhat more detailed description of this program is given in my study: *The United States Investment Guaranty Program and Private Foreign Investment*, Princeton Studies in International Finance, No. 9 (Princeton, 1959) from which this discussion is taken.

[2] *Economic Cooperation Act of 1948*, 62 *Stat.* 137.

[3] *Ibid.*, pp. 144-145.

paid-in-investment, not to exceed $15 million during the first year nor a total of $300 million during the 14-year lifetime of the program. A maximum annual fee of 1 per cent was designed to "limit the use of the guaranty feature to those who most need it,"[4] and reserves had to be set aside in an amount equal to the full face value of all guaranties issued. Since guaranty reserve funds were not to be separately earmarked but to come from the over-all loan appropriation, any money used as backing for guaranties would reduce by an equal amount the sums available for low-cost loans under the Marshall Plan.

The Guaranty Program was designed to apply to all ERP countries, but actual participation required the negotiation of a bilateral treaty spelling out procedures to be followed. Guaranty clauses, providing for consultation between the U.S. Government and that of the host country regarding projects for which guaranties were requested and for recognition of the U.S. Government's ownership of any currency or credits transferred to it by a private investor upon payment of a guaranty claim, were included as Article III of the ECA Agreements with 14 European countries.[5] The actual granting of a guaranty, however, required the implementation of this clause with a more detailed agreement, designed to reduce the U.S. Government's own risk by obtaining, in advance, agreement on definite procedures in the event that a claim should be honored. These treaties were negotiated with members of the European Recovery Program gradually over the following few years.

The brief legislative provisions for the Guaranty Program left the establishment of criteria for investment eligibility and the development of operational procedures to administrative discretion. ECA interpreted Congress's

[4] *U.S. Code Congressional Service*, 80th Cong., 2nd Sess., 1948, II, 1387.

[5] U.S. Economic Cooperation Administration, *First Report to Congress*, Washington, 1948, p. 82.

intention as covering only new investments with an expected lifetime of five years or more, which would contribute to the objective of European recovery, and in which the investor was a United States citizen or a "company organized under American law and predominantly owned by American citizens."[6] To be eligible for a guaranty, an investment had to be regarded as a substitute for a possible loan or grant, and proposals were examined in this light with respect to the recipient country's need for the proposed products, the amount of dollar imports saved, the creation of new exports, and the soundness of the investment from the point of view of European recovery as a whole.[7]

The Export-Import Bank was immediately named by the first ECA Administrator as the liquidating or contractual agent for the Program, to ensure administrative continuity after the expiration of the ECA guaranty authority. Regulations for guaranty applications and processing procedures were issued in July 1948, although their use had to await the signing of bilateral treaties. A prospective investor, in addition to securing the approval of the host country, was required to submit to the guaranty administrator an exhaustive description of his plans, including engineering and economic surveys, balance sheets and income statements, and a statement showing the ex-

[6] U.S. Mutual Security Agency, *Investment Guaranty Manual*, Washington, 1952, p. 2. In general, this meant a company in which more than one-half (originally, 85 per cent) of the total value of all classes of stock is owned by United States citizens. The requirement that the company be organized under United States law meant that a foreign subsidiary of a U.S. corporation, even if wholly owned, was not eligible to receive guaranties for its investments in other enterprises. In October 1961, however, as part of a considerable expansion of the Guaranty Program under the Agency for International Development, this rule was relaxed to permit guaranty coverage for the dollar investments made by foreign subsidiaries of U.S. companies.

[7] U.S. Economic Cooperation Administration, *Third Report to Congress*, Washington, 1949, pp. 47-48.

pected effect of the investment on the foreign exchange position of the host nation.[8]

Inevitably, in view of the lack of precedents for such a guaranty scheme, its early administration was uncertain, overcautious, and therefore too slow and complicated to attract the maximum interest from potential users. In part for this reason, public reaction to this new form of public protection for private foreign investment during its first year was largely one of indifference. Early in 1949, with one guaranty and 12 applications to the Program's credit, ECA Administrator Paul Hoffman said: "The primary reason for the low volume of applications appears to be the uncertain conditions in Western Europe, which are not attractive to new dollar investments even with a guaranty of convertibility. A secondary factor affecting the magnitude of applications to date is the relatively short period since the inauguration of the investment guaranty program."[9]

The fact that the Program's total for the year was "far below anticipations"[10] was a matter of considerable concern to its supporters in the Administration and in Congress, particularly in the House.[11] A number of suggestions

---

[8] U.S. Economic Cooperation Administration, *First Report to Congress*, Washington, 1948, p. 11.

[9] U.S. Economic Cooperation Administration, *A Report on Recovery Progress and United States Aid*, Washington, 1949, p. 112.

[10] U.S. Economic Cooperation Administration, *Fourth Report to Congress*, Washington, 1949, p. 56.

[11] Actually, there was considerable difference of opinion within the Administration regarding the value of the Program. The view of the State Department that the Program was "perhaps the most effective possibility for altering the prospects now facing U.S. private investors in foreign areas" (Wilfred Malenbaum, "America's Role in Economic Development Abroad," *Department of State Bulletin*, xx [March 27, 1949] 374) was countered by Secretary of the Treasury Snyder's opinion that "I doubt seriously whether any extensions of the guaranty provisions would be very effective in actually attracting more private investment to Europe." (U.S. Congress, House, Committee on Foreign Affairs, *Extension of the European Recovery Program, Hearings*, 81st Cong., 1st Sess., 1949, p. 377.)

for broadening the Program had been made in the 1949 European Recovery Program Hearings by the American Bar Association, including: an increase in the guaranty authorization to $1 billion and its separation from the ECA loan authorization; the extension of guaranty coverage to the convertibility of earnings and profits as well as of the capital originally invested; the extension of risk coverage to seizure or confiscation, destruction through riot or revolution, and "forced abandonment by the investor as a result of discriminatory policies of the foreign government. . . ."[12] All but the first of these suggestions were adopted by the House, despite the opposition of the ECA itself, but the Senate would not consent to such broadening of coverage, and convertibility remained the only insurable risk in the 1949 legislation.

The 1949 amendment to the Economic Cooperation Act of 1948 did, however, reflect some liberalization of policy. The definition of eligible enterprises was broadened to include the "expansion, modernization or development of existing enterprises," as well as the "furnishing of capital goods items and related services, for use in connection with projects approved by the Administrator," if these were not to be paid for entirely within the same fiscal year.[13] Coverage was also extended, within limits, to earnings and profits on tangible investments, as well as to profits from techniques or processes, if the latter were based on a tangible property investment. Specific limitations on earnings guaranties were left by Congress to the ECA, which set an over-all limitation of 175 per cent of the original capital invested, with more detailed restrictions applying to the first six years of the life of an investment.[14]

[12] Statement by Norman M. Littell, *ibid.*, p. 645.

[13] *An Act to Amend the Economic Cooperation Act of 1948*, 63 *Stat.* 51 (1949).

[14] Convertibility guaranties were limited to 100 per cent of the original capital invested during the first year of operation, and

The total guaranty authorization was reduced to $150 million by the 1949 legislation[15] (of which less than $3 million had been used when the bill was passed), but it was now separate from the ECA loan authorization, thus eliminating the "competitive" disadvantage from which the Program had suffered as long as guaranties issued reduced by their face amount the sums available for loans. Finally, the legal position of the United States with respect to claims was clarified in this bill, which provided that, after the payment of a claim, any currency or credits forthcoming from the investment should become the property of the U.S. Government *and* that the U.S. Government should be subrogated to any right, title, or claim in connection with these assets.[16]

In his message to Congress of June 24, 1949, on the implementation of the Point Four Program, President Truman recommended that the Guaranty Program be expanded to include underdeveloped areas and that it be administered entirely by the Export-Import Bank: "Since the development of underdeveloped economic areas is of major importance in our foreign policy, it is appropriate to use the resources of the Government to accelerate private efforts toward the end. I recommend, therefore, that the Export-Import Bank be authorized to guarantee United States private capital, invested in productive enterprises abroad which contribute to economic development in underdeveloped areas, against the risks peculiar to those investments."[17] Extensive hearings were held on this proposal in the House Banking and Currency Committee, both in 1949 and during the decade following.

---

could then increase by 15 per cent annually until the maximum total coverage of 175 per cent was reached.

[15] Ten million dollars of this was earmarked for informational media guaranties.

[16] *An Act to Amend the Economic Cooperation Act of 1948*, 63 *Stat.* 51-52 (1949).

[17] U.S. Department of State, *Point Four*, Washington, 1950, pp. 101-102.

But the House Foreign Affairs Committee effectively opposed such a transfer of authority to a "conservative" banking institution, and industrial guaranties remained the responsibility of ECA.

The House Foreign Affairs Committee continued its efforts to make the Guaranty Program an effective instrument in 1950 in the face of continued apathy and considerable opposition, not only from segments of the business community but from within ECA itself; spokesmen for ECA stated publicly their opposition to broadened guaranty coverage and the conviction that the Program should be transferred to the Export-Import Bank.[18] The Senate once again defeated in Conference the House's efforts to add war and revolution guaranty clauses and to increase the total guaranty authority to $300 million. The House Committee was successful, however, in extending guaranty coverage to loss through expropriation or confiscation, and in increasing the authority from $150 million to $200 million. Furthermore, the repatriation of royalties paid for the contribution of patents, processes, or techniques to a foreign enterprise, whether accompanied by a cash investment or not, was now made eligible for guaranty coverage.[19] And finally, the importance placed by Congress on the successful operation of the Program was incorporated into the legislation itself, at the insistence of the House Committee, in a phrase stating ". . . the intent of Congress that the guaranty herein authorized should be used to the maximum practicable extent and so administered as to increase the participation of private enterprise in achieving the purposes of this Act. . . ."[20]

[18] U.S. Congress, House, Committee on Foreign Affairs, *To Amend the Economic Cooperation Act of 1948, as Amended, Hearings*, 81st Cong., 2nd Sess., 1950, pp. 19, 58.
[19] *The Economic Cooperation Act of 1950*, 64 *Stat.* 198-199; and *U.S. Code Congressional Service*, 81st Cong., 2nd Sess., 1950, II, 2441-2463.
[20] *The Economic Cooperation Act of 1950*, 64 *Stat.* 200.

FROM EUROPE TO THE UNDERDEVELOPED WORLD

American involvement in the Korean hostilities in 1951 completely shifted the emphasis of the foreign aid program from the economic recovery of Europe to the military strengthening of the entire free world. With the expiration of the ECA and the Administration's failure to muster sufficient support for transferring investment guaranties to the Export-Import Bank, the program seemed doomed. But, during hearings on the new Mutual Security Act, several members of Congress favored widening the geographical coverage of the guaranties and, despite the Administration's lack of enthusiasm, they were authorized under the Mutual Security Act of 1951 "in any area in which assistance is authorized by this Act."[21] Although Administration policy called for the avoidance of "strings" on foreign aid, Congress nevertheless attached to the Mutual Security Act a number of criteria for aid. One of these was the controversial Benton Amendment, which made the extension of aid, including the Guaranty Program, conditional upon agreement to certain general actions to foster free private enterprise. The provision, as adopted, stated that the Act should be administered so as "to eliminate the barriers to, and provide the incentives for, a steadily increasing participation of free private enterprise in developing the resources of foreign countries consistent with the policies of this Act. . . ."[22]

On December 31, 1951, with the expiration of ECA, the Investment Guaranty Program was turned over to the Mutual Security Agency. The Paley Commission's Report to the President, issued in June 1952, gave its guarded approval: ". . . the present guaranties against inconvertibility and expropriation should be viewed as experimental pending longer and geographically more extended experi-

21 *Mutual Security Act of 1951, 65 Stat.* 384.
22 *Ibid.,* p. 382.

ence."[23] But the opposition spoke with a stronger voice; representative of a major segment of business opinion was the view that "there is now considerable agreement that this [Guaranty Program] has done little to stimulate investment overseas and it has probably lessened the feeling of responsibility which other governments should have towards U.S. investors."[24]

During the four years that followed, the legislative history of the Investment Guaranty Program was marked primarily by the continuing and frustrating struggle between the efforts in the House of Representatives to broaden and strengthen the Program and the unyielding, generally successful opposition in the Senate. Every year, the House legislation contained provisions for broadening the Program in area, time limit, and types of risk covered, stressing particularly the importance of extending risk coverage to war, revolution, and civil disorder. And every year the Senate forces, led by Senator Walter F. George of Georgia, nullified or drastically limited these extensions. Senator George's chief objection, as phrased by a Congressman who had supported expansion in the long wrangle, was apparently that "if you have a big American company over there that has a big investment and is losing money on it, some companies are ruthless enough that they will organize an insurrection so they can get their money back through the guaranty."[25] Whether

[23] U.S. President's Materials Policy Commission, *Resources for Freedom*, Washington, 1952, I, 69.

[24] Walter L. Lingle, Jr. (Vice-President, Procter and Gamble), "A Corporation's Approach to Overseas Investment," *Report of the 40th National Foreign Trade Convention*, New York, 1953, p. 160.

[25] Representative Walter H. Judd, U.S. Congress, House, Committee on Foreign Affairs, *Mutual Security Act of 1957, Hearings*, Washington, 85th Cong., 1st Sess., 1957, p. 1271. Steuart Pittman who, as Assistant General Counsel of ECA, was closely concerned with the Program's development, suggests that Senator George also regarded the Program as a possible source of discrimination against domestic investment. (From a letter dated Nov. 19, 1958.)

all the opponents of the Program's extension based their opposition on such an extreme view of the operation of perverse incentives is uncertain but, in any case, the quarrel had by 1955 reached such proportions that one particularly outspoken originator and supporter of the Program, Congressman Vorys of Ohio, complained that "anything that will make this guaranty effective will run into trouble in the Senate Foreign Relations Committee. We have marched up the Hill and down, year after year . . . they are dead set against making this guaranty work."[26]

The pressure of the House Foreign Affairs Committee for the introduction of war and revolution guaranties received support in 1954 from the findings of the Randall Report, which approved the Guaranty Program both because it removed obstacles to the initial consideration of private investment abroad and because, unlike a public loan, it required the private investor to judge the commercial risk attached to a proposed undertaking. The Report warned against the tendency of the Program to conceal the extent of the Government's stake in a project, but it recommended that the experimental program be continued and broadened by a war-risk guaranty.[27]

Although the findings of the Randall Commission were endorsed by the President as official government policy, the Congressional supporters of the Program expressed dissatisfaction several times during this period with the attitude of the executive branch, as reflected in the administration of the Investment Guaranty Program: "The Committee is not satisfied that 'broad criteria' have been applied by the executive branch to the guaranty provisions nor that the participation of private enterprise is being facilitated to the maximum extent practicable . . .

[26] U.S. Congress, House, Committee on Foreign Affairs, *Mutual Security Act of 1955*, *Hearings*, Washington, 84th Cong., 1st Sess., 1955, pp. 707-708.

[27] U.S. Commission on Foreign Economic Policy, *Report to the President and the Congress*, Washington, 1954, pp. 22-23.

the interpretation placed by the executive branch on the type of investment covered has been unduly narrow, contrary to the intent of Congress, . . . that the executive branch exercise the utmost imagination and effort to expand the investment guaranty program. . . ."[28]

Despite all the wrangling, some legislative extensions of the Guaranty Program did take place during this period. The Mutual Security Act of 1953 extended the Program's issuing authority to mid-1957, and lengthened the maximum term of guaranties from April 1962 to "twenty years from the date of issuance." It also extended the geographical scope of the Program to its ultimate limits, providing that guaranties might be issued "in any country with which the United States has agreed to institute the guaranty program," whether or not it was eligible for aid under the Mutual Security Act.[29] The following year, some broadening of coverage was provided by a seemingly minor change in the wording of the legislation: in the provision for expropriation guaranties the phrase "action of the government of a participating country"[30] was amended to read "by action of the government of a foreign nation."[31] The effect of this alteration was to provide for protection against expropriation by the government of an invading or occupying nation, i.e., protection against one possible source of loss as a result of war.[32]

The administration of the Investment Guaranty Program changed hands twice between mid-1953 and mid-1955. With the termination of the operations of the Mutual Security Agency on August 1, 1963, the industrial

[28] *U.S. Code Congressional and Administrative News*, 84th Cong., 1st Sess., 1955, ii, 2369.

[29] *Mutual Security Act of 1953*, 67 *Stat.* 158, 161; and *U.S. Code Congressional and Administrative News*, 83rd Cong., 1st Sess., 1953, ii, 1931, 1934.

[30] *Economic Cooperation Act of 1950*, 64 *Stat.* 199.

[31] *Mutual Security Act of 1954*, 68 *Stat.* 847.

[32] Arnold Rivkin, "Investment Guaranties and Private Investment," *Federal Bar Journal*, xix (Oct. 1959), 358.

guaranty program was transferred to the new Foreign Operations Administration (the informational media guaranties had been turned over to the State Department in mid-1952). Less than two years later, on June 30, 1955, the Mutual Security Program was divided, the military aspects to be administered by the Department of Defense and the economic by the Department of State. The Investment Guaranties staff came under the direction of the International Cooperation Administration, a newly established and semi-autonomous agency within the Department of State.

Throughout this administrative reshuffling, the Investment Guaranties staff managed to maintain continuity, and to concentrate on acquainting non-European countries with the Program and thus to increase the number of participating countries. Special efforts were directed toward the rather difficult negotiations for the first bilateral agreements with Latin American countries, eight of which were signed before the end of 1955.

Within the existing legislative framework, the Guaranties staff also introduced a number of administrative changes intended to increase the incentive effect of the Program:

1. Fees, which had ranged as high as 1 per cent for convertibility and 4 per cent for expropriation, were reduced to one-half of 1 per cent.

2. Convertibility insurance, previously limited to 175 per cent of the original investment, was raised to a maximum of 200 per cent.

3. The eligibility requirement that 85 per cent of the stock of an investor company be owned by the United States citizens was reduced to 51 per cent.

4. Conversion rights would no longer be reduced by the amount of earnings withdrawn without resort to the guaranty.[33]

[33] (U.S. President's) *Report to the Congress on the Mutual Security Program*, for the six months ended December 31, 1954, Washington, 1955, pp. 62-63.

Finally, several operational changes were made to shorten the processing time and simplify the procedure of obtaining a guaranty, the most important of which was the application of a single standard for investment proposals in both Europe and underdeveloped areas. The applicant no longer had to prove that his proposal would contribute directly to the specific objectives of the Mutual Security Program; indication of its value to the development of production or trade or to mutual defense in general was now sufficient.

LEGISLATIVE BROADENING AND RESTRICTION

The Mutual Security Act of 1956 brought, at last, a number of important legislative changes to increase the effectiveness of the Program.[34] The most important of these was that risk coverage for losses "by reason of war" was at last provided for; the House Foreign Affairs Committee had won part of its battle. But the new legislation restricted coverage to direct losses from war damage, and specifically excluded revolution and civil strife. Indeed, these latter risks were to remain excluded from the Program for another five years, despite the strong recommendations of the 1959 Boeschenstein and Straus reports to the President that such expanded coverage be provided.

The 1956 legislation extended the authority to issue guaranties by ten years, to June 30, 1967. It also provided in a number of ways for an increase in the maximum permissible dollar volume of guaranties. The statutory limitation on the total face value of the guaranties was increased from $200 million to $500 million and, for the first time, the media guaranty authorization, covering investments in the production or distribution abroad of American informational media, was no longer included in this sum. Furthermore, the amount of issuing authority, which represented the effective limitation on the dollar

[34] *Mutual Security Act of 1956*, 70 *Stat.*, 558-559; and *U.S. Code Congressional and Administrative News*, 84th Cong., 2nd Sess., 1956, II, 3235-3244.

volume of guaranties, might now be increased by the dollars received by the U.S. Government for any assets or foreign currency of an investor whose claim it had paid. Formerly the issuing authority could be increased only by the amounts of guaranties reduced, expired, or cancelled. Much more important for the expansion of the effective issuing authority was the provision that as of June 30, 1956, all guaranties could be issued on a fractional reserve basis. Previous legislation had required that the total face amount of guaranties be backed by the Administrator's notes purchased by the Treasury plus income from fees; now, in accordance with accepted banking and insurance practice, only 25 per cent need be held in notes and fees against the face value of the guaranties.[35]

The next two years were devoted to efforts to consolidate the Program's effectiveness under its existing legislative mandate. During this period the staff worked out bilateral agreements covering war risk guaranties; these were somewhat complicated because, unlike the convertibility and expropriation agreements, they required the provision for special (either national or most-favored-nation) treatment of guarantied enterprises in the event of war—a requirement which was dropped in 1962, as part of a general move toward simpler guaranty agreements. At the same time, the staff continued its emphasis on the movement

[35] The rationale underlying the provision for fractional reserves was given in the *Mutual Security Act of 1956*: "All guaranties issued after June 30, 1956 . . . shall be considered . . . as obligations only to the extent of the probable ultimate net cost to the Government of the United States of such guaranties" (70 Stat. 559). The reasons offered for regarding such reserves as sufficient were: 1) guarantied projects are widely dispersed geographically; 2) the United States takes over the investor's currency or claims after making payment under a guaranty; it is therefore not expected that such payments will represent total losses; 3) guarantied investments are "double counted" when an investor obtains both convertibility and expropriation guaranties; it is unlikely that both guaranties would ever be invoked to their face amounts, yet they are both charged in full to the guaranty authority.

of private capital to underdeveloped countries; although the Program was instituted with only one such country—Ghana—during 1958, negotiations were proceeding with about 30 more, and the first guaranty contracts ever issued in Iran, Bolivia, Ecuador, and India were concluded. "The education of foreign countries on climate matters and of potential United States private investors on investment opportunities,"[36] was also regarded as an essential aspect of the geographical expansion effort, and the chief of the Guaranties staff pointed out in the 1959 hearings that "a small information center on country investment is maintained for the benefit of the investor."[37]

In view of the fact that nearly $450 million in guaranties had been issued by mid-1959, and applications pending totaled nearly $1 billion, an increase in the issuing authority from $500 million to $1 billion was requested and received in the 1959 legislation. This doubled authorization was accompanied by a geographical restriction which completed the shift in focus which the Program had been undergoing since 1951: a Senate amendment adopted in the final bill effectively limited the Program after January 1, 1960 to the protection of investments in projects which are expected to be instrumental in "the development of the economic resources and productive capacities of economically underdeveloped areas."[38] Although, as Table 2 shows, the word "underdeveloped" was interpreted broadly enough to include several European countries which are not generally included in that term (i.e., Greece, Portugal, Spain, Yugoslavia), the more advanced coun-

[36] Testimony of Charles B. Warden, Chief, Investment Guaranties Staff, U.S. Congress, House, Committee on Foreign Affairs, *Mutual Security Act of 1957*, *Hearings*, 85th Cong., 1st Sess., 1957, p. 1260.

[37] Testimony of Mr. Warden, U.S. Congress, House, Committee on Foreign Affairs, *Mutual Security Act of 1959*, *Hearings*, 86th Cong., 1st Sess., 1959, p. 891.

[38] *Mutual Security Act of 1959*, 73 *Stat.* 251.

tries of Western Europe and Japan were thus rendered ineligible for future guaranties.[39]

The reasoning underlying this geographical limitation was made clear in the Foreign Relations Committee Report on the 1959 bill: "The committee was disturbed . . . by the fact that, of the $400 million in guaranties issued to date, $321 million have been to cover investments in the countries of Western Europe. . . . The program was originally established to encourage private investment in Western Europe, but that was at a time when Europe was prostrate from the war and was receiving massive Government economic assistance. This condition no longer exists. The focus of efforts to encourage private investment is now on underdeveloped countries. These efforts should certainly be pursued, but there is no reason to give this further encouragement to private investment in Europe."[40]

FOCUS ON THE DEVELOPING WORLD

It was in 1961, after the Investment Guaranty Program had experienced a year of sharply reduced activity resulting from the fact that guaranties for economically developed countries were no longer permitted and the Program was not really equipped to handle many of the complexities involved in guarantying investments in underdeveloped nations, that the legislative breakthrough finally came. The war-risk guaranty, which had gone virtually unutilized because investors found its coverage too narrow to be useful, was at last broadened to include revolution and insurrection. The Administration had, in fact, asked Congress to go even farther, and specifically authorize guaranty protection for all types of civil strife and for certain forms

[39] Countries which had signed guaranty agreements no longer eligible for further guaranties included: Austria, Belgium, Denmark, Finland, France, Germany, Ireland, Italy, Japan, Luxembourg, Netherlands, Norway, and United Kingdom.

[40] U.S. Congress, Senate, *The Mutual Security Act of 1959*, Report No. 412, 86th Cong., 1st Sess., 1959, p. 31.

of "creeping expropriation" as well.[41] Congress refused to extend the specific-risk guaranty coverage quite this far, but it did authorize an experimental, highly selective *all-risk* guaranty for high priority projects, which will be described more fully in Chapter IX on the Development Loan Fund and AID. But for the specific-risk program, the new legislation expanded not only the types but also the scope of guaranty coverage: eligibility for guaranties was now extended to wholly owned foreign-chartered subsidiaries of U.S. corporations, an extension for which American companies with investments abroad had long been pressing.[42]

The 1961 legislation provided directly for the expansion of the types of risks covered and of the types of enterprise eligible for coverage by the Investment Guaranty Program. It also provided indirectly for its geographical expansion by liberalizing the requirements for agreements with foreign governments instituting the Program. The rigid requirements that foreign governments recognize the U.S. Government's right to subrogation to claims and succession to ownership rights after claims have been paid were replaced by a phrase requiring simply that "the President shall make suitable arrangements for protecting the interests of the United States Government."[43] This change was expected to reduce the obstacles encountered in negotiating agreements to institute the Program with many Latin American nations, either because their insistence on legislative ratification of such agreements often led to delays of many months or years, or because constitutional or statutory provisions barring ownership of real property

[41] U.S. Department of State, *An Act for International Development, Fiscal Year 1962. A Summary Presentation*, Washington, 1961, p. 106.

[42] *Foreign Assistance Act of 1961*, 75 Stat. 429. In the 1963 legislation, the requirement of 100 per cent U.S. ownership was modified to allow for outside ownership of not more than 5 per cent of the shares where such ownership was required by law.

[43] *Ibid.*, p. 430.

by a foreign government prevented them from recognizing the succession rights of the U.S. Government. Although the intention was that agreements specifically recognizing these subrogation and succession (or "turnover") rights should still be negotiated whenever possible, "This new provision will allow alternative agreements suited to the particular circumstances of the case where legal obstacles in less-developed countries inhibit their entry into standard form bilateral agreements."[44]

After the extensive changes of 1961, the legislation on the Investment Guaranty Program remained substantially the same for two years. Except for a provision in the Foreign Assistance Act of 1963 that the issuance of any guaranty should "consider the possible adverse effect of the dollar investment under such guaranty upon the balance of payments of the United States,"[45] the only changes in the Program's legislative authorization were financial. The ceiling on the face amount of guaranties issued was raised from $1 billion to $1.3 billion in the 1962 legislation, and to $2.5 billion the following year, in recognition of the Program's sudden and rapid increase in activity. Concurrently, the requirements for reserves against guaranties outstanding were steadily reduced. The 1961 legislation set up a single reserve for both specific-risk and DLF (later AID) extended-risk guaranties, and provided that both types of guaranty should be considered as obligations only to the extent of their "probable ultimate net cost" to the Government.[46] The administering agency first interpreted this requirement by putting *all* guaranties on a 25 per cent reserve basis, but later reduced the requirement for specific-risk guaranties to 12 per cent. The 1963 legislation, formalizing a ruling of the Attorney General the year be-

[44] U.S. Congress, House, Committee on Foreign Affairs, *Mutual Security Act of 1961*, *Report*, 87th Cong., 1st Sess., House Report No. 851, Washington, 1961, pp. 36-37.

[45] *Foreign Assistance Act of 1963*, 77 *Stat.* 382.

[46] *Foreign Assistance Act of 1961*, 75 *Stat.* 431.

fore, provided that all guaranties "shall be considered contingent obligations backed by the full faith and credit of the Government of the United States of America."[47] Although obligated funds and fee income were retained as a primary reserve for the payment of claims, the necessity for any particular ratio of reserves to guaranties was thus abolished, leaving the legislative ceiling of $2.5 billion as the only limitation on the permissible volume of guaranties.

In November 1961, the International Cooperation Administration and the Development Loan Fund both went out of existence, and their functions were absorbed by the newly created Agency for International Development (AID) within the Department of State. The Guaranties Division, now a part of the Office of Development Finance and Private Enterprise, remained essentially intact and continued to concentrate on the extension of the Guaranty Program. One major aspect of its work was the negotiation of new or expanded agreements instituting the Program.

Between the beginning of 1962 and March 31, 1964, agreements were signed with 18 countries which had not heretofore participated in the Program, bringing the total number of participating countries to the 58 shown in Table 2. Thirteen of these were in Africa, including Egypt, Ethiopia, and a number of newly independent states, and 4 in Latin America. In addition, 13 agreements, including 4 with such important Latin American nations as Argentina, Bolivia, Chile, and Colombia, were amended to permit expanded risk coverage; in many cases, possible coverage was extended from convertibility risk only to expropriation, war, revolution, or insurrection and extended risks. The new legislation proved particularly useful in the difficult and important negotiations of agreements or amendments with Latin American nations. In the cases of Colombia and Venezuela, for example, it made possible the

[47] *Foreign Assistance Act of 1963*, 77 *Stat.* 382.

TABLE 2

Countries Where Investment Guaranties Are Available,
as of March 31, 1964

Country	Type of Guaranty		
	Converti-bility	Expropri-ation	War, Revolution, Insurrection, Extended Risk
Afghanistan	X	X	X[a]
Argentina	X	X	X
Bolivia	X	X	X
Chile	X	X	X
China, Republic of	X	X	X
Colombia	X	X	X
Congo (Brazzaville)	X	X	X
Congo (Leopoldville)	X	X	X
Costa Rica	X	X	
Cyprus	X	X	X
Dominican Republic	X	X	X
Ecuador	X	X	X
El Salvador	X	X	
Ethiopia	X	X	
Gabon	X	X	X
Ghana	X	X	
Greece	X	X	X
Guatemala	X	X	
Guinea	X	X	X
Haiti	X	X	
Honduras	X	X	
India	X	X	
Iran	X	X	
Israel	X	X	X
Ivory Coast	X	X	X
Jamaica	X	X	X
Jordan	X	X	X
Korea	X	X	X[a]
Liberia	X	X	X[a]
Malagasy, Rep. of	X	X	X
Malaya, Fed. of	X	X	
Morocco	X	X	X
Nepal	X	X	X
Nicaragua	X	X	X[a]
Niger	X	X	X
Nigeria	X	X	

TABLE 2—continued

Country	Type of Guaranty		
	Converti-bility	*Expropri-ation*	*War, Revolution, Insurrection, Extended Risk*
Pakistan	X	X	
Panama	X	X	Xa
Paraguay	X	X	
Peru	X		
Philippines	X	X	
Portugal	X	X	
Senegal	X	X	X
Sierra Leone	X	X	X
Somali Republic	X	X	X
Spain	X	X	
Sudan	X	X	X
Tanganyika	X	X	X
Thailand	X	X	Xa
Togo	X	X	X
Trinidad-Tobago	X	X	X
Tunisia	X	X	X
Turkey	X	X	
U.A.R. (Egypt)	X	X	X
Uruguayb	X	X	
Venezuela	X	X	X
Vietnam	X	X	X
Yugoslaviac	X	X	

And the underdeveloped overseas dependencies of the following countries:

Denmark	X	X	
France	X	X	
Netherlands	X	X	
Norway	X	X	
United Kingdom	X		

a War risk only; revolution, insurrection and extended risk guaranties not available.

b Although applications will be accepted for Uruguay, guaranties cannot be processed until agreement is ratified by the country's legislative body.

c Available only under special Presidential waiver.

Source: Agency for International Development, Investment Guaranties Division.

institution of interim agreements, permitting the provisional issuance of guaranties on a unilateral basis by the United States before the agreements were ratified, and it also made possible the long-desired negotiation of an agreement with Venezuela despite the fact that legal and political difficulties here made the recognition of U.S. subrogation and turnover rights impossible.[48]

Much of the Guaranties Division's effort in this period was devoted simply to keeping up with the remarkable increase in demand for guaranties. This boom in demand, which originated in the Cuban expropriations of U.S. private investments during 1960—including some investments which had no guaranty protection because their owners had thought such protection unnecessary in such a "safe" country—was intensified by the broadening of guaranty coverage to include revolution and insurrection risks and the extension of eligibility to wholly owned subsidiaries in 1961. As a result, the Division was soon swamped by a backlog of guaranty applications, reflected in the figures in Table 5, and devoted considerable effort to the search for methods of streamlining the guaranty-issuing procedure. A special department was set up just to screen and process applications, and lawyers embarked on the complex problem of working out standard forms for guaranty contracts in order to obviate the necessity of writing a new contract for each investor. These standardized contracts were put into use during the first half of 1964.

THE GROWTH OF THE PROGRAM

During the decade following its inception in 1948, the Investment Guaranty Program grew steadily, not without pauses, but with an upward trend of increasing accelera-

[48] Statement by Hon. Frank M. Coffin, Chairman, Program Development Group of the President's Task Force on Foreign Economic Assistance, and Managing Director, Development Loan Fund, June 26, 1961 (Mimeo.), and discussions with members of the Investment Guaranties Division.

tion which reached a peak in 1958. During the three years that followed, the value of guaranties issued dropped off sharply, for reasons we shall consider later. But then, in 1962 and 1963, it bounced back to set new records; the total face value of guaranty contracts issued in those two years alone was greater than the value of all contracts issued during the 14 preceding years. By the end of 1963, as Table 3 shows, the face value of all guaranties issued since the Program's inception totaled $1,399.1 million, of which $1,070.7 million was outstanding. Of this total $744.2 million was for convertibility, $594.6 million for expropriation, and $59.2 million for war risk. These guaranties covered investments in 47 countries; of the total issued, more than $1 billion had been for investments in 38 different underdeveloped areas. Guaranty applications totaling another $5,756.1 million, all for underdeveloped countries, were in process as of the end of 1963.

All but a handful of these guaranties had been issued in the years after 1955. For, as Tables 4 and 5 make clear, the Guaranty Program had initially gotten off to a slow start. Only one convertibility guaranty, for an $850,000 investment in a carbon-black plant in Great Britain, had been issued by the end of 1948, although the Program had been instituted with 12 European countries and 12 applications totaling over $5 million were pending. By the end of 1949 the Program included 14 signed contracts with a combined value of $3.9 million; by the end of the following year the tally had jumped to 26 contracts totaling $24.9 million, of which more than half was accounted for by the $14.5 million guaranty issued to Standard Oil of New Jersey for investment in an Italian subsidiary. The first expropriation guaranties were issued in 1951 for two investments in West Germany which had joined the list of participating countries the previous year. By the time the Program passed from ECA to the Mutual Security Agency at the end of 1951 it had issued 37 contracts for investments and earnings valued at $33.5 million, $1.3

million for expropriation and the rest for convertibility risks.

Three non-European countries—Nationalist China, Israel, and the Philippines—signed bilateral agreements instituting the Guaranty Program during 1952. The total value of guaranties issued increased rather slowly during that year and those immediately following, equaling $39.8 million at the end of 1952, $42.4 million a year later, and $48.5 million by the close of 1954. By the latter date 21 countries, 6 of them non-European, were Program participants, 18 of them having signed agreements covering expropriation as well as convertibility guaranties.

During 1955, the Foreign Operation Administration's second full year, bilateral convertibility agreements were signed with 10 new countries, 6 of them in Latin America, which had until then refused to negotiate such agreements. All but 2 of the new Program members also consented to

TABLE 3

Specific-Risk Investment Guaranties
Authorized and in Effect, as of December 31, 1963[a]

Country	Guaranties Authorized	Balance Outstanding
Afghanistan	$ 800,000	$ 800,000
Algeria	15,750,000	3,500,000
Argentina	284,961,100	271,309,790
Austria	2,030,000	0
Belgium	552,000	120,000
Bolivia	21,264,448	7,138,928
China, Rep. of	64,371,603	57,006,200
Colombia	1,010,000	1,010,000
Congo (Leopoldville)	950,000	730,991
Costa Rica	1,397,996	1,061,771
Denmark	182,500	0
Ecuador	7,695,465	7,678,065
El Salvador	2,400,000	2,400,000
France	50,288,831	16,129,719
French Guiana	200,000	200,000
Germany	58,731,231	40,964,807

TABLE 3—continued

Country	Guaranties Authorized	Balance Outstanding
Greece	5,894,700	5,647,088
Guatemala	3,219,000	2,400,000
Guinea	72,000,000	65,000,000
Haiti	4,623,360	2,660,000
Honduras	5,046,700	4,660,700
India	92,487,032	87,005,390
Iran	20,918,351	20,867,758
Italy	159,221,326	24,205,592
Ivory Coast	4,331,000	4,331,000
Israel	171,390	171,390
Jamaica	206,000	150,000
Japan	5,294,000	2,000,000
Jordan	8,000,000	0
Korea	91,678,116	91,678,116
Liberia	21,404,500	21,404,500
Malaya	1,934,250	1,934,250
Morocco	6,297,696	6,297,696
Netherlands	11,327,891	187,750
Pakistan	76,721,000	76,721,000
Paraguay	10,824,000	6,254,000
Peru	13,420,857	10,531,239
Philippines	11,670,850	9,514,554
Portugal	8,000,000	8,000,000
Thailand	13,350,160	12,775,460
Trinidad	17,749,125	14,472,615
Tunisia	11,697,400	9,797,400
Turkey	133,760,136	121,273,663
United Kingdom	32,381,099	9,869,412
Venezuela	31,174,000	31,174,000
Vietnam	7,680,238	7,680,238
Yugoslavia	4,000,000	2,000,000
Total	$1,399,069,351	$1,070,715,082

ª These figures differ slightly from those given in the *Cumulative Report of All Specific Risk Investment Guaranties Issued Since the Beginning of the Program through December 31, 1963*. The figures given there were: Guaranties issued, $1,434,454,335; balance outstanding, $1,125,215,090.

Source: Agency for International Development, *Financial Summary of the Investment Guaranty Program*, Quarterly Issue, as of December 31, 1963.

TABLE 4

Investment Guaranties Issued, 1948-1963[a]

(in millions of U.S. dollars)

Calendar Year	Developed Countries	Underdeveloped Countries	Total
1948	2.0	—	2.0
1949	3.9	—	3.9
1950	19.6	—	19.6
1951	8.5	—	8.5
1952	3.0	2.8	5.8
1953	2.6	—	2.6
1954	6.1	—	6.1
1955	37.7	8.3	46.0
1956	21.2	7.8	29.0
1957	45.4	18.6	64.0
1958	98.7	113.3	212.0
1959	67.7	29.8	97.5
1960	.2[b]	63.6	63.8
1961	—	71.1	71.1
1962	—	440.8	440.8
1963	—	362.4	362.4
1964 (to March 31)	—	88.4	88.4
Total	316.6	1,206.9	1,523.5

[a] Slight discrepancies between the figures given here and those cited in the text for the early years of the Program are due to the fact that the latter come from annual or semiannual reports to Congress of the agency administering the Program, while the data in this table are cumulative figures, adjusted as of the end of 1963 for a variety of minor discrepancies in the annual data.

[b] Amendment of existing contract.

Source: Agency for International Development, Investment Guaranties Division.

the institution of expropriation guaranties in their countries. Agreements now existed with 12 European, 6 Latin American, 4 Far Eastern, and 4 Near Eastern countries. During 1955 also, the number of contracts issued increased from 69 to 98 and their total value from $48.5 million to $94.5 million. The Program had picked up considerable

TABLE 5

Applications Pending for Investment Guaranties, 1948-1963,
Active as of December 31
(in millions of U.S. dollars)

Calendar Year	Developed Countries	Underdeveloped Countries	Total
1948	5.4	—	5.4
1949	32.0	2.3	34.3
1950	36.2	12.9	49.1
1951	27.9	10.3	38.2
1952	36.0	17.2	53.2
1953	41.2	46.1	87.3
1954	98.0	34.0	132.0
1955	113.0	160.0	273.0
1956	182.4	327.7	510.1
1957	154.9	476.7	631.6
1958	429.0	611.0	1,040.0
1959	[a]	1,072.5	1,072.5
1960	[a]	1,440.1[b]	1,440.1
1961	[a]	3,173.6[b]	3,173.6
1962	[a]	3,173.2[b]	3,173.2
1963	[a]	5,756.1[b]	5,756.1

[a] Developed countries not eligible for guaranties after December 31, 1959.

[b] Does not include applications for non-participating countries or countries where particular type of coverage desired is not available.

Source: Agency for International Development, Investment Guaranties Division.

momentum. By the end of 1956, after the ICA's Investment Guaranties staff had taken over, there were 144 contracts in 15 countries, with coverage of $92.5 million for convertibility and $31.0 million for expropriation. Applications pending at that time had reached the then unprecedented sum of more than half a billion dollars, representing 25 countries.[49]

[49] Guaranties issued in any given year, as Tables 4 and 5 show, are always a rather small proportion of guaranties pending. This is due to the fact that many applications may be pending over

War risk agreements were signed with 6 countries during 1957, 5 of them underdeveloped, and by the end of the year applications for this type of guaranty had been processed, but various delays, often involving investors' disappointment at the limitations of the guaranty, prevented the actual completion of any such contracts during the year. The number of participant countries had by now reached 31 and the total face value of all guaranties $187.5 million, $151.9 million of which were still in effect, after reductions and cancellations had been subtracted. Pending applications, even after more than $100 million of them had been culled out as inactive or abandoned, stood at $632 million, representing 29 countries.

In terms of both new guaranty contracts completed and of applications received, the Program did more business during 1958 than in all the previous 9 years of its existence. Guaranties issued rose by $212 million to $400 million, while pending applications jumped from $632 million to more than $1 billion, and for the first time in the Program's history, more than half of the completed contracts as well as the applications were for investments in underdeveloped areas. Guaranties were written for the first time in 4 such countries, and 2 of the largest contracts yet issued—a $72 million expropriation guaranty for an Olin-Mathieson bauxite development project in Guinea and a $17.8 million convertibility contract for the W. R. Grace Company's fertilizer plant in Trinidad—were concluded for investment projects in less-advanced areas. In these transactions, for the first time, a significant proportion of the American investment was obtained from insurance companies and other institutional lenders. This was an important sign that one of the nation's largest sources of investment capital was at last becoming available, at least

---

several years while an investor completes his plans and also to the fact that numerous others, representing only tentative investment plans that are subsequently changed or abandoned, never become final guaranty contracts.

under the protection of public guaranties or participations, for projects contributing to the development of backward economies. In addition, in the case of the Olin-Mathieson enterprise, guaranties were provided for the first time to a project developing a country's basic resources, including port facilities, a railroad, hospitals, and schools.

Program participation, in terms of dollar volume, dropped off sharply in the three years following the 1958 peak. Guaranties issued totaled $97.5 million in 1959, of which $29.8 million were for less-developed areas. The 1960 total, representing such areas exclusively, was $63.8 million; in 1961 it rose slightly, to $71.1 million. A part of this decline, particularly that which took place after 1959, was due to the fact that developed countries became ineligible for the issuance of new guaranties at the beginning of 1960. In fact, this legislation had begun to have an anticipatory effect even during 1959, after it was passed but before it went into effect. But the apparent decline of that year is sharpened by an essentially random factor: the fact that during the peak year 1958, 5 exceptionally large investments, some of which had been under negotiation for as long as 3 years, reached the stage of contract issuance and, in fact, accounted for $179 million of the $212 million in guaranties issued during that year. In terms of the number of contracts issued, the total actually rose from 60 in 1958 to 103 in 1959, dropping down to 46 only in 1960, when new guaranties were restricted to investments in less-developed areas. During early 1961 the Program showed some signs of picking up again, but its recovery was limited by the fact that the latter half of the year was a period of considerable confusion created by the combination of a change in Administration, important changes in authorizing legislation, and the administrative reorganization as ICA expired and AID took its place. But while contract issuance lagged, interest in the Program did not, and the result was a near doubling in applications pending, from $1.1 billion in 1959 to $2.0 billion at the end of

1961, all for investments in less-developed countries. Thirteen such countries joined the Program during these three years, including 6 in Latin America, 5 in Africa, and 2 in the Far East. And war-risk guaranties were written for the first time, for a total of slightly less than $2 million, a little over $1 million of it in Asia.

The changes which had caused confusion in 1961 bore fruit in 1962; during that year 144 guaranty contracts were issued for the unprecedented total of $440.8 million. Even so, the volume of applications pending at the end of the year rose again, to $3.2 billion. During 1963 the pace was maintained even though the dollar volume was not; the face value of the 171 contracts issued totaled $362.4 million, and the sum of applications pending at the end of the year spiraled upward to $5.8 billion. Among the major investments for which guaranties were obtained during these two years were: a) The $72 million PASA petrochemicals project in Argentina, which also received funds from the IFC and the IDB; 29 different investors in the United States, both business and institutional, acquired convertibility guaranties totaling $77.3 million[50] and expropriation guaranties totaling $52.5 million, and in addition, extended risk guaranties totaling $7 million were issued by AID. b) The Gulf Oil Company's investment in an oil refinery in Korea, for which it acquired $32 million of convertibility coverage, an equal amount for expropriation, and $27 million against war risk; this investment alone accounted for much of the increase in war-risk guaranties and by the end of 1963 such contracts totaled about $60 million, including also $14 million in China (Taiwan) and $11 million in Venezuela. c) The Eregli integrated steel mill in Turkey, a $245 million project to be constructed by three U.S. firms, for which the DLF

[50] A figure for convertibility guaranties larger than the entire cost of the project is explained by the fact that convertibility contracts can cover capital and earnings up to 200 per cent of the original investment.

had provided $129.6 million of the financing; U.S. investors obtained convertibility guaranties for $21 million and expropriation guaranties for $20 million.

A geographical breakdown indicates even more clearly than do the over-all figures the fact that 1958 marked a turning point in the utilization of the Investment Guaranty Program for projects in underdeveloped areas. As of mid-1958, less than 20 per cent (in dollar volume) of all guaranties ever issued were for such investment; one year later, even before legislation had restricted the program to less-developed areas, the proportion had doubled. By early 1964, guaranties issued for projects in a total of 39 underdeveloped countries and dependencies accounted for nearly four-fifths of all guaranties ever issued; the 9 advanced countries for which guaranty contracts had been issued prior to 1960 accounted for only 21 per cent of the total dollar volume of contracts. As of March 31, 1964 contracts with a total face value of $441.0 million had been acquired for investments in Latin America; the comparable figures were $383.6 million for the Near East and South Asia, $326.7 million for Europe, $198.6 million for the Far East, and $132.4 million for Africa.

THE FLOW OF PRIVATE FUNDS

All the figures cited so far refer to the face value of guaranty contracts issued, while what we really want to know is the amount of American private funds that have been invested abroad in conjunction with the operations of the Investment Guaranty Program. The total of private funds invested is a good deal smaller than the total face value of guaranty contracts issued in the same period, because a single investment is double counted in the face value figures whenever both convertibility and expropriation guaranties are held for the same investment. If the investor held a war-risk guaranty as well, his investment would actually be triple counted. In some cases, on the other hand, the face value figures include only part of a given investment. This happens, for example, when guaranties have been taken out on the equity but not the loan portion of an investment, or vice versa, but this incomplete coverage is a much smaller factor than the double counting.

The total value of all investments of cash, loans, or equipment abroad through the Guaranty Program as of March 31, 1964, is estimated by the Guaranties Division at $719 million, plus $75 million in the form of contributions of techniques, processes, or other services for which royalties or other payments are received. Of this total, Latin America received $246 million, more than $200 million of it since 1960, with $151 million accounted for by Argentina alone. The Near-East—South Asia region received the next largest share, $212 million, with over half this total accounted for by two countries: India and Turkey. Investments in Europe, which until 1955 gave the Guaranty Program virtually all its business, came to $180 million, or less than one-quarter of the total, in early 1964. Guarantied investments in Africa, a relative latecomer to the Program, totaled $90 million, $51 million of it in Guinea, while only $66 million had been invested through the Program in the Far East, almost all of it in China (Taiwan) and Korea.[51]

Table 6 suggests that the flow of private funds abroad through the Investment Guaranty Program followed roughly the same chronological pattern as did the dollar value of guaranties issued, with a relatively gradual growth at first, considerable acceleration from 1955 through 1958, a drop-off in 1959-1961, and then a spurt to new heights in 1962 and 1963. Roughly half of the dollar value of all the guarantied investments which have been made during the lifetime of the Investment Guaranty Program appears to be accounted for by these last two

[51] Unpublished study provided by the Investment Guaranties Division, June 1964. By December 31, 1964, the figure for total value of all investments had reached $1 billion.

TABLE 6

U.S. Private Funds Which Have Gone Abroad
through the Specific-Risk Investment Guaranty Program,
as of March 31, 1964

(in millions of U.S. dollars)

Calendar Year[a]	Amount
1948	$ 2.0
1949	3.3
1950	15.6
1951	8.2
1952	4.8
1953	2.0
1954	3.9
1955	21.5
1956	16.8
1957	41.3
1958	109.3
1959	61.1
1960	40.1
1961	50.0
1962	226.3
1963	160.1
1964 (through March 31)	27.3
Total	$793.6[b]

[a] Date of contract issuance.

[b] Includes $74.9 million of investments in the form of processes, techniques, or technical assistance, for which royalties or fees are received.

Source: Agency for International Development, Investment Guaranties Division.

years. This time-path is a tentative one, however, since our annual figures are based entirely on the date of contract issuance, while in reality the flow of investment funds under a guaranty issued in a given year may be spread out over a number of years. Very little is known about this flow-of-funds pattern, but the Guaranties Division estimates that the bulk of an investment generally takes place during the period, averaging about 18 months, immediately preceding the actual issuance of a guaranty contract, unlike the private flows associated with the five lending agencies under study, which generally take place after the loan authorization date. This is because of the Guaranty Program's "waiver letter" procedure, which permits a guaranty applicant to go ahead with his investment in advance of signing a contract, and postpones the actual issuance of a contract until "investment arrangements are finalized and can be fully described in the contract."[52]

All the figures so far cited concerning the flow of private funds refer to the amounts of American investment actually covered by guaranties. The total funds from all sources invested in projects financed at least in part by guarantied investments would, of course, total considerably more. Complete figures of this sort are not available, but data from two questionnaire surveys of investors who had obtained guaranties, together covering the period from June 1960 to December 1963, suggest that the total amount of U.S. investment in projects covered by investment guaranties is between 30 and 50 per cent greater than the figures given here. This same sample indicates that a substantial amount of non-U.S. funds—perhaps between 50 and 100 per cent of the American total—have also been invested in these projects.[53]

BUSINESS OPINIONS

The attitudes of the American business community toward the concept of government investment guaranties exerted a powerful influence on the speed and direction of the Investment Guaranty Program's growth. Like the Program itself, business enthusiasm for it grew very gradually at

[52] Letter from Mrs. Ellen C. Hughes, Investment Guaranties Division, dated April 26, 1961.

[53] AID, "Surveys of Investment Projects Covered by Investment Guaranties," 1962 and 1964 (Mimeo.). Available summaries included a 95 per cent sample, by dollar amounts of guaranties, from the first survey and a 50 per cent sample from the second.

first. Initial reactions were not encouraging; some typical answers to a poll of executives conducted by *Business Week*[54] just after the Program was announced in 1948 were:

"We're too busy trying to supply the domestic demand for our products to worry about the opportunities in Europe."

"The guaranty against losses through exchange controls doesn't make up for the other risks involved in investing today in Europe. The guaranty doesn't cover any increase in the value of investment."

"This guaranty is just more government paternalism; the taxpayers' money should not be used this way."

At the same time, two powerful business associations, the National Association of Manufacturers and the National Foreign Trade Council, expressed unequivocal opposition to the guaranty idea. Both groups feared that the Program would entail undue government regulation of or involvement in business, and felt strongly that the provision of guaranties was the responsibility of the host, not the United States, government.[55]

The United States Council of the International Chamber of Commerce, although it favored giving the Program a trial in the hopes that it would reduce the amounts expended in "give-away programs" stated at its very inception the four objections which business groups have voiced most often ever since, that guaranties might:

1. Weaken the incentive to foreign countries to improve the investment climate.

2. Involve undesirable government intrusion into the affairs of private business concerns, particularly since some

[54] " 'Invest in Europe,' says ECA," *Business Week*, June 19, 1948, p. 118.

[55] Austin T. Foster, "Legislative Implementation of the Point Four Program," *Report of the Thirty-Sixth National Foreign Trade Convention*, New York, 1949, p. 152.

screening of "desirable" from "undesirable" investment projects would be necessary.

3. Result in unfair discrimination against existing investments.

4. Result in the loss of billions of dollars by the government and, ultimately, the American taxpayer.[56]

This general problem of perverse incentives, implied in the first point above and stated more strongly by Secretary of Commerce Charles Sawyer in 1952, when he said "Guarantees offered by the United States against occurrences which are the result of policies pursued in other countries would tend to encourage rather than discourage unsound policies, and to promote the very thing which the businessman is afraid of,"[57] is one which every commercial insurance scheme also must face. And, just as in the private case, its seriousness depends very largely on how the guarantor administers cases involving claims. If either the guarantied investor or the host country felt that it could profit from a situation in which the U.S. Government paid off under a guaranty contract, such a danger might be one to consider. But, as far as investors are concerned, arrangements for procedures to be followed prior to the payment of claims make it highly unlikely that a firm would find a guaranty payment more profitable than continued operation of the enterprise or its disposal by more conventional methods. And, with respect to the host governments, numerous provisions of the Program are specifically designed to avoid the inclination to such behavior, chief among them the requirement of host approval for all guarantied projects and the provision that the U.S. Government acquire title to all assets and claims for which it makes payment to an American firm under a guaranty contract. The fact that, between

[56] U.S. Council of the International Chamber of Commerce, *Intelligent International Investment*, New York, 1949, pp. 9-12.

[57] "Europe's Business Tasks: How U.S. Can Help," *U.S. News and World Report*, Dec. 26, 1952, p. 71.

1948 and 1963, the U.S. Government has had to pay only one investor under a guaranty contract suggests that these countries recognize, too, the adverse effect which irresponsible actions leading to guaranty claims would have on their international credit standing.[58]

From the beginning the Program also had its supporters in the business community. Representatives of the important Detroit Board of Commerce and of some of the country's most powerful giant corporations appeared regularly at Congressional hearings with suggestions for improving the Program, which they regarded as an important aspect of the Government's over-all effort to increase foreign investment. And, over the years, with legislative broadening, administrative improvements, and the favorable experiences of individual participants, the fears which lay behind much of the opposition have abated. Experience has shown that participating countries almost always offer a more favorable investment climate than non-participants; the gradual reduction in the amount of information required of a guaranty applicant and the absence of any interference by the Guaranties Division in the management of a guarantied investment has convinced many skeptics that government support need not mean government control; and the obvious inclination of host governments to treat all foreign investments alike, whether guarantied or not, has allayed fears of discriminatory advantages for new investments. Indeed, by 1959, the U.S. Chamber of Commerce had completely reversed its "perverse incentive" position, saying: "Apparently the Investment Guaranty Program has done much to impress participating nations with a sense of responsibility in recognizing the international morality of contracts. At any rate, the presence of

[58] These arguments, of course, might not hold in cases where a group hostile to all private enterprise seizes power through revolution. It is highly doubtful that either U.S. Government claims on assets or fear of the loss of international credit standing would have prevented seizures of U.S. owned private property in Cuba.

agreements has had a healthy effect on the investment climate. Applications for insurance are not only on the rise, but also coming in for underdeveloped countries once considered too unstable and risky."[59]

General feelings toward the Program do not always dictate the course of individual action in regard to it, as is demonstrated by the fact that a number of those expressing strong opposition to the general principle of public insurance of private risk are nevertheless participants in the Guaranty Program.[60] In its effort to discover the effect of investment guaranties on action rather than opinion, a 1953 Department of Commerce Study came up with the following results: of its 366 respondents (247 of whom were foreign investors), about half were acquainted with the Program. Of the foreign investors, 52 per cent said that guaranty insurance had a generally encouraging effect on foreign investment and only 5 per cent said it did not. But 65 per cent replied that this insurance had had no effect on their own investment decisions, though some had or felt they might acquire insurance after the decision had been made. Only 8 per cent said that the existence of the Program had encouraged their decisions, while 9 per cent more felt that they might make use of the guaranties. But not one executive interviewed felt that, in any single investment decision, the existence of guaranties had tipped the scales.[61]

That business enthusiasm for and utilization of the Guaranty Program increased greatly with the passage of time is made clear by several more recent surveys of business opinion. Of the 55 corporations, all of them Program participants, who answered a questionnaire distributed in connection with a study made in 1957-1958

[59] The Chamber of Commerce of the United States, *Spotlight on Foreign Aid*, Washington, 1959, pp. 21-22.

[60] U.S. Department of Commerce, Bureau of Foreign Commerce, *Factors Limiting U.S. Investment Abroad*, Washington, II, 1954, 26.

[61] *Ibid.*, pp. 26-30.

by a group of students at the Harvard Business School, 50 per cent replied that their investments would have been made even without guaranties, 20 per cent were not sure, and 20 per cent said definitely that the investments would not have been made if guaranties had not been available.[62] By 1958-1959, the group of foreign investments made possible by the existence of the Investment Guaranty Program, which did not seem to exist at all in 1953, had grown still further; of the 41 Program participants who responded to a Commerce Department questionnaire regarding private investment abroad, half said that "their decision to invest abroad was based upon the availability of a guaranty."[63] And by the early 1960's the swing of the pendulum seemed clear; of 91 respondents to two surveys conducted by the Investment Guaranties Division, 59, or nearly two-thirds, stated that they would not have made their investments without the guaranty. Only 23 said that they would have done so, and 9 gave uncertain replies.[64]

The 1958-1959 Commerce Department Survey also indicated a growing sense of the importance of investment guaranties among the larger business community, whether currently Program participants or not. Of the 110 respondents, all with international business interests, whose plans for expansion were based on the assumption that they would receive some type of government assistance,

[62] Peter Strauss *et al.*, *The Investment Guaranty Program*, Cambridge, Mass., 1958, p. 45.

[63] U.S. Department of Commerce, *Reportorial Review: Responses to Business Questionnaire Regarding Private Investment Abroad*, Washington, 1959, p. 9.

[64] AID, "Surveys. . . ." Of 54 U.S. business respondents to a similar query in the World Bank's 1961 survey 13 called the availability of guaranties a "significant factor" in their investment decisions, 6 said it was "not a significant factor," and 35 gave no reply. This respondent group included firms which had not invested in less-developed countries as well as some which had, either with or without guaranties. IBRD, *Multilateral Investment Insurance*, Washington, 1962, pp. 39-40.

the largest number indicated that they would probably seek ICA guaranties. When asked what sort of increases or changes in government assistance would encourage their own expansion plans still further, 50 of 184 respondents cited increased availability and widened coverage of ICA investment guaranties. Only tax concessions were mentioned more often (51 instances) in reply to this query. Similarly, in response to a question asking what government inducements were considered necessary, in general, to encourage greater private investment abroad, investment guaranties again ranked second only to tax incentives. They were mentioned by 49 per cent of 358 respondents "as a stimulant to increased private participation in the economic growth of underdeveloped countries," and only 8 respondents opposed an expansion of the Guaranty Program.[65]

QUESTIONS OF COVERAGE

There is little question that by the early 1960's the Investment Guaranty Program had at last begun to have a growing incentive effect, at least collateral and sometimes decisive, on the movement of American capital abroad. But some problems remained as obstacles to the Program's expansion. Among the difficulties most often cited by foreign investors, both participant and non-participant, were those of inadequate coverage, both functional and geographical.

Because of the generality of the enabling legislation, the task of defining, in advance, the exact conditions under which guaranty claims will be honored has fallen to the staff administering the Guaranty Program. The *Investment Guaranty Handbook* gives the guidelines developed by the Guaranties Division; these are spelled out in more detail in the specimen guaranty contracts provided to prospective investors.

Convertibility guaranties assure that, if an investor is

[65] U.S. Dept. of Commerce, *Reportorial Review* . . . , p. 15.

prevented from transferring earnings or capital into U.S. dollars for a period of 30 to 60 days, conversion of foreign funds can be made at 95 per cent of the "reference rate" of exchange in effect at the time the transfer is attempted. This reference rate is the free market exchange rate or, where none exists, some substitute defined in the guaranty contract. This reference exchange rate system means that, where multiple exchange rates exist or partial convertibility restrictions are in force, the investor is protected against any deterioration in his *relative* position between the time he makes the contract and the time he withdraws his receipts. It quite specifically does not protect the investor, however, against depreciation of the foreign currency in terms of United States dollars subsequent to the signing of the guaranty contract.

This depreciation threat is a major obstacle to many potential investors in less-developed countries. In some cases the internal inflation which so often accompanies depreciation may provide protection for business in the form of rapidly increasing prices and profits, but this is by no means always the case, and certainly cannot operate in cases where profits are regulated by the host government. Furthermore, the necessity for excess depreciation reserves (in dollar terms) and for write-offs of working capital values as a result of devaluation is likely in any case to be a serious problem for investors. In addition, since most countries today "peg" their currencies, the depreciation threat would seem to fall into the category of political rather than commercial risks, and thus be appropriate for public guaranty coverage. There is the inescapable fact, though, that if devaluation were an insurable risk, the liability incurred by the United States Government in the event of a runaway inflation and depreciation in a country with sizable guarantied investments might be extremely large.

Potential investors have also complained that the Guaranty Program's definition of expropriation fails to face the realities of "creeping expropriation," which many fear more than the outright variety. The definition of expropriation given in the latest (1964) version of the *Investment Guaranty Handbook*, which is spelled out in considerably greater detail in the specimen Contract of Guaranty, reflects an effort to allay investors' concern on this point; it is broader and less restrictive than any previous administrative definition of the term, providing: "In *equity investments*, 'expropriation' will be deemed to have occurred if, for a period of one year, the foreign government prevents the exercise of substantial control over the investment property. Taxation or regulation by the foreign government will not be considered expropriatory unless it can be shown to be arbitrary and not reasonably related to constitutionally sanctioned objectives of the host country. . . . In *loan investments*, expropriation will be deemed to have occurred if, for a period of one year, the foreign government directly prevents any repayments of principal or any payments of interest or causes a prevention of such payments as a direct consequence of expropriation. . . ."[66]

The newest definition of expropriation also includes an extension specifically authorized in the 1961 legislation, which provided that "the term 'expropriation' includes but is not limited to any abrogation, repudiation, or impairment by a foreign government of its own contract with an investor, where such abrogation, repudiation, or impairment is not caused by the investor's own fault or misconduct, and materially adversely affects the continued operation of the project."[67] In addition, the expropriation

[66] AID, *Investment Guaranty Handbook* (preliminary draft), Washington, 1964, Chap. v-1. The previous definition had stipulated that "Taxation or regulation by the foreign government will not be considered expropriatory unless it can be shown that the government's primary objective is to divest the owners of their investments. . . ." ICA, *Investment Guaranty Handbook*, Washington, 1960, pp. 17-18.

[67] *Foreign Assistance Act of 1961*, 75 Stat. 432.

guaranty now makes explicit its coverage of expropriatory or confiscatory action by any governmental subdivision (e.g., a state) of the host government.[68]

Possibilities for "creeping expropriation" not covered by guaranty contracts certainly remain, and it is not difficult to imagine "constitutionally sanctioned objectives of the host country" which would appear expropriatory to the American investor. But the current definition of expropriation, at once broader and more precise than any of its predecessors, should meet many objections by reducing the wide area of administrative discretion in deciding whether a given loss is covered by the guaranty. A provision for arbitration of disputes concerning claims under guaranty contracts, recently introduced in response to suggestions from investors and the legal profession, should also alleviate fears concerning unduly restrictive interpretation of the expropriation guaranty provisions by the administrative body responsible for the payment of claims.

The war, revolution, and insurrection guaranty "covers injury or destruction of the [investor's] tangible property directly caused by insurrection, revolution or war. . . ," including defense action. Consequential damage, such as the inability to conduct business and other intangible losses, is excluded from coverage, as is damage "caused by civil strife of a lesser degree than revolution or insurrection."[69] Coverage was limited to 90 per cent of the investor's ownership in physical property until early 1964, when the protection limit was raised to 100 per cent.[70]

The necessity for precise *a priori* definition of the situations covered by guaranty contracts was particularly acute when the responsibility for contract negotiation and the decision-making authority with respect to claims were

[68] AID, *Investment Guaranty Handbook* (preliminary draft), Washington, 1964, Chap. v-1.

[69] *Ibid.*, Chap. vi-1.

[70] *Ibid.*, Chap. vi-2.

administratively separate, the first vested in the Investment Guaranties Division and the second in the Export-Import Bank as contractual agent for the Program. When these two functions were merged in AID in mid-1962, the problem was somewhat alleviated, but there was still a certain amount of concern, particularly among lawyers, about the absence of precise, written definitions of the conditions under which claims would be honored. The actual experience of claimants is not very helpful since, whether because of the desire of foreign governments to maintain their credit standing with the United States or because of investors' reluctance to press claims and thereby impair their relations with the host government in a situation which might prove soluble, only two investors had made claims under guaranty contracts as of the end of 1963. In one case, the U.S. Government paid promptly three separate claims made under the convertibility contract of an investor in the Congo; in the other case, the claim of an investor in the Philippines under a convertibility contract was denied, and the case is currently in the Court of Claims. Not until a larger body of experience has been acquired will it be clear whether the definitions and distinctions provided by the Guaranties Division are adequate. Nonetheless, the broadened and yet more precise definitions of guaranty coverage set forth in the standard Contract of Guaranty and summarized in the 1964 version of the *Handbook* should help to avoid many cases of disagreement or misunderstanding, while the provision for arbitration offers a generally acceptable procedure for settling those disagreements which do arise.

The most obvious geographical limitation on the Guaranty Program's coverage is its restriction, since the beginning of 1960, to investments in less-developed areas only. But, even before the legislative restriction on new guaranty contracts came into force, applications for contracts covering European investments had been dropping off. As of June 30, 1959, only about a third of the dollar volume of applications pending for investment guaranties were for European countries, and of these, two-thirds were for convertibility contracts covering investments in France—reflecting a situation which has since stabilized. In several European countries which had guaranty agreements for a number of years, there was a considerable volume of American investment with little or no use of guaranties. And toward the end of the 1950's, several companies canceled as no longer necessary earlier guaranties in such countries as Germany and the United Kingdom. Although the immediate result of the geographic restriction on the Program was a sharp drop in the issuance of guaranties, applications pending continued to rise steadily, and the volume of contracts issued soon turned upward again as the negotiation of new agreements with non-European countries was completed.

Another type of geographical limitation on the Guaranty Program stemmed not from legislative restrictions but from the difficulties encountered by the Guaranties Division in negotiating agreements instituting the Program with a number of important countries, particularly in Latin America and the Middle East. The conflict of such agreements with the principles of the Calvo Doctrine adhered to by many Latin American nations is one source of difficulty. In addition, many countries which desire foreign investment nevertheless fear foreign domination to such an extent that they regard the potential claims of the U.S. Government to assets on their soil, until recently provided for in all guaranty agreements, as an unacceptable threat to their national sovereignty. Others fear that participation in the Program would be regarded as submission to United States leadership and treason to the cause of nationalism by their neighbors, and so are unwilling to take the first step.

In such cases, the completion of a treaty with one or a few key countries—such as the institution of guaranty agreements with Argentina and Chile in 1961—may make the institution of the Program with their neighbors much easier. More important, the increased flexibility in negotiating guaranty agreements provided for in the 1961 legislation, and particularly the freedom to omit the clause concerning the subrogation and turnover rights of the U.S. Government in particular cases, has eliminated many of the constitutional objections just cited, and has already eased the process of negotiation with a number of countries. But some key nations, such as Brazil and Mexico, still remain outside the scope of the Program. Considerable pressure to join the Program will soon be brought to bear on these countries, under a provision of the Foreign Assistance Act of 1963 that "No assistance shall be provided under this Act after December 31, 1965, to the government of any less-developed country which has failed to enter into an agreement with the President to institute the investment guaranty program . . . providing protection against the specific risks of inconvertibility . . . and expropriation or confiscation. . . ."[71]

PROCEDURAL PROBLEMS

A number of procedural matters have also brought complaints from potential, actual or past Program participants. The annual fees, reduced in 1954 from between 1 and 4 per cent to one-half of 1 per cent annually for each guaranty are still regarded as too high by a number of Program participants, and have evidently been the cause of several drop-outs.[72] They were also cited as the reason for not purchasing guaranty coverage by almost half the respondents to this query in the World Bank's 1961 questionnaire survey on international investment insurance.[73]

[71] *Foreign Assistance Act of 1963*, 77 *Stat.* 388.

[72] The Harvard Business School questionnaire cited 68 per cent of the respondents as saying that the present rates were reasonable, while 38 per cent termed them too high. However, very few (only 10) of the respondents to the 1958-1959 Commerce Department Survey felt that the fees should be substantially reduced.

[73] IBRD, *Multilateral Investment Insurance*, Washington, 1962, p. 40.

There is, unfortunately, no basis for determining objectively whether the present fee schedule is too high or too low to make the Program just self-supporting, neither a tax on nor a subsidy to the investor in the long run. No losses were sustained by the Program during its first 16 years of operation; 3 claims totaling $69,008.41 were paid under a convertibility contract held by the Pluswood Industries in the Congo, but the Congolese francs thus obtained were subsequently sold for $70,521.31, leaving the U.S. Government with a net gain of $1,512.90.[74] But there are good reasons for not using this experience as the basis of expectations concerning the Program's future loss experience, since it has only quite recently begun to operate on a large scale in the less-developed countries. The opinion of the American Actuarial Association emphasizes the point: ". . . you are not really selling insurance. It might look like insurance, but there is no actuarial basis. You are constantly intensifying your risk,"[75] by shifting operations from "safe" countries, such as those in Western Europe, to the relatively unsafe developing areas.

The complete lack of any actuarial basis for determining potential liability makes it impossible to tell whether the ratio of accumulated fee-reserve to maximum outstanding liabilities ($15.1 million to $1,125.2 million at the end of 1963)[76] is adequate or not. To a commercial

[74] AID, "Claims Paid under the Investment Guaranty Program (Specific Risk)," memorandum dated Feb. 25, 1964.

[75] Quoted by George Rublee, Assistant General Counsel for AID, in: U.S. Congress, Joint Economic Committee, Subcommittee on Inter-American Economic Relationships, *Private Investment in Latin America, Hearings*, 88th Cong., 2nd Sess., Washington, 1964, p. 179.

[76] This fee income represents only a small portion of the primary reserve for guaranties. The major part is provided by a $199.1 million authorization to expend from public debt (Administrator's notes), plus an additional appropriation to reserves of $30 million under the Foreign Assistance Act of 1962 and $27.7 million of appropriated funds transferred from DLF when a single reserve fund for all guaranties was set up in 1961. Total outstanding

insurance expert it might appear dangerously low, yet the fact that no losses have been sustained to date has led a number of investors to regard it as too high. The experience of the British Export Credits Guarantee Department reminds us, however, that a substantial reserve fund of fees built up over a number of years free of claims can be wiped out by a single crisis. A working capital of $36 million, maintained from 1931 to 1952, was wiped out by Brazilian transfer claims and the Department had to have help from the Treasury to meet its commitments.

On the other hand, if investment guaranties are regarded as a substitute for loans by the U.S. Government itself, the picture is quite different. It has been pointed out that in the case of loans the U.S. Government takes all the risks, and frequently charges a lower rate of interest than it has to pay on borrowed funds, while in the case of guaranties the Government takes only some of the risks and has net earnings equal to the fees charged, since it need not use borrowed funds at all.[77] Whether or not the present fee schedule should be lowered or not may depend in part on which of these views one takes: whether one feels that the Guaranty Program should be self-supporting in the long run or regards it as an alternative to the direct lending of public funds. But in either case, there is a strong argument for reducing the fees for investors who purchase a "package" guaranty for all three types of coverage since, as has already been pointed out, such coverage involves a good deal of double or triple counting; an investor cannot collect twice for the same loss, and it is difficult to imagine a situation in which the Government would have to pay out in full on all three contracts held for a single investment.

---

liabilities for all guaranties, including DLF, extended-risk, and Latin American housing guaranties, were $1,143.0 million at the end of 1963.

[77] Bruce E. Chubb and Verne W. Vance, Jr., "Incentives to Private U.S. Investment Abroad under the Foreign Assistance Program," 72 *Yale Law Journal* 3 (1963), 490.

It has often been suggested that the system of uniform fees be replaced by a more equitable system of adjusting them according to the riskiness of the investment's location.[78] Freedom to do so was provided in the 1961 legislation, but AID has rejected the idea, arguing that "professional actuaries who have examined the problem say that there is no actuarial basis for employing different fees, that variations would have to be arbitrary."[79] And even if one could quantify the differences in risks of exchange stringency, expropriation, or revolution which doubtless do exist among countries, the administrative difficulties of making such differentiations would be difficult enough to interfere seriously with the efficient operation of the Program. Since no objective basis exists for any of the guaranty fees, such a system would inevitably produce a negative reaction among actual and potential participants in countries deemed high-risk areas. Furthermore, the countries so designated, especially in the case of expropriation, would unquestionably take offense, and the Program's efforts at geographical expansion would be severely impeded. Worse, it might thus hinder rather than aid United States efforts to establish and preserve friendly relations with underdeveloped nations. The argument for varied rates may be economically sound but, in the absence of a body of quantitative information on which differential rates could be based, the probable repercussions of such a system on the Program's effectiveness offer a more telling argument for retaining the present practice of charging uniform fees. Finally, as AID has pointed out

[78] The Guaranties Division did initially attempt to vary its fees for the expropriation guaranty between 1 and 4 per cent, depending upon the riskiness of the investment location. In October 1954 both convertibility and expropriation rates were reduced to a uniform one-half of 1 per cent, and one-fourth of 1 per cent for stand-by coverage on unutilized portions of guaranties.

[79] U.S. Congress, Joint Economic Committee, Subcommittee on Inter-American Economic Relationships, *Private Investment in Latin America, Hearings*, p. 181.

". . . with fees at the present levels . . . significant variations could not be made without raising the fees."[80]

The considerable time which generally elapses between initial application and the signing of the guaranty contract has often been cited as an obstacle to the Program's effectiveness, particularly since in many cases a project's profitability is heavily dependent upon getting there ahead of the competition. The size of the backlog has varied greatly during the Program's lifetime but in recent years, with the great spurt in activity, it has been considerable. A member of the Guaranties Division staff estimated early in 1964 "that the present backlog is equivalent to a 30 to 36 month backlog," and stated that "the existence of a backlog of this size is the most serious problem facing the specific risk program."[81]

The Program's "waiver letter" procedure, permitting an investor to go ahead with his project in advance of receiving a guaranty contract without jeopardizing its eligibility as a "new" investment, is designed as a partial solution to the backlog problem, but it is not a complete one, since it gives no assurance that the guaranty will eventually be issued. Since less than one-third of all applications for investment guaranties are ultimately consummated as contracts, improvements in the application-screening procedure in order to reduce the volume at an early stage of processing might seem to offer an answer, and a special department has recently been established in the Guaranties Division to make this process more efficient. But this is not likely to bring any dramatic improvement, since only a very small proportion of the unconsummated applications can be attributed to the refusal of the Guaranties Division to issue a contract; in the vast majority of cases it is the prospective investor who changes his mind. Much more hopeful is the new Standard Contract of Guaranty, which should greatly streamline the time-consuming process of contract negotiation.

[80] *Ibid.*   [81] Unpublished memorandum of January 7, 1964.

There is little doubt that the requirement of foreign approval lengthens appreciably the processing time required in most cases, and a number of investors have said that the Program would be more interesting to them if it were abandoned. To eliminate completely the provision for host government approval of a guaranty applicant would raise a number of serious problems: it would require the renegotiation of all bilateral agreements instituting the Program on terms which would doubtless be unacceptable to many participants, and it would destroy the insurance afforded by the prior approval provision to the U.S. Government, which becomes liable in the event of certain hostile actions by the host government against a guarantied investment. There is, however, a change which should prove much easier to negotiate, and which would retain the protective aspect of the present procedure while substantially reducing the time and complications involved. This would make proposed investments subject to the veto of the host country rather than to the requirement of positive approval; failure to veto the project within a specified time after it was presented for consideration would be regarded as constituting official approval. Such an alteration in the operational provisions of the Investment Guaranty Program should improve its usefulness to foreign investors without impairing the interests of either the host or the United States Government.

Whatever their criticisms of the coverage and the procedures of the Investment Guaranty Program, few in the business community today quarrel with its basic purpose. Most agree on the necessarily public nature of such an undertaking if it is to exist at all. For a number of reasons, private insurance of this nature would be a practical impossibility. Lack of actuarial experience with this type of risk, combined with the enormous potential liability, would force a commercial insurer to charge prohibitively high rates. The preventive function of government insurance would be lost. A private company would be less likely than the Government to be able to utilize the local currency acquired after payment of a convertibility claim, nor would it have at its disposal the diplomatic and other resources available to our Government in negotiations regarding the realization of assets following payment under an expropriation guaranty. These considerations, plus the fact that no private company can have the staying power which the Government could exercise in unfavorable situations, would increase the necessary reserves still further.

That this view is shared by influential segments of the business community is evident in the statement of the American Enterprise Association that "It seems clear, however, the private enterprise cannot provide insurance against these risks and that the Federal Government is not displacing private activity in this regard,"[82] as well as by Standard Oil of New Jersey's opinion "that its investments conceivably could absorb most of a private group's guarantying ability."[83] Except in the case of firms whose size and geographical dispersion of investments serve as adequate self-insurance, the function of providing foreign investment insurance against political risks must clearly be provided by the government if it is to be provided at all.

[82] American Enterprise Association, *American Private Enterprise, Foreign Economic Development, and the Aid Programs.* (Study No. 7 for the Senate Special Committee to Study the Foreign Aid Program, 85th Cong., 1st Sess., Washington, 1957, p. 56.)

[83] Strauss *et al.*, p. 44.

V · THE INTERNATIONAL BANK FOR RECONSTRUCTION AND DEVELOPMENT

THE GROWTH OF THE IDEA

The IBRD, better known as the World Bank, represents the first institutional recognition of collective international responsibility for the economic betterment of nations other than one's own and, as such, has written an important chapter in world history. Much can be—and has been—written about its wartime origins, the evolution of its lending policies, the effects of its loans (a total of $7 billion by the end of 1963), on borrowing nations, and the achievements and difficulties of its economic survey and technical assistance missions. Here, however, we will concentrate on the Bank as borrower rather than as lender, on its efforts to channel funds from capital-exporting to capital-importing nations.[1]

The two leading allied nations, the United Kingdom and the United States, began postwar monetary and financial planning as early as 1941, with Lord Keynes guiding the efforts on one side of the ocean and Harry Dexter White doing the same on the other. By early 1944, tentative plans for two complementary institutions—the International Monetary Fund to deal with members' short-term foreign exchange needs and the IBRD to concern itself with the international flow of long-term capital—had been drawn up, and on July 1, 1944, 44 participating nations completed final drafts of the Articles of Agreement for the

[1] Probably the best concise source book on the World Bank is: International Bank for Reconstruction and Development, *Policies and Operations of the World Bank, IFC and IDA*, Washington, 1964. A less detailed but more analytical study is: Alec Cairncross, *The International Bank for Reconstruction and Development* (Princeton Essays in International Finance, No. 33), Princeton, 1959. This section relies heavily on both these works, as well as on the *Annual Reports* of the IBRD.

Fund and the Bank. By the end of 1945, the Articles had been accepted by a majority of the Bretton Woods participants, and the Bank opened for business on June 25, 1946. Its early loans were for the purpose the Bretton Woods planners had emphasized, the reconstruction of the war-devastated countries of Western Europe. But it quickly became apparent that Europe's long-term capital requirements were far greater than the Bank could hope to meet or the Western European countries could borrow with hope of repayment.[2] The Marshall Plan brought a way out of this impasse, and when the European Recovery Program came into operation the Bank began to concentrate on its other responsibility—the economic development of the backward nations of the non-European free world.[3] By mid-1963, as Table 7 shows, nearly three-fourths of its loans had been for projects in less-developed areas.

During the early planning days, the World Bank was viewed less as an international public lending institution than as "a safe bridge over which private capital could move into the international field."[4] This emphasis is nicely reflected in section ii of Article I of the Articles of Agreement, which states the purpose of the Bank: "ii) to promote private foreign investment by means of guarantees or participations in loans and other investments made by private investors, and when private capital is not available on reasonable terms, to supplement private investment by providing, on suitable conditions, finance for productive purposes out of its own capital, funds raised by it and its other resources."[5] It was obvious to the Bretton Woods conferees and the officers of the new Bank that conditions were highly unsuitable for the restoration of

[2] IBRD, *Policies and Operations. . . ,* p. 6.

[3] Since the end of the European Recovery Program, this has also included the less-developed areas of Europe itself, e.g., Southern Italy.

[4] IBRD, *Policies and Operations. . . ,* p. 3.

[5] IBRD, *First Annual Report,* Washington, 1946, p. 4.

TABLE 7

IBRD Loans Classified by Purpose and Area, as of December 31, 1963
(in millions of U.S. dollars, net of cancellations and refundings)

Purpose	Total	Africa	Asia and Middle East	Oceania	Europe	Western Hemisphere
Grand Total	7,486	924	2,498	426	1,699	1,939
Development Loans: Total	6,989	924	2,498	426	1,202	1,939
Electric Power	2,581	259	568	129	534	1,091
Transportation	2,452	443	1,098	140	171	600
Communications	46	4	—	—	—	42
Agriculture and Forestry	561	59	187	103	88	124
Industry	1,144	120	570	53	319	82
Iron and Steel	380	—	314	13	23	30
Pulp and Paper	138	—	4	1	113	20
Fertilizer and Other Chemicals	82	—	25	—	57	—
Other Industries	97	—	5	24	59	9
Mining	204	101	55	14	12	22
Water Supply	2	—	—	—	2	—
Development Banks	240	19	167	—	54	—
General Development	205	40	75	—	90	—
Reconstruction Loans: Total	497	—	—	—	497	—

Source: IBRD, *Policies and Operations of the World Bank, IFC and IDA*, Washington, 1964, p. 53 and NAC, *Semiannual Report, July 1—December 1, 1963*, p. 12.

private foreign lending at that time, and that the Bank "must serve during the transitional postwar period to do what private banking facilities cannot do yet."[6] Yet the ultimate goal remained in the foreground; the Bank's first President insisted that: "The essential objective of the Bank is to promote the international flow of long-term capital . . . the Bank ought to make every effort, even in the early stages of its operation, to help borrowers obtain from private sources the funds they need."[7]

The men who initiated the plans for the Bank and the national representatives who met at Bretton Woods to complete them expected and intended that the chief means by which the Bank would mobilize private funds for foreign lending would be the guaranty; the Secretary of the United States Treasury stated at the closing plenary session of the Conference that "The chief purpose of the Bank is to guarantee private loans made through the usual investment channels."[8] Indeed, Lord Keynes had fought at the Conference for a scheme under which the Bank's member nations would make only token contributions to it but would commit themselves to quotas which would be called only if needed to cover losses on loans. Under this plan, the Bank would not loan its own funds at all, but simply guaranty development loans arranged through its auspices but floated in private investment markets.[9]

Although Keynes' idea was modified to permit the Bank sufficient funds to make loans from its own resources, particularly during the early years of its operations, its capital structure as finally evolved (and as it remains

[6] Eugene Meyer, "The International Bank for Reconstruction and Development," *Proceedings of the Academy of Political Science*, XXII (Jan. 1947), 40.

[7] *Ibid.*

[8] Allan Fisher, "The International Monetary Fund and the International Bank for R. & D.," *Foreign Economic Policy for the United States*, Seymour Harris (ed.), Cambridge, Mass., 1958, p. 241.

[9] Robert W. Oliver, "The Origins of the IBRD" (unpub. Ph.D. dissertation Princeton University, 1957), pp. 428-429.

today) still reflected the primary emphasis on the guaranty function. Of the original authorized capital stock of $10 billion, 2 per cent of each member's quota was payable in gold or United States dollars and was to be freely available to the Bank for any of its operations. Another 18 per cent was payable in the currency of the member country (with a maintenance-of-value clause) and could be lent only with the consent of that member. The remaining 80 per cent of each subscription was not to be paid in or used for lending at all; it was subject to call if necessary to meet the Bank's obligations on borrowings or loan guaranties, and was payable in gold, dollars, or the currency needed to discharge the obligation. This last provision represented a guaranty of the Bank's obligations by its members, who shared in the risks of its loans and guaranties in proportion to the uncalled portions of their capital subscriptions.[10]

Even before the Bank had actually begun operations, it became obvious that the assumption of the Bretton Woods conferees ". . . that by virtue of the guaranties of the Bank's obligations provided by its capital structure, the Bank would have ready access to the private investment market"[11] had been naively optimistic. Since the Bank itself was an unknown and untried quantity to investors, the securities it guarantied would have sold at varying interest rates depending upon the credit of the borrower, which would have been a serious inconvenience and would have injured the Bank's own credit.[12] In February 1946, American bankers informed the National Advisory Council that the Bank's own bonds would sell more readily than foreign bonds guaranteed by it.[13] Since it was obvious that, for some time to come, the Bank would have to rely entirely on the U.S. investment market for private funds, this information made it clear that the Bank could help its

---

[10] IBRD, *Policies and Operations.* . . , pp. 23-24.
[11] *Ibid.* (1960 edn.), p. 7.   [12] Cairncross, p. 7.
[13] Oliver, p. 616.

borrowing members to acquire funds more cheaply and readily by selling its own securities and making loans to them from the proceeds. Accordingly, the Bank modified its view of its own primary function and began preparations for the marketing of its own securities.

Although the funds available from the "hard" 2 per cent (in the United States' case, 20 per cent, amounting to $635 million) of members' capital subscriptions were more than adequate for immediate lending needs, it was obvious that the problem of marketing the Bank's securities would be a complicated one. For one thing, private investors, whose memories of interwar experiences made them reluctant to embark upon any kind of foreign lending, knew little about the Bank or the resources behind its obligations and were therefore bound to be additionally hesitant at the prospect of purchasing unseasoned securities. For another, at the time the Bank came into existence, the largest potential purchasers of its securities, United States institutional investors, were almost all subject to federal or state laws prohibiting or restricting the purchase of any foreign securities, which would include those of the Bank. Therefore, it was decided to embark immediately upon the widespread information program and intensive efforts towards legislative changes that would obviously be the necessary precursors of the establishment of a broad market for IBRD bonds in the United States.[14]

LENDING POLICIES AND PROTECTIVE DEVICES

Among the provisions of the World Bank's Articles of Agreement designed in part to make its operations acceptable to the private financial community are requirements that it pay "due regard to the prospects that the borrower . . . will be in a position to meet its obligations under the loan,"[15] and that it satisfy itself, before mak-

[14] IBRD, *Policies and Operations. . .* , p. 82.
[15] *Ibid.*, p. 5.

ing or guarantying any loan, "that in the prevailing market conditions the borrower would be unable to obtain the loan from private sources under reasonable conditions."[16] In addition to these general and somewhat rhetorical strictures, the IBRD has in common with the Eximbank a number of more specific provisions regarding loans: they must be for productive purposes (as opposed to such social overhead areas as health and education), generally to finance direct foreign exchange costs only, and for specific reconstruction or development projects specified in advance. But, again like its sister institution in the United States, the World Bank has in practice interpreted at least the last two of these apparently restrictive provisions so liberally and with so many exceptions that they do not appear to offer a serious bar to any loans it might wish to make. It has, in fact, made a number of general-purpose reconstruction or stabilization loans,[17] as well as several "impact" loans to cover the indirect foreign-exchange costs resulting from the effect of a project on the national economy as a whole.[18]

Although the Bank's lending directly to private enterprise is limited by the requirement of a government guaranty and by administrative considerations which make it impractical for it to handle small loans, it tries to stress the growth and expansion of the private sector in borrowing countries. It has made a number of loans directly to private enterprise in the heavy industry and power fields, including loans totaling more than $155 million to two Indian steel companies and a series totaling about $150 million to the Japanese steel industry. Among the larger loans to private power have been almost $120 million to the Brazilian Traction Company and $37 million to the Mexican Light and Power Company. The Bank has also laid increasing stress in recent years on the indirect financing of private projects through loans to development

---

[16] *Ibid.*   [17] Cairncross, p. 16.
[18] *Ibid.*, e.g., to Italy and Japan, p. 21.

banks; its loans to such institutions totaled $225 million by the end of 1963.

Another aspect of IBRD's emphasis on the development of private enterprise is its reluctance to lend money to governments for the development of areas, such as competitive industries, which it feels should be left to private hands. While there is no absolute bar on loans to government-owned industry, the Bank maintains that it will make them only when it is satisfied that private capital is not available and that the government's participation will be compatible with efficient administration and will not hinder the general expansion of private enterprise.[19] On occasions, this view has led to an impasse— the Bank has refused to loan funds for a project that it felt should be financed privately, while the borrowing country has been unwilling to borrow private funds, either on cost or on sociopolitical grounds. This type of situation has arisen, for instance, in cases where countries attempted to borrow from the Bank to develop their own oil deposits and were refused.[20]

Also central to the attraction of private participation are a number of protective devices intended to minimize the possibility of losses. Aside from the government or central bank guaranty required on all loans not made directly to such a public body, the World Bank activities entail also two other types of "guaranty." While the Bank as lender generally does not require any positive security for its loans (except in the cases of loans to private borrowers), it usually exacts a "negative pledge clause" in loan agreements signed with member governments which provides that the Bank will share proportionally in any positive security or priority on governmental assets that may in the future be created to secure external debt.[21] This insures that, with a few specified exceptions, the ob-

[19] IBRD, *Policies and Operations.* . . , p. 37.

[20] Cairncross, p. 27.

[21] IBRD, *Ninth Annual Report*, Washington, 1954, p. 53.

ligations to the Bank will not be placed in a position junior to that of some subsequently contracted debts. The Bank's own bonds sold to private investors, which are general obligations unsecured by specific assets, contain a similar negative pledge clause.

Much more crucial, from the point of view of U.S. private participants in World Bank loans, is the ultimate "guaranty" provided by the United States Treasury in the form of the uncalled 90 per cent of the United States' capital subscription, which is subject to call should it ever be necessary to meet any obligations issued or guarantied by the Bank. Bank obligations up to the full amount of this subscription are covered by the full faith and credit of the United States Government, under section 7 of the Bretton Woods Agreements Act, which gives the Secretary of the Treasury the authority, without further Congressional action, to make payments on the United States subscription to the Bank as required from time to time.[22] Although the uncalled portions of the capital subscriptions of all 102 member nations, including several with strong convertible currencies, are part of the ultimate guaranty to the Bank's creditors, that provided by the United States is, not surprisingly, of overriding importance to the United States investment market.

Just how important this particular U.S. Government guaranty is to private purchasers of Bank securities became clear early in 1959 when it was noted that, at its current rate of borrowing, the Bank's outstanding obligations could be expected to exceed the uncalled portion of the U.S. capital subscription, amounting to $2,540 million, in the next two years. In his letter to Congress transmitting a Report of the NAC which recommended approval of a proposed increase in this country's total capital subscription from $3,175 million to $6,350 million, the President noted that "At present, and in the foreseeable future, the ability of the Bank to raise funds in the capital market of

[22] *59 Stat.* 512ff.; 22 U.S.C. 286ff. (1945).

the United States will depend largely upon the guarantee inherent in this country's subscription."[23] Earlier, the Bank's own Executive Directors had pointed out that: "While the Bank's dollar bonds . . . are being purchased in increasing measure by investors outside the United States, U.S. institutional investors are the main source of the Bank's long-term funds. . . . Although the soundness of the Bank's loans and the guarantees of other members have been of great importance, the existence of the U.S. guarantee is still in many instances decisive."[24]

As part of an increase in the Bank's total authorized capital stock from $10 billion to $21 billion, the U.S. subscription was indeed raised by the amount cited in 1959 and, since the entire increase was to remain uncalled, the guaranty now afforded by the U.S. subscription totals $5,715 million, or more than twice the total outstanding funded debt of the Bank ($2,510 million) at the end of 1963.[25] The maintenance of some such "margin of safety," although not necessarily such a large one, is important. For, despite a marked increase in recent years in the proportion of dollar bonds held outside the United States and in the number of IBRD issues denominated in currencies other than dollars, access to the New York investment market remains crucial to the Bank's effective operation, and the underlying U.S. Government guaranty continues to be important to many of the Bank's creditors outside the United States as well.

Besides the $18,656 million in uncalled capital subscriptions of its members, which provide ultimate and contingent backing, the Bank's obligations are directly

[23] U.S. National Advisory Council, *Special Report on Increases in the Resources of the International Monetary Fund and of The International Bank for Reconstruction and Development*, Washington, 1959, p. v.

[24] *Ibid.*, p. 34.

[25] IBRD, *Eighteenth Annual Report*, Washington, 1963, p. 45, and IBRD, "Financial statements for six months ending December 31, 1963," Bank Press Release No. 6412, Feb. 4, 1964.

secured by two major types of assets. The first is its entire outstanding portfolio of disbursed loans, which exceeds the Bank's indebtedness by the amount of loans made from members' paid-in capital subscriptions, and which amounted to $3,315 million at the end of 1963. The second is represented by two liquid reserve accounts, held mainly in the form of cash and U.S. Government obligations. One is the Special Reserve Fund, derived from a 1 per cent commission on the outstanding portion of all loans, provided for in the Articles of Agreement, which amounted to $271 million as of December 31, 1963. The other is the Supplemental Reserve Against Losses on Loans and Guarantees, to which the net income of the Bank is allocated, which totaled $558 million on the same date. At the end of 1963, after nearly 20 years of operation, the Bank had not suffered a single loss on any of its loans. But, should losses occur, funds from both these reserve accounts will be available to cover them. In addition, the Bank has available at all times varying amounts of working capital, held in the form of cash and short-term liquid investments, as well as demand notes representing national currency subscriptions not currently needed in operations. At the end of 1963 total resources behind Bank obligations, including uncalled capital subscriptions, came to approximately $25 billion.[26]

As a final measure of protection, the Bank attempts to do a good deal of "policing" of borrowers, both before and after loans are made. On occasion, it will require as a condition of Bank financing that the borrowing country institute measures to restore stability to its economy. The Bank also normally informs applicants in default on foreign obligations that it cannot help them "unless and until they take appropriate steps to reach a fair and equitable settlement of their debts."[27] The Bank's member countries have made such progress in clearing up defaults that this

[26] IBRD, *Policies and Operations. . .* , p. 29.
[27] IBRD, *Policies and Operations. . .* , p. 42.

problem has been reduced from serious to almost negligible proportions during the postwar years.

Once a loan is made, the Bank's practice is to maintain a close relationship with the borrower throughout the life of the loan. It takes steps to ensure that loan funds are spent only for authorized goods and services and follows closely the progress of the project being financed. In addition, it keeps in continuous touch with general economic and financial developments in the borrowing country. By these contacts, the Bank attempts "to ensure that the maintenance of service on Bank loans is not jeopardized by the emergence of conditions which might be prevented."[28] These paternalistic procedures have in some cases yielded valuable technical assistance and planning advice, and thus doubtless contributed to the preservation of the Bank's loss-free loan record. But they have also led on occasion to severe friction and resentment on the part of the borrowing country, indicating the need for a process of gradual adjustment in which the lender as well as the borrower learns to adapt to the new forms and vehicles of international lending.

THE MARKETING OF IBRD BONDS

For the World Bank, more than for the Export-Import Bank, the participation of private capital is essential not only in order to fulfill its primary purposes as laid down in its charter, but also in order to have sufficient funds at its command to carry on its lending activities. The Bank's

[28] *Ibid.*, pp. 42-43. The paragraph continues: "But the Bank also has a broader objective in view. By keeping closely in touch with the progress of its members, the Bank hopes to be of some assistance to them in meeting important economic problems." In this effort, the Bank goes a good deal further than simply supervision of loan projects. It has given substantial assistance, both in general development programming and in more specific problems, such as the mobilization of local capital, to those members requesting it. It has also conducted various training programs for officials of less-developed countries.

principal sources of funds, indicated in Table 8, are the proceeds of bond issues in the world's private investment markets, the paid-in portions of its members' capital subscriptions, and sales from portfolio; loan repayments provide a much smaller but growing portion of total funds. "From the Bank's point of view, however, the only really elastic source of funds is the issue of fresh bonds. It may cajole members to respect their obligations; it may plough back all it earns; it may sell from its own portfolio to a widening circle of clients. But if lending spurts as it did from 1956 onwards, the Bank is forced to borrow in the market."[29]

TABLE 8

Summary of Funds Available for IBRD Loans,
up to June 30, 1964
(in U.S. dollar equivalents)

Portion of subscriptions of all members paid in gold or U.S. dollars	228,543,000
National currency portion of subscription of the U.S.	571,500,000
National currency portion of subscriptions made available by other members	904,593,000
Total available capital subscriptions	1,704,636,000
Funds available from operations	655,571,000
Funds available from outstanding debt (including amounts not yet drawn)	2,491,844,000
Funds available from principal repayments	772,746,000
Funds available from loans sold and agreed to be sold	1,778,588,000
GROSS TOTAL	7,403,385,000
Disbursed on loans	5,973,530,000
BALANCE AVAILABLE FOR DISBURSEMENT	1,429,855,000

Source: IBRD, Treasurer's Department, Securities Division.

[29] Cairncross, p. 12.

For this reason, "it took some years before the Bank could claim with assurance that its lending would not be limited by the funds at its command and that it could undertake to lend to any country as much as that country, in its judgment, could hope to repay."[30] And even in the 1960's, its ability to fulfill its first function ("to assist in the reconstruction and development of the territories of members . . .") as well as its second ("to promote private foreign investment . . .") under the Articles of Agreement is heavily dependent upon its success in attracting private funds to share its loan burden.

Since, for the reasons alluded to above, the establishment of a broad market for World Bank bonds in the United States was obviously going to take time, the Bank decided almost as soon as it was organized to take any favorable opportunity to introduce its securities even before the national currency portions of its capital had been fully utilized. It accordingly began its information campaign in the spring of 1947, endeavoring through pamphlets, speeches by Bank officers, and invitations to representatives of lending institutions to acquaint the American public with its organization and purposes. It also worked intensively to obtain the enactment in several states of legislation permitting insurance companies, commercial and savings banks to invest in its securities. On July 17, 1947, the Bank made the first public offering of its bonds, consisting of $100 million ten-year 2¼ per cent bonds and $150 million 25-year 3 per cent bonds. The offering was made through more than 1,700 securities dealers, who received a commission nearly twice that offered for comparable corporate bonds. Apparently the Bank had laid its ground well; both issues, sold originally at par, were heavily oversubscribed and went immediately to a premium.[31]

[30] *Ibid.*, p. 7.
[31] IBRD, *Second Annual Report*, Washington, 1947, p. 20.

Since that auspicious beginning, the Bank has succeeded in creating a steadily broadening market in the United States and, since 1950, in other major capital markets as well. Crucial to such success in this country was the passage of appropriate legislation. In 1949, Congress amended the National Bank Act and the Bretton Woods Agreements Act to permit national banks and members of the Federal Reserve System to deal in and underwrite Bank securities and to exempt these securities from certain provisions of the Securities Act of 1933 and the Securities Exchange Act of 1934, thus in effect according them the same general treatment as U.S. Government, state, and municipal bonds. Because of this enabling legislation, U.S. banks have been able to aid materially in developing the market for the Bank's bonds. Equally important, appropriate legislation had by mid-1963 made the Bank's bonds legal investments for commercial banks in every state but one, and for savings banks, insurance companies, and trust funds in all but a few.[32] Thus, the largest potential source of loan funds in this country has been progressively opened to the Bank, and by mid-1953, it could report that ". . . the Bank's bonds were firmly established among a wide range of institutional investors."[33] Even in their unseasoned days the obligations of the Bank showed considerable price stability in the U.S. market (often going to a premium, in fact), and by mid-1960, well seasoned and with an "AAA" rating, their market action compared favorably with high-grade corporate and U.S. Government issues. The system of negotiated underwriting, adopted in 1952 after several other methods of marketing had been attempted, has proved most satisfactory ever since, and the delayed delivery provisions and protection against early redemption, included in all public issues since January 1957, have clearly enhanced the attractiveness of the Bank's obligations to

[32] IBRD, *Policies and Operations. . .* , pp. 82-84.
[33] IBRD, *Eighth Annual Report,* Washington, 1953, p. 41.

institutional investors.[34] Impressive evidence of this popularity was given in February 1960, when an issue of 25-year 5 per cent bonds originally planned for $100 million was increased to $125 "to meet heavy demand, particularly from institutions which had not previously bought Bank bonds."[35]

Of the 78 note and bond issues, totaling $4.1 billion, which comprise the Bank's entire borrowing record to December 31, 1963, 43, amounting to about $3.3 billion were denominated in U.S. dollars.[36] Of the $1,893 million in dollar borrowings outstanding on that date, the Bank estimated that approximately 42 per cent was held abroad, by private and governmental investors in about 40 countries, including some of the less-developed nations of Latin America, Asia, and Africa.[37] Most of these foreign-held obligations were dollar issues purchased in whole or in part by investors outside the United States at the time they were originally offered for sale, the rest were securities bought originally in this country which gradually moved

[34] IBRD, *Policies and Operations* . . . (1960 edn.), pp. 89-91. Under delayed delivery provisions, institutional investors may delay delivery of and payment for securities purchased for periods up to two years, thus coordinating their expenditures on them with their projected cash positions. Protection against early refunding is provided by making the bonds non-redeemable in the first ten years of their life. A number of Bank bond issues contain sinking fund provisions, but in issues since 1957 these operations do not begin until ten years after issuance.

[35] IBRD, *Fifteenth Annual Report*, Washington, 1960, p. 14.

[36] "Facts about the World Bank," information sheet provided by IBRD. Bond and note issues denominated in foreign currencies as of December 31, 1963 include 16 in Swiss francs, 7 in Deutsche marks, 3 each in Canadian dollars and pounds sterling, 4 in Netherlands guilders, and 1 each in Belgian francs and Italian lire.

[37] Estimated from figures in "Facts about the World Bank," IBRD, *Policies and Operations*. . . , pp. 95-96, and information provided by Raymond E. Deely of the Treasurer's Office. The major part of the dollar obligations held outside the United States are the shortest maturities, from one to three years, held mainly in the portfolios of central banks. IBRD, *Policies and Operations*. . . , p. 86.

abroad in subsequent trading transactions. In any case, at the close of 1963, United States investors held approximately $1,090 million of the direct obligations of the World Bank.[38]

To try to estimate American investments in Bank obligations on a year by year basis by applying the 58 per cent estimate for outstanding issues to annual data on dollar issues would be futile, since in some years dollar securities were purchased exclusively in this country while in others entire issues were placed abroad. An independent estimate of the Bank's dollar obligations bought initially by U.S. purchasers, pieced together from information in the *Annual Reports*, yields a gross total of $1,515 million, distributed annually as indicated in Table 9. The ratio of this estimate to the total sum of dollar obligations issued is 46 per cent, or about 12 per cent less than the U.S.-held proportion calculated by the Bank for issues outstanding in 1960. This relationship seems reasonable, since the foreign-held share of the gross total is given a somewhat spurious boost by the heavy proportion of notes and short-term bonds purchased by foreigners, only a small fraction of which were outstanding at the end of 1963. If each issue were weighted by its average lifetime, the gross and net figures for shares of dollar issues held in the United States would doubtless be much closer together.

Except for a definite, although by no means regular, increase in the proportion of dollar obligations held outside the United States, the annual variations in U.S. purchases of IBRD obligations depicted in Table 9 reveal no discernible pattern. When one considers the combination of factors which have together determined the pattern of World Bank security sales in the United States, this lack of a systematic trend is not surprising.

[38] These holdings were distributed approximately as follows: pension and trust funds, 62 per cent; life insurance companies, 23 per cent; savings banks, 14 per cent; commercial banks and other investors, 1 per cent.

TABLE 9

Purchases of IBRD Dollar Bond Issues
(in millions of U.S. dollars)

Fiscal Year	*Total Issue*	*Purchased by U.S. Investors*
1948	250	250
1949	—	—
1950	100	100
1951	50	20
1952	150	110
1953	60	40
1954	175	125
1955	50	—
1956	—	—
1957	275	170
1958	650[a]	375
1959	303[a]	100
1960	282.5[a]	125
1961	508[a]	—
1962	200	100
1963	110[a]	—
July 1 - Dec. 31, 1963	100	—
Total	3,263.5[b]	1,515

[a] Figures for these years include a total of $753.5 million of IBRD notes, denominated in dollars and privately placed in Europe, chiefly in Germany.

[b] These figures include a number of refundings, including the $100 million issue of 1950, which was used to redeem a 1948 issue of the same amount, and several note issues in recent years.

Source: Totals obtained from the *Annual Reports* of the IBRD; U.S. figures estimated from information contained in these same *Reports*, with the assistance of the IBRD Treasurer's Department, Securities Division.

The scale and timing of the Bank's issues of its own obligations is, initially, determined by the amount of loans made in a given period. In the early years of its operations the Bank felt it must have sufficient funds on hand to cover all its loan commitments, even though disbursements are normally spread out over a three-to-four year period. As the Bank's credit became established and the market for its bonds improved, this requirement was relaxed to permit the keeping of sufficient cash to cover only one year's disbursements.[39] This change in policy was one factor which offset the generally rising trend in loan commitments, as far as U.S. bond sales were concerned. Another offsetting factor was the fact that private participations in the Bank's loan portfolio, reducing its own commitments, increased steadily. Perhaps even more important was another shift: in the immediate postwar years the only functioning investment market was that of the United States, but, beginning in 1951, the Bank was able to sell parts of its dollar issues to a widening market outside the United States and, since that same year, has also found increasing scope for sales of issues denominated in currencies other than dollars. Since the Bank is extremely anxious to reduce its dependence on the U.S. investment market, it has tended to favor these non-dollar issues whenever possible, and they have consequently cut sharply into the Bank's need and desire for U.S. bond sales. Recently, in support of the United States' efforts to reduce the strain on its balance of payments, the Bank has also marketed several dollar-denominated issues outside the United States. Finally, decisions concerning issues on the U.S. market in a given year depend heavily upon the Bank's estimate of the rate at which they can be sold and the reception they will get, which are in turn closely related to the fluctuating state of market liquidity reflected in the cash positions of American banks and other institutional investors.

OTHER FORMS OF PARTICIPATION

The preceding discussion has focused on only one of the three types of private participation in the lending activities of the World Bank, namely, the purchase of the Bank's

[39] IBRD, *Policies and Operations* . . . (1960 edn.), p. 86.

own obligations. A second and increasingly important form of such activity is the sale to private investors of the obligations of the Bank's borrowers, either through simultaneous private participation in a World Bank loan commitment or by subsequent purchase from the Bank's portfolio. "Starting as a modest source of replenishment of funds, these transactions have become an important adjunct to the financing of the Bank's loan operations . . ."[40] amounting by the end of 1963 to $1,727 million. Of this total, nearly $566 million had come from U.S. investors, $123 million of it during fiscal year 1963 alone.[41]

As just indicated, Bank sales from its portfolio can be made in two ways: "In some cases the sales are made after the loan contract between the Bank and the borrower is signed and disbursements have been made; in others the sales are arranged about the time of the signing of the contract and the funds are called when disbursements are made."[42] United States institutions have made more than half of their purchases by the second method; purchasers abroad have generally preferred the first. The first such transaction took place in August 1948, when a group of 10 United States Banks purchased a block of $8.1 million of the notes received by the Bank from Dutch shipping companies in connection with a $12 million dollar loan. Since that time, the market in the United States and, since 1950, abroad as well, has steadily broadened; during fiscal year 1955 such sales in the U.S. totaled more than they had over the entire period until then; five years later, the year's sales were double this previous peak, and by fiscal 1963 they had reached a record high of $123 million. In 1955-1956, when the Bank's *Annual Reports* began to list the private participation as a routine part of the individual loan descriptions, such loans included among others, 4 Asian and 7 Latin American countries. By 1959-1960,

[40] IBRD, *Policies and Operations.* . . , p. 92.
[41] Figures provided by the Treasurer's Department of the IBRD.
[42] IBRD, *Policies and Operations.* . . , p. 93.

Africa was also displayed prominently in the list: 6 nations or territories on that continent received private funds through World Bank loans during that year. In fact, the great majority of loans in which participations were taken during the eight-year period ending with 1963 were to less-developed countries.

The market-broadening which has taken place over the years has not been simply a matter of increasing volume. Indeed, the annual figures for such transactions shown in Table 10, heavily dependent as they are on market conditions, are characterized more by fluctuation than by a consistent upward trend. One sign of increasing acceptance of such participations is the increase in the length of maturities private lenders are willing to take. At first, the demand was exclusively for the shortest maturities of any issue, always five years or less, and more often three

TABLE 10

U.S. Private Participations in IBRD Loans
(in millions of U.S. dollars)

Fiscal Year	Participations	Portfolio Sales	Total
Prior to 1952	24.1	4.6	28.7
1952	3.5	2.4	5.9
1953	1.0	0.5	1.5
1954	10.1	1.9	11.9
1955	32.8	15.5	48.3
1956	12.3	10.7	23.0
1957	14.5	0.2	14.7
1958	37.5	1.8	39.3
1959	26.2	0.9	27.1
1960	66.7	27.9	94.6
1961	12.9	21.2	34.1
1962	25.5	69.3	94.8
1963	9.7	113.1	122.8
July 1—			
Dec. 31, 1963	12.4	6.5	18.9
Total	289.2	276.5	565.6

Source: IBRD, Treasurer's Department, Securities Division.

years or under. But about 1955 a market began to develop for maturities of ten years and more, chiefly among insurance companies,[43] and in several instances "strips of maturities from the first to last—as much as 20 years ahead—have been sold."[44] And, although many banks whose liabilities are largely in the form of demand deposits feel that only the shortest maturities are appropriate to their portfolios, a number of them have begun to use their World Bank participations as a means of entering the long-term foreign financing field, taking maturities of five years or more.[45] Most private lenders continue to insist that their portion of a loan be repaid before the Bank's, but, within the limits of this protection, their receptivity to longer-term lending is growing with their confidence in the Bank's lending record. And finally, the growing status of such participations among institutional investors is showing itself in the expanding "core" of institutions, chiefly commercial banks, which have come to participate in Bank loans on a repeat and almost routine basis, subject always, of course, to the domestic demands on their cash supply. A majority of these 75-odd participants are the very large banks situated in New York and other major cities, but an increasing number of smaller institutions are also beginning to play an active role.

Initially, all participations in World Bank loans were taken with a full and unconditional repayment guaranty granted by the Bank itself. The first sales from portfolio without guaranty were made in fiscal year 1951; from then on those sold with guaranty formed a steadily declining proportion of the total until they ceased altogether after 1955-1956. In all, of the $1,727 million of private participations in Bank loans, $69 million were with the

---

43 IBRD, *Tenth Annual Report*, Washington, 1955, p. 14.

44 IBRD, *Sixteenth Annual Report*, Washington, 1961, p. 9.

45 Indicated in several letters to the author from officers of commercial banks which participate in Eximbank and World Bank loans.

guaranty, of which perhaps $45 million were purchased by investors in the United States.[46] Investment under a full repayment guaranty is not strictly speaking private investment at all, as the Bank's statement concerning guarantied participations recognized: "Such loans, of course, do not constitute private international investment in the usual sense of the term, but they do establish a direct relationship between lender and borrower which may lead to other credit operations without the Bank's intervention."[47] And the guarantied participations did, in fact, prove themselves a strictly transitional phenomenon, leading directly and in a relatively short period of time to the establishment of a flourishing system of participation without guaranties.

The third and loosest form of relationship between the Bank's lending activities and American private investors are joint Bank-New York market operations. These are in no sense participations, but simply arrangements with United States investment houses ". . . whereby a World Bank loan is made to coincide with the raising of additional funds from private investors, either by means of a public offering of the borrower's bonds on the investment market, by private placement of securities with institutional investors, or by a combination of the two."[48] They do, however, fall clearly within the purview of this study as private funds which have moved abroad as a direct result of the operations of a public lending institution. For not only are the funds raised from the two sources applied to financing the development of the same borrower, and sometimes even to the same project or program, but "agreement on the use of the funds is reached beforehand by representatives of the borrowing country or agency, the investment banking firms concerned and the World

---

[46] "Facts About the World Bank." The estimate of the United States' share was provided by Mr. Deely of the Treasurer's Office.
[47] IBRD, *Third Annual Report*, Washington, 1948, p. 21.
[48] IBRD, *Policies and Operations . . .* , p. 94.

Bank."[49] For example, although the Bank has no liability for the bonds or notes sold to private lenders, in general the latter are protected by final maturities on the Bank's loans running well beyond those of the privately held obligations.[50] Generally the terms on the obligations in private hands have ranged from 3 to 15 years, on those held by the Bank in such operations, from 3 to 25 years.

Fifteen such joint operations took place between December 1954 and December 1963; these borrowings totaled $561.8 million in all, with $309.8 million coming from private lenders and the rest from the Bank (see Table 11). The first such transaction was a $50 million loan to Belgium—$20 million from the World Bank and $30 million from the investment market—for a large port and waterways development program. During the following five years, 10 governments or government agencies, at the rate of one or more a year, used this means to raise development funds for hydroelectric power, transportation, industrial and other projects. In 1959, Denmark, Italy, and Japan raised a record total of $130 million in this fashion.

The advantages of this type of joint public-private lending are succinctly set forth by the Bank itself, which points out that: "(1) The call on its own resources is reduced by the amount made available by the market, thereby lowering the amount the Bank must raise through the sale of its own obligations; (2) the resources of institutional investors are directly enlisted in the financing of development; and (3) opportunities are presented to member countries to establish their credit in the investment market which ultimately may enable them to finance future development without recourse to the World Bank or other governmental agencies."[51] Of the 10 countries which borrowed

[49] *Ibid.*

[50] *Ibid.* (1960 edn.), p. 105. The exceptions are the loans to South Africa and one of the loans to Belgium, in which the final maturities of the Bank's loans and of the bond issues coincide.

[51] *Ibid.*, p. 94.

in this manner, the 3 African nations thus issued their first publicly offered bonds in the United States, and 5 European countries and Japan floated public issues here for the first time since the 1930's.

TABLE 11

Joint IBRD—New York Market Loan Operations
(in millions of U.S. dollars)

Year	Country	World Bank Loan	Bond or Note Issue	Total Financing
1954	Belgium	20	30	50
1955	Norway	25	15	40
	Union of South Africa	25.2	25	50.2
1956	Australia (Qantas)	9.2	17.8	27
1957	Air India International	5.6	11.2	16.8
	Belgium	10	30	40
	Union of South Africa	25	35	60
1958	Fed. of Rhodesia and Nyasaland	19	6	25
	Union of South Africa	25	25	50
	Austria	25	25	50
1959	Japan	10	30	40
	Denmark	20	20	40
	Italy (Cassa per il Mezzogiorno)	20	30	50[a]
1960	Japan Development Bank and Kawashi Steel Corp.	6	4	10
	Japan Development Bank and Sumitomo Metal Industries	7	5.8	12.8
		252.0	309.8	561.8

[a] Does not include a loan of $20,000,000 to the Cassa per il Mezzogiorno (Italy) by the European Investment Bank made at the same time as the World Bank loan and the public offering of the Cassa's Bonds on the U.S. investment market.

Source: IBRD, *Policies and Operations of the World Bank, IFC and IDA*, Washington, 1964, p. 95.

Finally, there is the elusive category of what might be termed concurrent or parallel equity investments, investments which bear no formal relationship whatsoever to the operations of the IBRD, but which are made in enterprises receiving IBRD funds at roughly the same time (or at least as part of the same project) as the Bank loan commitment. It is difficult even to track down such investments, and it is quite impossible to determine the degree of causal relationship which exists between a World Bank loan and the concurrent investment of private equity funds. In some cases it is the Bank loan which makes a particular undertaking, and thus the private equity investment in it, possible, in others the investment would probably have taken place even without the IBRD funds.

Those cases of concurrent investment of U.S. equity capital which we have been able to trace total roughly $50 million. Most of this sum is attributable to a single enterprise, COMILOG in Gabon, which received a $35 million loan from the World Bank in mid-1959. The share capital of this manganese mining company is owned 51-49 per cent by French and American shareholders, whose investments provided the rest of the estimated $89 million cost of the project, which included not only the operation of the mine but also the construction of transport facilities to carry the ore to the coast. Institutional investors in the United States also took participations totaling more than $20 million in the IBRD loan itself.[52] The remaining cases of concurrent U.S. equity investments are relatively small —between $100,000 and $1,000,000—shareholdings in the development banks of 7 different countries: Finland, Iran, India, Malaya, Morocco, Pakistan, and the Philippines. Five of these investments were made during 1963, and involved both IBRD and IFC funds.[53]

Although sufficient information is not available to com-

[52] IBRD, *Fourteenth Annual Report*, Washington, 1959, p. 18, and unpublished data provided by the IBRD.
[53] IBRD, press releases and unpublished data.

pute exactly an over-all ratio between public and U.S. private funds in IBRD loans in which both types of funds have participated (as we have done for the other lending agencies), it is possible to determine such a ratio for those loans that have involved some private participation, from both United States and European sources. Since there have been very few World Bank loans which attracted European participations only, the discrepancy between the ratio calculated here and the one which would be exactly comparable to those computed for the other lending agencies is insignificant.

When participations and portfolio purchases alone are considered, the ratio between private U.S. funds and net IBRD commitments is 13/100 or 13 per cent. When joint operations with the New York market are included the figure rises to 20 per cent, and remains approximately the same when enterprises involving both IBRD loan funds and concurrent investments of U.S. equity are also added to the total.[54]

This average of one U.S. private dollar for every five IBRD dollars invested in undertakings which have attracted both types of funds has held relatively stable in recent years; it was the same when calculated as of mid-1963 as it had been three years earlier. But the average masks an enormous range in the individual items; U.S. private participations have varied from substantially less than 1 per cent of the net IBRD commitment in a given transaction to several cases, all in Africa, in which they exceeded the portion ultimately held by the Bank. More

[54] IBRD, *Eighteenth Annual Report*, Washington, 1963, Appendix K; IBRD, *Policies and Operations. . .* , p. 95, and unpublished data provided by the IBRD. The ratios here cited were obtained by dividing, for all loans involving some private funds, the amount of such participation from U.S. sources by the net amount of the IBRD commitment after subtraction of the portion taken over by private lenders. Non-U.S. participations and portfolio purchases were subtracted from both numerator and denominator, that is, not counted at all, in obtaining these ratios.

than half the simultaneous participations have been for less than 10 per cent of the net public funds invested. In all but one of the 15 joint operations with the New York market, on the other hand, the private investment was equal to or greater than the IBRD loan. The largest private-public ratio was in a transportation loan to Belgium, in which the private investment was three times that of the Bank; the smallest was in a railway loan to the Federation of Rhodesia and Nyasaland, in which the sum loaned from private sources was approximately one-third as large as the Bank's commitment.

The Bank's stated purpose at the time of its inception was that it should ultimately obtain the bulk of its funds from the sale of its securities to private investors. Fourteen years after it started operations with members' capital subscriptions as its only source of funds, it had achieved this goal with notable success. Of the $7.9 billion in loans authorized as of December 31, 1963,[55] $6.3 billion, or approximately 80 per cent, had been financed by private investors in one of the ways described above. About 40 per cent ($2.6 billion) of this latter sum had come from investors in the United States, $1.5 billion in the form of purchases of the Bank's own securities, which carry the ultimate guaranty of the U.S. Treasury. The other $1.1 billion was almost equally divided between portfolio participations or purchases and joint operations, neither of which (except for a small amount of guarantied participations in the early years) are backed by any such security, but depend entirely upon the credit of the foreign borrower. These figures do not include, of course, the private funds mobilized indirectly: the private foreign investment which resulted from improved investment climates growing

[55] This figure includes $7.6 billion in loans authorized by the Bank itself, plus $.3 billion representing the private portion of joint Bank-market operations. The latter component was included in the "authorizations" figure here to provide comparability with the figures on the proportion coming from private sources, in which joint operations are included.

out of the Bank's efforts or from broadened contacts stemming originally from participation in Bank loans, or the local private money mobilized by new development institutions and projects brought into being by Bank funds.

RELATIONSHIP WITH THE BUSINESS WORLD

Throughout most of its first two decades, the World Bank has enjoyed the almost unanimous support of the American business community. When the Bank first began operations one heard, to be sure, misgivings: past experience proved that World Bank loans would result in heavy losses; if conditions were sound, private investors would supply a market for foreign bonds without the Bank's aid. A letter to the Editor of the *Commercial and Financial Chronicle* in June 1947 insisted that ". . . this time there can be no doubts that the majority of the nations that are going to receive our dollars are bankrupt." The author went on to say that, individually, the member nations were poor credit risks, not worthy of our trust, and were not much better collectively except insofar as the U.S. Treasury provided security. He concluded that investment dealers would be doing "a patriotic service" by advising their customers against buying the Bank's debentures.[56]

Once the Bank was a going concern and its conservative lending standards and resulting loan record became known, such criticism ceased. The prevailing view was, rather, represented by the opinions of the Citizens' Advisory Committee, composed largely of representatives of large banks and manufacturing companies. While citing the usual arguments about the dangers of government financing in the commercial sphere, the Committee acknowledged that, in this interim period, government financing of the "infrastructure" sectors was a necessary prerequisite to attracting private capital. It commented

[56] Henry Schouten, letter to the editor, *Commercial and Financial Chronicle*, 165 (June 5, 1947), 6, 35.

that "In recent years, the two banks [World Bank and Eximbank] have been among the few instruments by which capital from the United States, or elsewhere, available for international investment has been channeled into productive, worthwhile, self-liquidating projects."[57] The Committee went on to praise the Bank for helping to create a better climate for foreign investment in borrowing countries and for using its position to establish high standards for both borrowers and lenders in international finance.[58] A few years later praise came from a representative of the United States Council of the International Chamber of Commerce, who testified that: "This bank has earned the admiration of businessmen in countries of all stages of development, and it has been an effective instrument in mobilizing private capital for large projects to provide the basic economic facilities for underdeveloped countries."[59]

In letters to the author, commercial banks which regularly participate in Bank loans have cited its "outstanding contribution towards the solution of the international liquidity problem and the free flow of trade and capital."[60] Citing the Bank's loss-free loan record, the same writer attributes it (in a sentence cited more fully later with reference to the Eximbank) to "a strict adherence to sound banking principles, . . . and a complete knowledge of economic conditions. . . ." Other bankers pointed out that "involvement in such loans helps us to generate other business in the borrowing countries." Clearly, during the

[57] U.S. Citizen's Advisory Committee to the U.S. Congress Senate Committee on Banking and Currency, *Study of the Financial Aspects of International Trade and of the Export-Import Bank and the World Bank, Report*, Washington, 1954, p. 41.

[58] *Ibid.*, pp. 45-46.

[59] U.S. Congress, House, Committee on Ways and Means, Subcommittee on Foreign Trade Policy, *Private Foreign Investment, Hearings*, 85th Cong., 2nd Sess., Washington, 1958, p. 479.

[60] Mr. Flemming Kolby, Vice-President, Central National Bank of Cleveland, letter of November 11, 1960.

years of its operation, the World Bank has won the growing respect of the private business and financial community.

This general attitude does not mean, of course, that the Bank has escaped a wealth of criticism of specific policies from that same business community. Until the mid-1950's, one of the complaints heard most often concerned the Bank's requirement of a government guaranty of any loan not made directly to a member government itself. This requirement hampers severely the Bank's usefulness as a direct source of funds for private enterprise, since businessmen are generally extremely reluctant to seek a government guaranty for fear of thus inviting political interference, and governments are equally loath to grant them because such action might be construed as favoritism or, at the very least, involve them undesirably in judging the merits of a given enterprise. The Bank itself has long recognized these limitations but finally decided, rather than change its own charter and increase substantially the risk and expense of its loans, to establish a separate subsidiary, the International Finance Corporation, to make investments in private enterprises without government guaranties. The merits and limitations of this organization will be discussed separately in the next chapter.

PROBLEMS OF POLICY

The general question on which the Bank has received the most criticism in recent years is that of its lending policies. Its critics often assert that its effectiveness as an aid to development is severely curtailed by its insistence on making "sound" loans by banking standards. The criteria by which the Bank judges "reasonable assurance of repayment" are, they say, so harsh as to eliminate a large number of worthwhile projects and cut off from the Bank's help those very borrowers who most need it. At the same time, a number of opinions cited earlier made it clear that these restrictive standards, and the loss-free record attributed in part to them, are the chief conditions on which private investors are willing to participate in Bank loans or purchase its own securities.

The problem of trying to meet two different and often conflicting sets of demands is one faced in varying degrees by every international lending agency which tries to attract private capital to participate in its activities, but one which has proved particularly troublesome for the World Bank and the Export-Import Bank. The conflict has probably been most acute in the case of the World Bank since, unlike the Export-Import Bank, it has adhered quite consistently to strict economic lending principles, and its record of no losses and no loans in arrears has generally been maintained without the assistance of the repayment-adjustment and refunding arrangements utilized by its sister institution. Furthermore, the forms of private participation available to the international institution make it dependent almost entirely upon the institutional investors who are most likely to adhere to conservative lending standards; its U.S. counterpart is free to attract a variety of more venturesome investors, including those with equity funds.

The Bank has also been criticized frequently on the grounds that its interest rates—which generally range from 4 to 6¼ per cent—are too high and its repayment terms too inflexible to be appropriate for the type of basic development projects, often slow to reach the income-producing stage, which are most essential for backward economies. At the same time, the Bank is urged to establish "interest rates and maturities attractive to sources of private finance,"[61] implying that its present rates are too low and its terms too long to attract such investors. Some partial solutions to the dilemma thus posed have been worked out, including the introduction of serially maturing issues, of which private investors can choose the shorter maturities. But the Bank continues to be plagued by the

[61] U.S. Citizen's Advisory Committee, *Study of the Financial Aspects. . .* , p. 40.

problem of serving two masters—borrowers and lenders—at the same time.

These criticisms indicate that the Bank faces conflict at many points between the first and second functions set forth in its Articles of Agreement. How can it devise means better "to assist in the development of the territories of its members" without relinquishing its effectiveness as an instrument "to promote private foreign investment"?

In part, the Bank has sought a solution to this dilemma through a series of measures aimed at improving the climate for foreign investment by bringing closer together the often divergent views of borrowers and lenders. A major effort along these lines is the Bank's sponsorship of consortia and consultative groups for "the international coordination of financial assistance to a developing country" in order to insure its most effective use.[62] The first such group, the Consortium for Aid to India, was organized in 1958; a similar organization was formed for Pakistan in 1960. More recently, consultative groups have been organized to coordinate aid to Colombia, Nigeria, and Tunisia. As part of its search for ways of alleviating investors' fears of "abnormal" risks in developing countries, the Bank published a study of various proposals for a multilateral investment insurance scheme. This study, while thorough in its investigation of proposals and existing national schemes, was noncommital and inconclusive. The Bank itself has given more positive endorsement to another approach, which would grow naturally out of the successful use of its good offices to settle disputes between investors and host governments on several occasions in the past. This is a proposal, under study by the Bank's Executive Directors during 1963, to establish conciliation and arbitration services which foreign investors and host governments could utilize, on a voluntary basis, for the settlement of investment disputes.[63]

[62] IBRD, *Eighteenth Annual Report*, p. 7.   [63] *Ibid.*, pp. 6-7.

As far as its own operations are concerned, however, the Bank's answer so far to the conflicting demands of borrowers and lenders has not been to try to satisfy them within the framework of its own activities, but rather to create autonomous offspring specifically designed to meet one or another of the demands made on it. Thus, late in 1960 the International Development Association was established as an affiliate of the World Bank, to make development loans on easier terms and according to more liberal criteria than its parent institution. The IDA is not intended to mobilize private capital at all and, since it is a separate institution, its softer loan policies do not jeopardize the World Bank's effectiveness in attracting private funds. At the other end of the spectrum lies the Bank's other junior affiliate, the International Finance Corporation, which has been operating since 1957 according to strict private-investment standards, attracting private funds into carefully selected high-yield projects on the soundest of terms. The effectiveness of this organization in fulfilling the second function laid down in the Articles of Agreement of its parent institution is the subject of the next chapter.

VI · THE INTERNATIONAL FINANCE CORPORATION

WHY AN IFC

The International Finance Corporation was created to bridge certain important gaps in the powers of its parent institution. By the mid-1950's it had become clear that the World Bank's ability to carry out its Bretton Woods mandate—to spur economic development by aiding the restoration of private international capital flows—was severely limited by two of the operating rules set forth in its Articles of Agreement.

The first requirement limiting the World Bank's effectiveness as a source of financial assistance to privately sponsored enterprises is the requirement of a government guaranty on all loans not made to a government itself or one of its instrumentalities. Fears on the part of private borrowers that such a guaranty would lead to government interference in their affairs, and on the part of governments that their actions in granting or withholding guaranties might be construed as favoritism, has held IBRD loans to the private sector down to a relatively small proportion of its total loan activities.

The second limiting factor is the inability of the IBRD to provide equity capital, which is often the most crucial requirement in getting an enterprise started. The suggestion that the Bank should be able to provide equity as well as loan capital was originally advanced at Bretton Woods, but the "spirit of caution," led by Lord Keynes, ultimately prevailed, and the Bank was authorized to make only fixed-interest loans, which precluded the provision of venture capital in any form.

The International Finance Corporation came into being in mid-1956, after several years' battle against United States opposition,[1] with 31 members and capital subscrip-

[1] An account of the battle for the IFC's creation is provided by:

tions totaling $78 million, more than half of which was supplied by the United States. Its general aim was "to further economic development in its developing member countries by investing—without government guarantee—in productive private enterprises in association with private capital and management."[2] Alone among the United States and international lending institutions, the IFC's operations are aimed not just primarily but exclusively at the "private sector" of less-developed economies. Unlike the IBRD, it deals directly and almost exclusively with private business, making equity investments or loans with equity-type features and expecting a return commensurate with the greater risks it accepts. Its intended role is that of a catalyst; its aim is to use its limited funds to stimulate the creation of enterprises in which a minimum of half the capital is expected to come from private sources. As its first President repeatedly pointed out: "It is to increase the flow of private capital, and particularly of foreign private capital, into productive investment in the underdeveloped areas, that the IFC is now being created . . . in the last analysis, IFC's success must be measured, not so much by the amount and profitability of its own investments as by the amount of additional investment it succeeds in stimulating."[3]

According to Article I of its Articles of Agreement, the IFC is expected to carry out its purpose of encouraging the growth of productive private enterprise in less-developed member countries in three ways:

(i) By assisting in the financing, in association with private investors and without a government guarantee, of

B. F. Matecki, *Establishment of the International Finance Corporation and United States Policy*, New York, 1957.

[2] IFC, *International Finance Corporation* (leaflet), Washington, 1960.

[3] Robert L. Garner, *Statement on the International Finance Corporation* (at the Tenth Annual Meeting of the Board of Governors of the IBRD, Istanbul, 1955), Washington, 1956, pp. 5, 8.

productive private enterprises which will contribute to the development of member countries, in cases where sufficient private capital is not available on reasonable terms.

(ii) By seeking to bring together investment opportunities, domestic and foreign private capital, and experienced management.

(iii) By seeking to stimulate and create conditions conducive to the flow of domestic and foreign private capital into productive investment.

OPERATING CRITERIA

The major operating rule of the International Finance Corporation, and the one which ties it more closely than any other public lending institution to the encouragement of the flow of private funds into economic development abroad, is that "IFC is essentially an investing rather than a lending institution, and it judges projects on the basis of their merits as investments for private capital."[4] Rather than adhering to the "bankable" standards required by the other lending institutions under discussion, the IFC states that it stands ready to take the sort of risks generally assumed by private corporations or "venture capital" investors sending funds abroad. It expects, in return, the higher returns commensurate with such risks; it has stressed repeatedly its intention to avoid undercutting private capital by providing money at lower rates than the latter is willing to accept.

During the first five years of its operations, the IFC was prevented by the provisions of its charter from investing in equity shares, the most natural vehicle for carrying out its stated functions. Objections, chiefly of U.S. origin, to the idea of a public institution being in a position to exercise management functions, forced the inclusion in the IFC charter of a clause prohibiting investment in capital stock or shares.[5] As a result, the IFC was forced to ar-

[4] IFC, *International Finance Corporation.*
[5] IFC, *Articles of Agreement*, Washington, 1956, Article III, Section 2(a).

range more complicated forms of investment combining both debt and equity features, carrying not only fixed interest charges but also "some right to share in the profits and growth of the business. Such shares may take the form of a right to some additional income related to earnings, or an option to subscribe to share capital, and frequently a combination of the two."[6] Since the restriction on equity ownership was rescinded by an amendment to its charter in September 1961, the IFC has made most of its commitments in the form of equity or loan-equity combinations. It has also participated in a number of security issues through underwriting or standby arrangements.

Most IFC loans are denominated in U.S. dollars, while its equity investments are denominated in the currency of the country where the enterprise is located. Fixed interest charges vary with the risk entailed, the amount of IFC's participation, and the prospective return on the investment as a whole. In the past they have averaged about 6 to 7 per cent, the loan terms from 5 to 15 years, with a grace period determined by the time required before the project comes into profitable operation.[7]

The eligibility of an investment proposal for an IFC loan depends upon a number of considerations, aside from the primary ones of economic soundness and profit potential. A project must be located in a member country or one of its dependent territories and, for the present at least, the IFC will invest only in those areas designated as less-developed, which include Africa, Asia, Australia, Latin America, the Middle East, and a few areas in Europe. It will make no investment in a member territory to which the government of the member objects, thus giving the host government a veto power over proposed financings. It will invest only in enterprises which are es-

[6] IFC, *International Finance Corporation.*

[7] IBRD, *Policies and Operations. . .* , pp. 100-101 and John E. Loomis, *Public Money Sources for Overseas Trade and Investment*, Washington, 1963, pp. 187-195.

sentially private in character; that is, enterprises which are government owned and operated or in whose management the government participates significantly are ineligible, although the participation of some public funds does not necessarily preclude IFC investment. The IFC generally restricts its investments to predominantly industrial enterprises, including private industrial finance companies (development banks), and seeks to maintain reasonable diversification of its investments with respect to both geographical location and types of undertakings. Finally, although there are no formal limits on the amount IFC may invest in a single enterprise, practical considerations limit it to "a medium range." Administrative costs appear to dictate a minimum of about $100,000 while, at the upper end, it has not ordinarily considered single investments of more than $3 to $4 million, on the assumption that it will fulfill its intended function as a catalyst more effectively if it spreads its limited capital as widely as possible. The average size of IFC investments is about $1.25 million.[8]

GROWTH AND DIVERSIFICATION OF OPERATIONS

The IFC got off to a sluggish start, limited during its first few years of operations not by any lack of resources but by the inability to find a sufficient number of projects suitable for investment. Although its original capital of $78 million had swelled to $92 million, representing the subscriptions of 51 members, by September 1957, it had made only 4 loan commitments totaling $5.3 million as of that date. The remainder of its funds were invested in U.S. government securities. The organization had received a large number of loan proposals, but only a small proportion was regarded as falling within the scope of its operations and offering reasonable prospects of being suitable for investment.[9] During the years that followed,

[8] IBRD, *Policies and Operations. . .* , p. 100 and IFC, *Seventh Annual Report*, Washington, 1963, Appendix C.
[9] IFC, *First Annual Report*, Washington, 1957, pp. 6-7.

its commitments grew slowly, from $6.1 million in June 1958 to $44.4 million three years later.

Once the IFC acquired the freedom to invest in equity capital, its loan portfolio grew more rapidly. During fiscal 1962 its investment commitments increased by $18.4 million to $62.5 million, and in the following year it made another $18.0 million of new commitments. By December 31, 1963, although its paid-in capital had increased only slightly over the 1957 figure, to $98 million, its portfolio (including participations) had swelled to more than $80 million, representing 68 investments in 27 countries. These countries included 11 in Latin America, which accounted for $51.6 million of the investments, 6 in Asia and the Middle East, 5 in Europe, 4 in Africa, and 2 in Australia (see Table 12). Some $16.1 million of these funds had gone to industrial development finance companies for re-lending, the rest directly to industrial enterprises. The iron and steel industry was the major industrial recipient of IFC funds, and the chemicals, construction, and pulp and paper industries also accounted for substantial proportions of the portfolio.

The IFC's accelerated growth after mid-1962 was marked not only by a more rapid expansion of its investment portfolio, but also by a branching out into new areas. Once it was enabled to acquire share capital for its own portfolio, the Corporation was in a position to help finance industrial enterprises and at the same time contribute to the development of capital markets in less-developed countries through underwriting commitments and standby arrangements. The IFC made its first such commitment in June 1962, when it joined with Mexican, Swiss, and American financial institutions to underwrite an issue of capital shares of Mexico's largest private steel company. This first commitment was for $2.9 million; during the 18 months that followed, the IFC entered into 5 more such transactions, assisting in the marketing of the securities of

TABLE 12

Geographical Distribution of IFC
Investments and Commitments,
as of December 31, 1963

Area	Number of Investment and Standby and Underwriting Commitments	Net Investment Commitments[a]	Standby and Underwriting Commitments[b]
Australia	2	$ 975,000	$ —
Africa	4	7,795,774	1,400,000
Asia and the Middle East	14	15,461,970	5,149,016
Europe	8	7,960,846	158,644
Western Hemisphere	40	51,629,174	3,694,856
Total	68	$83,822,764	$10,402,516

[a] Original principal amounts of investment commitments totaled $91,630,232 of which $7,807,468 has been cancelled or expired.

[b] Of this amount, $5,276,452 was acquired by others.

Source: IFC, "Facts about IFC," Washington, 1964 (Mimeo.).

private development banks in Finland, Malaya, Nigeria, and the Philippines, and of a steel fabricator in Mexico. By the end of 1963, as Table 12 shows, the IFC's original standby and underwriting commitments totaled $10.4 million, more than half of which had already been acquired by private investors.

The IFC's entry into the field of security underwriting represents one major new technique for expanding its catalytic function; the announcement, early in 1962, of the creation of its Development Bank Services Department heralded another and closely related one. It is the responsibility of this department to plan and coordinate all assistance, both financial and technical, to private industrial development banks from the members of the World Bank Group—the IBRD, IFC, and IDA (International Development Association). By the end of 1963, the IFC had committed a total of nearly $16 million to the financing of new or existing institutions in Colombia, Finland, Malaya, Morocco, Nigeria, Pakistan, the Philippines, and Spain. In most of these instances the IFC joined with the World Bank in providing funds for these institutions, which also attracted capital from private investors in many nations and sometimes from other public lending agencies as well.

FORMS AND EXAMPLES OF PRIVATE PARTICIPATION

There are a number of ways in which IFC funds can join with private money in the financing of industrial enterprises in less-developed countries. Private banks and other institutional investors, generally investment companies formed to make portfolio investments of the "venture capital" type, may take up portions of IFC investment commitments, either by participation in the commitment at the time it is made or by later purchases from the IFC's portfolio. The first participation was taken by private investors during 1959, but the IFC did not begin to sell off its own loan portfolio, and thus revolve its funds, until late 1961, after it had had time to establish a loan record that would convince the private financial community of its creditworthiness and sound judgment. By the end of 1963, IFC investments had attracted participations and purchases from portfolio totaling nearly $20 million, all without the guaranty of the Corporation.[10]

Since 1962, after it was enabled to purchase equity securities, the IFC has utilized a second method of attracting private funds into development investment: underwriting new security issues or entering into standby arrangements to take up unsold portions of issues. During the first two years of these operations, the IFC entered into 6 such commitments, described earlier, totaling more

[10] Data provided by Mr. Deely of the IBRD, Treasurer's Department.

than $10 million. By March 31, 1964, more than $7 million of these issues had been taken up by private investors.[11]

Finally, of course, the IFC attracts private funds in the form of additional private investments, in both equity and loan form, in enterprises to which it is simultaneously making a commitment. There is no way of knowing how much private capital from all over the world has been channeled into development investment in this way, nor can we tell how strong a causal factor the IFC's involvement represented in any particular instance of such concurrent investment. But some idea of the magnitude of the private funds which have been invested in conjunction with IFC commitments can be gleaned from the organization's own estimate that, for each dollar of IFC funds committed, some 4 or 5 dollars of private funds (including participations) have been invested.[12]

Between 1959, when U.S. private capital first participated in an IFC commitment, and the end of 1963, private banking and investment institutions in the United States had taken as participations, or purchased from portfolio portions of 16 IFC commitments in 11 different countries, 6 of them in Latin America. These participations and purchases totaled just under $8 million, while the portion of these same commitments retained by the IFC amounted to $24 million. In addition, during 1962 and 1963, U.S. private investors acquired relatively small portions, totaling about three-quarters of a million dollars, in three security issues underwritten by the IFC, two issued by development banks in Finland and Malaya, the third by a Mexican steel fabrication firm.[13]

The first U.S. participation in an IFC investment was also, as of the end of 1963, the largest. This was a par-

[11] IFC, "Facts about IFC," Washington, 1964 (Mimeo.).
[12] IBRD, *Policies and Operations.* . . , p. 103.
[13] Data provided by Mr. Deely of the IBRD, Treasurer's Department.

ticipation totaling $3,175,000, taken in 1959 by the Bankers International Corporation, the Chemical Overseas Finance Corporation, and 13 private investors in a $4 million loan to Champion Cellulose, S.A., a Brazilian subsidiary of the Champion Fibre and Paper Company of Ohio for the construction of a wood pulp mill.[14] The only other participation involving more than $1 million of U.S. private capital was one taken in 1962 by 4 U.S. and 2 European investment companies in the IFC's $2 million commitment to COLTEJER of Colombia, Latin America's largest cotton textile manufacturer.[15] In both these instances, private investors in the U.S. and abroad together took up 80 per cent or more of the IFC's original commitment. The remaining 14 instances of U.S. participation were in the $100 to $500 thousand range, and generally represented a much smaller proportion of the original IFC commitment than the two cases just described.

Much more important than actual participations in IFC commitments have been investments of U.S. private capital, in both equity and loan form, in enterprises to which the IFC was simultaneously making a commitment. By the end of 1963, individuals and firms in the United States had invested an estimated total of more than $110 million in 24 such enterprises, of which, as Table 13 shows, a little more than half was in the form of equity funds. In most cases, the private investment was considerably larger than the IFC commitment.

By far the largest of these concurrent investments, accounting for more than half the total, was the financing provided by 5 sponsoring firms in the United States— Continental Oil Co., Cities Service, U.S. Rubber, Fish International Corp., and Witco Chemical—for PASA, a $72 million petrochemical industry in Argentina. The IFC's

[14] In the Champion Cellulose case, an equity investment was made by the U.S. parent company far exceeding the combined amounts of the IFC and private loans.

[15] IFC, *Seventh Annual Report*, Washington, 1963, p. 13.

TABLE 13

U.S. Private Funds Which Have
Accompanied IFC Investments
(in millions of U.S. dollars)

Calendar Year	IFC Commit-ment (net)[a]	U.S. Private Partici-pations	Concurrent Investment		
			Equity	Loan	Total
1957	0.6	—	0.8	—	0.8
1958	2.4	—	14.0	2.0	16.0
1959	6.4	4.0	16.6	6.2	26.8
1960	4.8	0.6	0.7	1.4	2.7
1961	7.1	0.2	19.0	38.0	57.2
1962	11.0	3.3	6.9	0.7	10.9
1963	9.0	0.9	3.2	0.5	4.6
Total	41.3	9.0	61.2	48.8	119.0

[a] These figures, unlike those in Table 12, are net of participations as well as cancellations and terminations.

Source: Compiled from information provided by officials of the IFC and IBRD, Treasurer's Department.

investment of $3 million helped to complete the financing for this operation, which included an equity investment of $18.5 million and loans of more than $30 million by the sponsoring companies.[16] A portion of the private investment was made under specific or extended-risk guaranties from AID as described in Chapter IX.

Among the other important, although much smaller, instances of this type of concurrent investment of IFC funds and private U.S. capital were:

(a) A $22 million expansion program for Willys-Overland de Brazil, S.A., a Jeep-manufacturing concern in which Willys Motors, Inc. of Ohio owns a large minority interest. Debt capital came from an IFC investment of $2,450,000 and investments totaling, $1,050,000 by the

[16] IFC, *Sixth Annual Report*, Washington, 1962, p. 8.

American Overseas Finance Company and the Chase International Investment Corporation. The larger part of the equity capital came from United States' sources, the largest single amount from Willys Motors, while the remainder was raised by the sale of stock to the Brazilian public.[17] (b) A $1.2 million loan by the IFC to Cementos Bio-Bio, S.A., a predominantly locally owned Chilean Company engaged in building a cement plant. Share capital for the project, whose total cost was estimated at $5 million, came from the Chilean public, the local subsidiary of the Koppers Company of Pittsburgh, and Transoceanic-American Overseas Finance Corporation Ltd., a U.S. investment corporation.[18] (c) A $3,757,000 expansion project for a pulp and paper mill owned and operated by Olinkraft S.A., a wholly owned subsidiary of the Olin Mathieson Chemical Corporation of the United States. Funds consisted of a $1.8 million equity investment by Olin Mathieson, a $1 million loan from Brazilian sources, and the IFC investment of $957,000.[19] (d) a $5,000,000 issue of convertible debentures by TAMSA, the Mexican manufacturer of tubular steel products mentioned earlier. The IFC purchased $250,000 of these debentures outright, and in addition took up $150,000 under a $750,000 standby agreement. More than $365,000 of this issue was placed with leading U.S. institutional investors and, at the same time U.S. investors purchased several million dollars of equity in the company.[20] (e) IFC investments originally totaling more than $6 million, plus $6.4 million in standby and underwriting commitments almost entirely taken up by others, in private development banks in Finland, Malaya, Morocco, Nigeria, Pakistan, Philippines, Spain, and Venezuela. Participations and equity in-

[17] IFC, *Second Annual Report*, Washington, 1958, pp. 10-11.

[18] IFC, *Fourth Annual Report*, Washington, 1960, p. 16.

[19] IFC, *Second Annual Report*, p. 10.

[20] IFC, *Seventh Annual Report*, pp. 15-16 and unpublished data provided by the IBRD and IFC.

vestments from U.S. sources in these same institutions totaled $5 million.[21]

In all, net IFC commitments to enterprises which had also attracted private loan or equity funds from the United States came to more than $40 million by the end of 1963, or almost two-thirds of its entire net commitment of funds to that date.[22] The U.S. private funds alone invested in these same enterprises are estimated at about $120 million, or nearly three times the IFC investment. Estimates of the types of funds composing this total are shown in Table 13: concurrent equity investments came to more than $60 million, concurrent loan funds to almost $50 million, and participations in IFC commitments to about $9 million. Unfortunately, no such detailed estimates are available of the amount of local and other foreign private capital which has also been invested in the enterprises which have received IFC money. But it must also be substantial in relation to the public funds committed, in view of the corporation's estimate that 4 or 5 private dollars have been invested for every dollar of IFC money.

BUSINESS SENTIMENT: FROM OPPOSITION TO INTEREST

Since the IFC, alone among the public lending agencies under discussion, deals directly and exclusively with private enterprise, the business community's views are in this case especially crucial to the organization's success. During the period of prolonged discussion and wrangling which preceded its establishment, the general opinion in government circles was that "American business is against the IFC." Closer investigation has revealed, however, that this is at least partly an illusion, caused by the fact that its opponents, though in the minority, "spoke out louder and more firmly than did its supporters."[23] Undoubtedly the

[21] Unpublished data provided by the IFC and IBRD.

[22] Table 13 and IFC, "Memorandum Relating to the Financial Statement," as of Dec. 31, 1963 (Mimeo.).

[23] Matecki, p. 91.

best organized and most vocal group to express an opinion on the question was the National Foreign Trade Council, which felt that the provision of equity capital is the function of private enterprise, and that any such "artificial" stimulation of equity investment as the IFC would provide is bound to result in uneconomic investments which could not, whatever the IFC's intentions, be later sold on their own merits to private investors.[24] Yet a survey of private investors in the leading capital-exporting nations made by the World Bank at about the same time indicated that a majority would be interested in using the facilities of the proposed corporation and regarded it as a good inducement to increased private investment in less-developed nations. A "strong minority" of those surveyed opposed the idea on the grounds that public funds should not be used for equity investment, and that where the investment climate was not attractive to private funds, public monies should not be invested.[25]

A similar division of opinion was apparent in testimony before Senate and House Committee hearings on the establishment of the IFC; the National Association of Manufacturers and a number of representatives of private firms shared the views of the National Foreign Trade Council, but a larger number of spokesmen for private business and trade groups and individual enterprises supported the creation of the IFC and, in some cases, indicated a personal interest in its operations.[26] Most impressive was the testimony of the representative of the Investment Bankers' Association: "There are several pools of capital that are to be devoted to foreign investment

[24] National Foreign Trade Convention, "Final Declaration," *Report of the 39th National Foreign Trade Convention*, New York, 1953, pp. 92-94.

[25] IBRD, *Report on the Proposal for an International Finance Corporation*, Washington, 1952.

[26] U.S. Congress, Senate, Committee on Banking and Currency, *International Finance Corporation, Hearings*, 84th Cong., 1st Sess., 1955, *passim*.

which are now in the process of formation. Each of these has been motivated in part by the prospect of entering into joint ventures with the International Finance Corporation."[27]

Also significant was the view of the United States Council of the International Chamber of Commerce that the IFC, unlike most proposals for supplementing private investment, would help to improve the investment climate in developing nations.[28]

Although the views of its most intransigent opponents did not alter radically once the IFC had come into being, the interest of the American business community in its operations increased as its aims and functions became more widely known. Its foundation coincided auspiciously with a greatly increased interest in foreign investment, particularly of the portfolio variety. The IFC's first President, Robert Garner, noted the importance of this resurgent interest to the work of his own organization in a speech to a bankers' group late in 1956: "We are aware also of new interest on the part of financial institutions in investment abroad. One indication has been more participation in World Bank loans by commercial banks and insurance companies. Another is that several of the most conservative banks in New York have begun to put certain of their investment accounts into stock of some of the leading foreign corporations . . . several new financial companies have been organized for foreign investment, and we in the International Finance Corporation have been told by them and by many of the leading investment banking houses in Wall Street of their interest in going along with us in deals."[29] And, indeed, a number of these new foreign investment companies are prominent among

[27] *Ibid.*, p. 97.

[28] *Ibid.*, p. 68.

[29] Robert L. Garner, *Foreign Investments in a Growing World* (Address to the 45th Annual Convention of the Investment Bankers Association of America, Hollywood, Fla., Nov. 29, 1956), Washington, 1957, pp. 5-6.

the private participants in the IFC investments described above. As far as the views of the business and financial community as a whole are concerned, as is so often the case with public programs, once the IFC's creation was an accomplished fact the hostile voices of its opponents faded noticeably, and arguments on grounds of economic principle yielded to a far more pragmatic interest in the actual services which the new corporation could perform for private groups or enterprises.

THE IFC: ITS POTENTIALITIES

In one sense, an evaluation of the difficulties and accomplishments of the agency under discussion should be simpler and more straightforward in this case than in any of the preceding ones. For, by making its avowed purposes at once narrower and more clearly defined than those of the other risk-sharing institutions, the IFC escapes the tension between two different and often conflicting sets of criteria characteristic of the other public lending agencies. By stipulating in advance that it will encourage economic development *only* by stimulating the investment of private funds, the IFC avoids having to choose between allowing easier lending terms and standards in order to assist a greater number and variety of development projects and maintaining more exacting ones in order to attract a maximum amount of private participation in its activities. We, in turn, are spared the necessity of judging it according to a double and therefore often confused standard. At the same time, just because the IFC has made its objectives a good deal more specific than the other lending agencies, there is a correspondingly greater chance for discrepancies between its aims and its actual accomplishments.

In encouraging the flow of U.S. direct investment funds to less-developed areas, the IFC's policy of dealing directly and exclusively with private enterprise is an advantage, since American firms are generally interested in foreign investment only where there is no significant public ownership or control. The situation is less clear-cut where portfolio investment is concerned; while the newer investment institutions created specifically to provide "venture capital" definitely prefer to lend in the private sector, some of the more cautious institutional investors such as commercial banks and insurance companies sometimes actually prefer that their foreign loans be to a government or one of its instrumentalities. On balance, however, there is no question that the IFC, by appealing to a different type of institutional investor than the older public lending agencies, has broadened the potentialities for channeling portfolio funds into economic development. Indeed, the IFC has put a special emphasis on the mobilization of what it terms "investment," as opposed to "business," capital.[30] Approximately half of the American funds invested in IFC enterprises through 1960 were of this portfolio type.

The fact that the IFC's investments are the "hardest" of any of the foreign-lending agencies, in terms of both lending standards and cost of funds, also increases its potentialities for attracting private capital. Its insistence on profit-potentiality as the dominant criterion for investment assures that the projects it selects should also be able to attract additional financing from private sources. At the same time, the high interest rates and profit-sharing provisions of its loan investments enhance its ability to turn over its funds through participations and portfolio purchases by private capital. And, although critics objected that by permitting the IFC to take equity as well as creditor positions "you are softening the loan,"[31] the fact is that this is the most common form of foreign investment for U.S. private capital, and the record shows

[30] IFC, *Third Annual Report*, Washington, 1959, p. 8.
[31] Testimony of Senator Symington in U.S. Congress, Senate, Committee on Foreign Relations, *The International Finance Corporation, Hearings*, 87th Cong., 1st Sess., 1961, p. 17.

that the IFC's movement into equity positions has enhanced rather than detracted from its ability to attract private funds into its commitments.

The similarity of the IFC's terms to those demanded by private investors also minimizes a problem which concerned several legislators during the hearings on the Corporation's establishment, namely, that by utilizing IFC funds for leverage purposes, private investors would be able to make large profits on a very small investment of their own funds.[32] The IFC's insistence on a rate of return commensurate with that which private capital would demand in a similar situation means that it offers very little scope for the operation of the leverage principle.

Of all the public lending agencies, the IFC seems uniquely suited to deal with several critical aspects of development investment stimulation. One is the attraction of newcomers into such investment. Ever since the controversy preceding its creation, both the IFC itself and outside observers have stressed that "its usefulness is importantly intended for inexperienced firms of medium and small size who want to go abroad."[33] To this end it not only offers financing and the increased confidence which is likely to accompany the very fact of its participation, but has also incurred ". . . substantial expense in such [investment project] investigations and in developing projects to the point where they are suitable for investment."[34] A number of IFC commitments have been directly to small and medium-sized enterprises, but much more important is the $16 million it has made available to private development banks in a number of less-developed countries. With the creation of the Development Bank Services Department in 1962, the IFC became the focal point of assistance from the international lending

[32] U.S. Congress, House, Committee on Banking and Currency, *International Finance Corporation, Hearings,* p. 86.

[33] A. Wilfred May, "New Era in Foreign Investing," *Commercial and Financial Chronicle,* 181 (June 16, 1955), 2753.

[34] IFC, *Third Annual Report,* pp. 10-11.

organizations to these institutions, which are generally the main, and in some cases almost the only, source of investment funds for small and medium-sized private industrial enterprise in the less-developed countries.

The three major functions of the IFC as stated in its Articles of Agreement are quoted at the beginning of this chapter; its President has stated them more succinctly as: first, to contribute to financing new or expanded ventures, in association with private investors, which are of high developmental priority to the economies of the countries where they are located; second, to contribute to the establishment or the development of capital markets in our member countries; and third, to stimulate the international flow of private foreign capital.[35] The first and third of these functions it shares with the other risk-sharing institutions, but for the second it bears the responsibility almost alone. Although small portions of World Bank bond issues have been taken by investors in the less-developed countries, only the IFC possesses the flexibility necessary to make a substantial contribution to the development of indigenous capital markets. The underwriting agreements and standby arrangements which the IFC has undertaken since the amendment to its charter permitting the purchase of equity securities are the major vehicle for such assistance. Although these contingent commitments have not been large—they amounted to only $10.4 million at the end of 1963—they represent potentially one of the most promising instruments for the mobilization of the capital resources of the developing countries themselves.

In its *Fourth Annual Report*, the IFC pointed out that "there is an unquestioned trend toward joint ventures under international and local sponsorship, based on growing evidence that the advantages outweigh the difficulties . . . IFC considers that where practicable joint enter-

[35] IFC, *Summary Proceedings*, 1962 Annual Meeting of the Board of Governors, Washington, 1962, p. 2.

prises are desirable."[36] Again, the operating criteria of
this organization are particularly well suited to the stimulation of such ventures; somewhere between a third and
a half of the enterprises which have received IFC funds
are under joint foreign-local ownership. Such ownership,
combined with the IFC's international character, can be
crucial in solving the capital-entry problem, as well as the
frequently more difficult one of capital-exit, in dealing
with reluctant host countries. The IFC hopes that it will
also serve as an important stimulus to the growth of an
experienced and responsible entrepreneurial group in developing countries.

GRADUAL REALIZATION AND ITS OBSTACLES

We have indicated several points of potential strength in
the IFC's structure; its critics have pointed out certain
weaknesses which they regard as inherent in this same
structure, and as likely to detract from the organization's
ability to mobilize private funds. One is the alleged tendency for "good" investments to be turned over to private investors while "bad" ones are left on the IFC's
hands; the other is the Corporation's inability until recently, under the rules of its charter, to exercise the normal
controls of equity management in the event of threatened
loss.[37] Although this stricture was removed by the 1961
amendment, which specifically empowered the IFC to
exercise voting and management rights in the event of
threatened or actual loss but at no other time, the question still applies to the majority of IFC investments, which
are in debt rather than equity form.

Whether or not the IFC finds itself "stuck" with the
bad investments depends entirely on the soundness of its
judgement. Unless this judgement is inferior to that of private investors, the profits it makes on the sale of "good"

[36] IFC, *Fourth Annual Report*, p. 5.
[37] U.S. Congress, House, Committee on Banking and Currency,
International Finance Corporation, Hearings, pp. 101-104.

investments should at least balance the losses it might suffer from being left with some "bad" ones. As far as risk of loss is concerned, the IFC as debtor is generally in a position similar to that of any middle-position (e.g., preferred stock) investor; its inability to exercise management functions is balanced by the protection afforded by the true equity capital subordinate to it. Indeed, the IFC has stated that, as a matter of policy, it "will not invest in projects where debt carrying fixed-interest charges are larger than the equity."[38] As an equity investor, the IFC may at times suffer from the fact that it cannot exercise day-to-day control, but only step in when calamity looms. On the other hand, an international organization like the IFC may well be in a position to make its wishes effective even where it does not possess legal management rights. Ultimately, in any case, the effect of its structural limitations on the IFC's over-all position is likely to depend less upon any of these considerations than upon the wisdom and astuteness with which its investment decisions are initially made.

Conjecture aside, the record of the IFC's first seven years offers little to substantiate these particular fears. As of the end of 1963, earnings on roughly $60 million of net effective commitments totaled more than $9 million. Profits and losses on the sale of securities balanced out to a net profit of more than $1 million. The IFC had suffered the loss of about $100,000 in the liquidation of one of its few investments in a developed country—Australia—and two of its smaller investments (totaling less than $600,000) were in difficulties which indicated the possibility of some ultimate loss by the Corporation. At the same time, the IFC's reserve against losses, to which its net income is allocated, amounted to more than $17 million.[39] Officers of the IFC anticipated that earnings on

[38] IFC, *Fourth Annual Report*, p. 9.
[39] IFC, *Annual Reports* and *Memorandum Relating to the Financial Statements* as of Dec. 31, 1963.

investments would drop off somewhat in the near future as the proportion of equity securities in IFC's portfolio rose, since equity investments do not normally pay out earnings in the early years, but that these investments would in the long-run greatly increase the organization's profit-making potential.

Finally, one of the most prevalent criticisms of the IFC during the period under discussion was that all its potential advantages are nullified by the fact that its utilization of the available funds has been slow, unimaginative, and incomplete. The slow growth of its commitments during the early years of operation has already been described, and even in mid-1964, a larger proportion of the IFC's total assets of $129 million was held in the form of time deposits and U.S. government obligations than in operational loans and equity investments.[40] Its capital subscriptions still exceeded net commitments by a substantial margin; it had just begun to augment its funds through sales from its portfolio and had not yet utilized sales of its own securities, a method for which some of the organization's original proponents had great expectations.

There are a variety of explanations one can offer for this apparent failure to live up to potential. One, propounded by the forces which fought for and eventually won an amendment to the IFC's charter, is that the organization, in addition to being a new and untried form of operation that would inevitably require time to build up expertise and contacts and win the confidence of private investors, was severely hamstrung by its inability to invest in capital stock. This argument stresses the many disadvantages of such a limitation: the complicated and unfamiliar forms which IFC investments were forced to take; its inability to strengthen the capital structure of enterprises by its own investments or to encourage private capital to join with it in making equity investments; the exchange risks accompanying fixed-interest loans denominated in

[40] IFC, *Eighth Annual Report*, p. 40.

dollars; the criticism of IFC lending terms as providing the "protection of a creditor and the rewards of a stockholder"; the difficulties encountered in selling off the hybrid securities in its portfolio and thus revolving its funds.[41] The 1961 abolition of the prohibition on equity investment should, in this view, unlock much of the IFC's potential and lead to a greater and more effective utilization of its resources.

Quite a different explanation of the same situation is given by the IFC's critics: that it has not lived up to its potential because it has not been sufficiently imaginative in seeking out investment proposals that meet its exacting lending standards and in utilizing the means at its disposal to secure funds for greatly increased lending activity. Finally, a third alternative explanation is that it is the underlying concept which is at fault; that the IFC's sluggish start and persistently small scale of operations are due neither to limitations on its powers nor to any lack of ability or effort on the part of its staff, but rather to the fact that the gap which it was created to fill simply does not exist. Its difficulty in finding suitable projects is due, in this view, to the fact that private investors do possess adequate information and that existing investment opportunities in the less-developed countries are in fact being taken up without the assistance of the IFC.

Although the case is not proven, and it would be foolish to regard equity investment as a complete panacea, the IFC's recent record does offer grounds for favoring the first and most optimistic possibility. Its investment rate did speed up after it was permitted to make equity as well as loan commitments; in fiscal year 1964 IFC commitments amounted to $21 million, "and there were more of them, in more countries, than in any earlier year."[42] "The accelerated rate of new commitments was

[41] U.S. Congress, Senate, Committee on Foreign Relations, *The IFC, Hearings. . .* , pp. 3-8.
[42] IFC, *Eighth Annual Report*, p. 7.

due not to any significant expansion of IFC's loanable resources but to a greater utilization of funds already available";[43] at the end of fiscal 1964, the IFC still had available more than $50 million of uncommitted funds. By late 1960, the IFC had attracted an estimated $46 million of U.S. private capital into its undertakings; three years later this figure had nearly tripled, and the ratio of private to public funds had also risen. Using the organization's own estimate of a three-to-one ratio between public and private funds, it appeared that as of 1960, about $100 million in private funds had been invested in developing countries in conjunction with the operations of the IFC. A similar calculation for 1963, using the IFC's revised, higher estimate of the public-private ratio, suggests that between $250 and $400 million of private capital had been invested, in addition to its own funds.

In sum, the amount of private capital mobilized by the IFC for economic development has been small, in relation not only to the needs of the borrowing nations but also to the sums actually sent abroad by the major capital-exporting nations during the same period. But the IFC's operations are growing at an accelerating rate, and a 1964 amendment to the charters of the IBRD and the IFC permitting the World Bank to make loans to its affiliate opened up a potentially important new source of funds. The important question is, with imaginative new investment techniques and a new source of funds at its disposal, how fast can the IFC continue to accelerate the growth of its commitments? The impressive ratio of private to public funds leaves no doubt that the organization is a catalyst; the question is simply whether it is to become a large catalyst or remain a small one. It is this matter of scale which, more than anything else, will determine whether the unique idea of the IFC is to be translated into an important vehicle for capital mobilization.

[43] National Advisory Council on International Monetary and Financial Problems, *Eighth Special Report*, 88th Cong., 1st Sess., House Doc. No. 175, Washington, 1963, p. 29.

VII · THE INTER-AMERICAN DEVELOPMENT BANK

A BANK FOR LATIN AMERICA: ORIGINS AND AIMS

The Inter-American Development Bank is unique among the risk-sharing institutions sponsored in whole or in part by the United States Government in that it has as its area of operations not the entire underdeveloped world but one particular geographic segment of it: Latin America. Of a number of regional development banks projected for various parts of the developing world, it was the first—and as of 1964, the only—one to come into operation. Patterned rather closely on the World Bank, it differs from the larger organization in two important respects: it is regional rather than worldwide in scope and membership, and it is "a bank of borrowers rather than of lenders." That is, while the capital structure and the voting power of the World Bank are dominated by the capital-exporting nations, the capital-importing nations contributed more than half of the initial capital of the Inter-American Bank and, since they also command more than half the voting power, assumed much of the responsibility for allocating and overseeing the utilization of the Bank's resources.

The notion of a hemispheric banking institution, which would concentrate solely on the needs of the Latin American nations, has been evolving for many decades; its origins can be traced back at least as far as a proposal made by Secretary of State Blaine at the First International Conference of American States in 1889.[1] But it was not until the late 1950's, against a background of intensified political urgency, that concrete steps for the creation of such an organization were taken by the nation whose sponsorship was essential for its effective operation—the United

[1] Inter-American Development Bank, *First Annual Report*, Washington, 1961, p. 1, and John E. Loomis, *Public Money Sources for Overseas Trade and Investment*, Washington, 1963, p. 197.

States. The consideration of proposals for an inter-American development bank was recommended at the 1957 meeting of the Economic Conference of the Organization of American States in Buenos Aires; in mid-1958, Under-Secretary of State Dillon announced at a special meeting of the Inter-American Economic and Social Council that the United States Government was willing to consider the establishment of such an institution.[2] After that, the practical steps necessary to bring the bank into existence were taken in short order: a committee composed of representatives of all the Latin American countries and the United States was set up to draft the agreement establishing an inter-American financial institution; the committee submitted the completed Agreement for ratification in April 1959; the first meeting of the Board of Governors was held in February 1960, and in October of that same year the Inter-American Development Bank (IDB) officially opened its doors for business.

The *Agreement* establishing the IDB, like the document promulgated for the IBRD nearly 15 years earlier, reflected the twin aims of promoting economic development and mobilizing private capital to do as much of the job as possible. The first three functions of the Inter-American Bank are set forth in the Agreement as:

(i) to promote the investment of public and private capital for development purposes;

(ii) to utilize its own capital, funds raised by it in financial markets, and other available resources, for financing the development of the member countries . . . ;

(iii) to encourage private investment in projects, en-

[2] IDB, *First Annual Report*, p. 1 and National Advisory Council, *Special Report of the National Advisory Council on the Proposed Inter-American Development Bank*, 86th Cong., 2nd Sess., House Doc. No. 133, Washington, 1959, pp. 9-10. Under-Secretary of State Dillon said that this decision was based in part on reports on the Latin American situation by Vice President Nixon, Secretary of State Dulles, and Milton Eisenhower.

terprises, and activities contributing to economic development and to supplement private investment when private capital is not available on reasonable terms and conditions.[3]

In addition, the functions of the IDB include specifically the provision of guidance in "orient[ing] their development policies toward a better utilization of their resources . . ." and "technical assistance for the preparation, financing, and implementation of development plans and projects. . . ." Here again, the founders of the Latin American bank were drawing on the experience of the World Bank. Although such non-financial activities were not originally envisaged as part of the IBRD's function, they gradually became an increasingly important part of its activities and one of the foundations of its success, both in mobilizing capital for economic development and in assuring that, in most cases at least, the borrowed funds are put to effective use.

The IDB's intended role as a bridge for the movement of international capital was made even more explicit in the organization's *First Annual Report*, which stressed its importance as ". . . an authentically inter-American financial organization to promote its interests on the international private capital markets and to serve as an adequate multilateral vehicle for channeling financial assistance from other nations."[4] Apparently the founders of the IDB envisaged a bridge across which not only foreign private but also foreign government capital could move into the developing nations of Latin America. This idea is elaborated in the *Second Annual Report*, which discusses the possible role of the IDB as financial agent for Latin American governments, and mentions "the possibility that the Bank might organize consortia of credit institutions

[3] IDB, *Agreement Establishing the Inter-American Development Bank*, Washington, 1963, Article I, Section 2(a).

[4] IDB, *First Annual Report*, p. 7.

and governments prepared to contribute to the continued and systematic financing of particular [national development] programs."[5]

FINANCIAL RESOURCES AND THEIR UTILIZATION

To enable the IDB to carry out its intended functions, the Agreement provided for initial capital resources of $1 billion, to be contributed on a prorated basis by the organization's member countries. Of this sum, $850 million constituted the authorized capital stock or "ordinary resources" of the Bank, $400 million of it to be paid in in three annual installments due in 1960, 1961, and 1962, the remaining $450 million to be callable "when required to meet the obligations of the Bank," that is, if funds should be needed to pay holders of the Bank's own securities or of guaranties issued by the Bank.[6] The other $150 million was segregated in a Fund for Special Operations, "established for the making of loans on terms and conditions appropriate for dealing with special circumstances arising in specific countries or with respect to specific projects."[7] Since the purpose of the Fund is to make "softer" loans than would normally be permitted under conventional standards of "bankability," its resources and its liabilities were carefully segregated from the IDB's ordinary capital, in order to avoid jeopardizing the Bank's ability to attract private capital into its ordinary operations through participations or the marketing of its own securities. Fifty per cent of the paid-in portion of each country's quota for both the ordinary resources and the Fund for Special Operations was payable in gold or U.S. dollars, the other 50 per cent in the members' own currency, but under a maintenance-of-value clause providing that "each payment of a member in its own currency . . . shall be in such amount as . . . is equivalent to the full value, in

---

[5] IDB, *Second Annual Report*, Washington, 1962, p. 4.

[6] IDB, *Agreement. . .* , Article II, Sections 2 and 4.

[7] *Ibid.*, Article IV, Section 1.

terms of United States dollars of the weight and fineness in effect on January 1, 1959, of the portion of the quota being paid."[8]

By the end of 1962, all of the member countries of the IDB had completed payment on their quotas for both ordinary resources and the Fund for Special Operations. The Bank's subscribed capital now consisted of $959.5 million: $381.6 paid in, $431.6 callable, and $146.3 paid in to the Fund for Special Operations. The remaining gap of $40.5 million represented the quota of Cuba, which failed to become a member of the Bank. The United States' subscription—$150 million paid in and $200 million callable—represented more than 40 per cent of the IDB's initial capital resources for ordinary operations, while its contribution of $100 million amounted to a little more than two-thirds of the total resources of the Fund for Special Operations.[9] In addition, the effective total resources of the IDB had been expanded in mid-1961, when it was made Administrator of the Social Progress Trust Fund, initially amounting to nearly $400 million. This fund was established by the United States, as a part of the Alliance for Progress, to make long-term, low-cost loans, repayable in local currency, for Latin American development in the areas of land settlement, low-income housing, water and sanitation facilities, and higher education.[10] And finally, the IDB had increased its resources during 1962 by the sale of two issues of its own securities, one for $75 million in the capital market of the United States and another for 15 billion lire ($24.2 million) to a consortium of Italian banks.[11]

The Inter-American Bank lost little time in putting its financial resources to use. Between the time it made its first loan in February 1961 and the end of that year, it

[8] *Ibid.*, Article IV, Section 3.
[9] IDB, *Second Annual Report*, pp. 14, 58.
[10] *Ibid.*, pp. 109-111.
[11] IDB, *Third Annual Report*, Washington, 1963, p. 14.

made 73 loans totaling almost $300 million in 18 of the 19 eligible member countries.[12] Of these loans $130 million were from the Bank's ordinary capital, $48 million from the Fund for Special Operations, and $116 million from the Social Progress Trust Fund. During the two years that followed the IDB maintained its brisk lending pace, and by the end of 1963 it had authorized a total of 192 loans amounting in all to $875 million. Eighty-two of these, totaling $386 million, had come from ordinary capital resources, 37 totaling $122 million from the Fund for Special Operations, and 73 amounting to $367 million from the Social Progress Trust Fund. Not surprisingly, the three largest countries in Latin America had received the largest single amounts; Argentina, Brazil, and Mexico had each received more than $100 million in loans.[13]

As of December 31, 1963, the authorized loans of the IDB were distributed as shown in Table 14, with the largest single share directed toward agricultural projects, and only slightly less substantial shares allocated to the areas of industry and mining, water supply and sanitation, and housing. But the loans made from ordinary resources alone, the only category which involves the direct mobilization of private funds either through the marketing of its own securities or through participations, fall into a somewhat different pattern. Industrial and mining projects received the largest single share of these funds, and agricultural enterprises were the direct or indirect recipients of a slightly smaller portion. The "infrastructure" areas of electric power, transport, water supply, and sanitation received much smaller portions of these funds while the areas which often yield no direct monetary returns, housing and education, received none at all. Looked at a little differently, more than half (54.2 per cent) of all loans from ordinary capital resources were made to govern-

[12] The Bank is not intended to make loans in the United States.
[13] IDB, *Activities 1961-63*, Washington, 1964, pp. 2-3.

TABLE 14

Distribution of IDB Loans by Purpose,
as of December 31, 1963
(in thousands of U.S. dollars)

Purpose	Ordinary Capital Resources	Fund for Special Operations	Social Progress Trust Fund	Grand Total
Industry & Mining	153.1	35.7	—	188.8
Agriculture	126.8	49.7	68.6	245.1
Electric Power & Transport	66.7	18.2	—	84.9
Water Supply & Sanitation	38.6	17.1	114.2	169.9
Housing	—	—	168.7	168.7
Advanced Education	—	—	16.2	16.2
Total	$385.2	$120.7	$367.7	$873.6[a]

[a] Excludes $1,451,000 for general planning studies.

Source: Inter-American Development Bank, *Activities 1961-1963*, Washington, 1964, p. 5.

ments and government entities, 28.5 per cent to development institutions for relending to private enterprise, and only 17.3 per cent directly to private enterprise.[14]

As a result of its brisk lending pace, the Inter-American Bank began very quickly to feel the pinch of shrinking funds, and during 1962 it took steps to increase its resources. By the end of 1963, the member countries had approved a $1 billion increase in the *callable* capital stock of the IDB, an additional increase in the authorized capital stock of $300 million to provide for the possible admission of new members, and a 50 per cent increase, amounting to $73.2 million, in the resources of the Fund for Special Operations. As a result of these increases, the total authorized capital of the Inter-American Bank rose

[14] IDB, *Fourth Annual Report*, Washington, 1964, p. 14.

to $2.15 billion, of which $475 million corresponded to paid-in capital shares and the rest to callable shares. The United States' participation in these increases amounted to an additional $412 million of callable capital and a new contribution of $50 million to the Fund for Special Operations. In addition, in December 1963 the U.S. Congress appropriated $131 million to replenish the nearly exhausted resources of the Social Progress Trust Fund.[15]

LENDING CRITERIA AND PROTECTIVE PROVISIONS

The "rules and conditions for making or guaranteeing loans," set forth in the IDB *Agreement*, like the corresponding provisions in the *Articles of Agreement* of the World Bank, are intended to create conditions under which IDB activities will attract private capital and at the same time to give assurance that the operations of the organization will not compete with private lending in Latin America. The Bank's general commitment to financial caution is contained in the statement "in making or guaranteeing a loan, the Bank shall pay due regard to prospects that the borrower and its guarantor, if any, will be in a position to meet their obligations under the loan contract."[16]

The IDB, again like its larger prototype the IBRD, has a specific project provision as part of its protective armor. But the wording, which is simply that IDB loans "shall be principally for financing specific projects," leaves a loophole through which any loan the Bank might wish to make could easily slip, and it makes specific exception for general loans to development institutions. Obtaining a government guaranty in the case of loans to non-governmental entities is optional rather than required in the case of the IDB, and the Bank has used this freedom to make a significant number of loans to private entities without

---

[15] *Ibid.*, pp. 12-13, 54, 84.
[16] IDB, *Agreement*. . . , Article III, Section 7(a).

government guaranty.[17] Finally, the *Agreement* provides that, "in guaranteeing a loan made by other investors, the Bank shall receive suitable compensation for its risk."[18] Since the Bank had never, as of the end of 1963, utilized its authority to guaranty loans made by others, it is not clear what its standard of "suitable compensation" would be.

The section of the *Agreement* which commits the IDB to avoid competing with private loan funds is even less specific than the provisions regarding protection of lending standards. It provides that in considering a request for a loan or a guaranty, the Bank shall take into account the ability of the borrower to obtain the loan from private sources of financing on terms which, in the opinion of the Bank, are reasonable for the borrower, taking into account all pertinent factors.[19]

It is difficult to imagine that a statement so hedged about with qualifications could ever serve as an effective barrier to any loan the Bank might wish to make. Subsequently, however, the IDB reemphasized and elaborated on its intention to avoid competing with other sources of external financing for Latin America, whether public or private, and added that "to encourage greater mobilization of public and private capital for economic development, the Bank will not normally lend more than 50 per cent of the total cost of the project to be financed."[20]

The terms of IDB loans from ordinary capital resources are roughly comparable with those of the IBRD or the Eximbank's development loans. That is, they are reasonably "hard" when the frame of reference is the practices of public lending organizations in general, but a good deal cheaper and more flexible than private funds would be under the same circumstances, even if such funds were

[17] *Ibid.*, and information provided by Dr. José Epstein, Deputy Director, Loan Division, IDB.

[18] IDB, *Agreement. . .* , Article III, Section 7(a).

[19] *Ibid.*   [20] IDB, *Second Annual Report*, p. 12.

readily available. The annual interest rate on loans from ordinary resources has recently been fixed at 5¾ per cent, including a 1 per cent commission for the Bank's special reserve against guaranty and borrowing obligations, plus a commitment fee of ¾ of 1 per cent on the undisbursed portion of loans. The amortization periods on loans to the private sector tend to fall between 8 and 12 years, while on loans for economic infrastructure works they may extend as long as 20 years, "including grace periods in both cases where justified." In the case of loans to private corporations, the Bank has generally protected its creditor position by placing some limitations on the payment of dividends. All loans from ordinary resources must be repaid in the currency borrowed, but the Bank generally requires maintenance-of-value when the loan, and therefore the repayment, are in currencies other than dollars.[21]

In reality, it is probably less the written rules and criteria of the IDB than the highly respectable record chalked up by the IBRD and the conviction that the regional bank would exercise the same sort of sound, rather conservative standards in making loans from ordinary resources which has given the private financial community the faith in its judgment that is the most important form of protection. For it is the soundness of the IDB's judgment which determines the adequacy of the various devices designed to protect the investment of a private participant in the Bank's activities. These include loan maturities held by the IDB itself which generally extend well beyond the maturities taken by private lenders; the liquid reserves against losses; and, finally, the Bank's loan portfolio itself, which is at present several times greater than the amount of private capital borrowed by the Bank. The size of the IDB's reserves against losses, for example, alone tells us very little. At the end of 1963, the general reserve

[21] *Ibid.*, pp. 12-13 and information provided by Mr. Epstein.

against losses (net income) amounted to more than $7 million, while the special reserve represented an additional half million.[22] This sum, which is certainly substantial when regarded in the light of the organization's zero losses so far, is nevertheless small in comparison with total loan authorizations of nearly $400 million from ordinary resources. But this reflects simply the fact that the IDB is a very young organization; less than a third of its commitments have even been disbursed as yet, and nearly all of its loans are still in the "grace period" which yields little income. What is important is private lenders' expectations about the IDB's loss record and earning power in the future and this, in turn, comes back again to the organization's soundness of judgment.

The foregoing discussion is relevant, of course, only to loans from the IDB's ordinary capital resources. The Fund for Special Operations makes loans on terms and criteria which would be far less acceptable to the private capital market. But the organizers of the Inter-American Bank were careful to provide that the operations of its "soft loan window" should in no way impinge on the ability of the "hard loan window" to mobilize private capital for its operations. Both participants in IDB loans and purchasers of the Bank's own securities are accordingly protected by the "Basic Principle of Separation," which provides that "The ordinary capital resources of the Bank shall under no circumstances be charged with, or used to discharge, losses or liabilities arising out of operations for which the resources of the Fund were originally used or committed."[23]

RELATIONS WITH PRIVATE CAPITAL MARKETS

There are several different ways in which the IDB was intended, and has already begun, to mobilize external private capital to help finance economic development in

[22] IDB, *Fourth Annual Report*, p. 32.
[23] IDB, *Agreement. . .* , Article III, Section 3(a).

Latin America. The one which has so far involved the largest amounts of money is the expansion of its ordinary loan resources through the sale of its own securities in some of the world's larger private capital markets. Although the IDB did not expect to begin such operations until it had had time to establish its reputation and acquire a substantial loan portfolio, it knew also from the IBRD experience that the laying of the groundwork was likely to be a time-consuming job, albeit eased by the fact that the World Bank had led the way and won the respect and confidence of the banking communities in the world's major capital-exporting nations. Accordingly, the IDB took initial steps during 1960, even before it had officially opened for business, to publicize its operations and to secure the legislation necessary to qualify its bonds for institutional investment in the markets where it expected to sell such securities.[24]

By the time the first issue of IDB bonds was marketed in the United States, late in 1962,[25] the groundwork had been well laid. These securities were by then legal investments for all national banks, for commercial banks in all but one state, and for savings banks, life insurance companies, and trust funds in a majority of the states, including most of the financially important ones. In addition, the IDB securities had been accorded many of the privileges enjoyed by U.S. Government bonds: member banks of the Federal Reserve system had been authorized to deal in and underwrite them; their use as security by Banks serving as a depository for U.S. Government funds had been authorized by the Treasury; and they were exempt from certain provisions of the Securities Acts.[26]

[24] IDB, *First Annual Report*, p. 17.

[25] This bond issue was preceded by one for 15 billion Italian lire ($24.2 million), sold to a consortium of Italian banks in April 1962.

[26] IDB (Executive Directors), *Proposal for an Increase in the Resources of the Inter-American Development Bank*, Washington, 1963, pp. 13-14.

The issue of December 11, 1962 consisted of $75 million of 20-year 4¼ per cent bonds, handled by an underwriting syndicate headed by three major New York investment firms and including a total of 102 commercial banks and investment banking firms located throughout the United States. The reception these bonds received made it clear that the fledgling organization was regarded as high quality investment by the U.S. private capital market. Offered at par, the Inter-American Bank bonds received an AAA rating and the issue was completely sold out on the first day of offering.[27]

At the same time, it was quite clear that however much the IDB stressed the soundness of its principles and the wisdom of its management in its efforts to create a market for its securities, it was the underlying "guaranty" of the U.S. Government that made the bonds attractive or even acceptable to U.S. investors. The Bank's own Board of Executive Directors pointed out that "After examining the matter with outstanding market specialists and taking into account the experience of other international institutions, the Bank believes that, for the time being, its capacity to sell its obligations in the international capital markets is in practice limited to the guarantee offered by the callable capital subscription of the United States which amounts to $200,000,000."[28] And pains had been taken to insure that the guaranty was airtight. Even though the callable portion of the U.S. capital subscription was only a contingent commitment, the full amount had been not only authorized but actually appropriated by Congress.[29] And in the 1962 bond issue, the IDB provided not only a negative pledge covenant, but also a com-

[27] National Advisory Council, *Special Report to the President and to the Congress on Increase in the Resources of the Inter-American Development Bank*, 88th Cong., 1st Sess., House Doc. No. 153, Washington, 1963, p. 39.
[28] IDB, *Proposal. . .* , p. 13.
[29] Public Law 86-213, 73 *Stat.* 445, Sept. 1, 1959.

mitment that so long as any of these bonds are outstanding it will limit the total amount of its outstanding borrowings and guaranties to "the amount of the subscription of the United States of America to the Bank's callable shares."[30]

In practice, it was felt that even this was not quite enough, that the "effective management of the Bank's borrowing program will be substantially aided by a sizeable margin of unused guarantee capacity in the form of callable capital,"[31] a reserve margin which the Bank set at about $25 million.[32] The fact that, by the beginning of 1963, this meant that only $75 million more could be borrowed by the IDB under its existing capital structure led to pressure for an increase in the organization's resources. The result was the increase of $1 billion in members' contributions to ordinary capital resources mentioned earlier, of which the United States' share was $412.8 million. The entire increase was made on a callable rather than a paid-in basis, on the grounds that ". . . it was always intended that after receiving a sizeable initial amount of paid-in capital, which would enable the Bank to establish its reputation as an effective lending institution, the ordinary capital loans would be primarily financed on the basis of the Bank's selling its obligations in the world's capital markets."[33] The Bank felt confident that, with the expanded margin provided by a total U.S. callable subscription of more than $600 million, it would be able to place bond issues in the U.S. and Western European capital markets in sufficient amount to support through 1967 its desired annual lending rate of $150 million from ordinary resources alone.[34]

[30] "Prospectus" for Inter-American Development Bank $75,000,-000 of 4¼ per cent Twenty-Year Bonds of 1962, Dec. 11, 1962.

[31] National Advisory Council, *Special Report. . .* , p. 24.

[32] IDB, *Proposal. . .* , p. 13.

[33] *Ibid.*, p. 20.

[34] *Ibid.*, pp. 19-20 and National Advisory Council, *Special Report. . .* , p. 25.

OTHER FORMS OF CAPITAL MOBILIZATION

In addition to buying the securities of the IDB itself, private banks can and do expand the organization's ordinary lending resources by taking participations in particular loan commitments. The IDB was prompt in establishing working relationships with commercial banks in the United States and Western Europe, and by the end of its first year of operations had attracted 73 participations totaling $4.5 million by 31 banks, all but 4 in the United States, in its $130 million of loans from ordinary resources.[35]

By the end of 1963, as Table 15 shows, the operations of the Inter-American Bank had attracted private partic-

TABLE 15

Private Participations in IDB Loans
(in thousands of U.S. dollars)

Calendar Year	U.S. Banks	European Banks	Total
1961	4,308.6	175.0	4,483.6
1962	2,850.1	430.0	3,280.1
1963	6,329.8	1,081.8	7,411.6
Total	13,488.5	1,686.8	15,175.3[a]

[a] Includes approximately $230,000 of sales from portfolio.
Source: Unpublished data provided by the IDB.

ipations totaling $15.2 million, or about 4 per cent of the $370.7 million of net loan authorizations from ordinary capital resources. Of this total, $13.5 million came from the more than 30 participating banks in the United States. During 1963, in fact, "participations actually allocated . . . totaled $7,381,518, but the applications from banks for participations aggregated a much higher figure."[36]

[35] IDB, *Second Annual Report*, p. 11.
[36] IDB, *Fourth Annual Report*, p. 5.

The IDB was forced to leave some of the private demand for participations unfulfilled because it did not want individual participations to be smaller than the size of borrower's disbursement drawings—generally, $100,000 or more—and it wanted to keep some of the early maturities for itself, in order to maintain a balanced portfolio and receive some earnings itself in the early years of the loans. And private participants apparently did not yet feel ready to take some of the longer maturities of IDB loans, as they have finally begun to do in the case of the World Bank. All participations in IDB credits have been taken without guaranty or any form of recourse on the organization, but the fact that, in each loan, the Bank holds securities with maturities extending well beyond those of the privately held portions provides a form of protection which the participating banks apparently regard as essential. As a matter of fact, it is less a change in the attitude of present participants than a broadening of the type of institution participating in IDB activities which can be expected eventually to overcome the present reluctance to take longer maturities. Commercial banks tend by their very nature to be confined, or to confine themselves, to fairly short-term investments; it is life insurance companies and similar institutional investors that find longer maturities more appropriate to their portfolios, and such organizations have not yet begun to participate on a significant scale in Inter-American Bank loans.

Participations in the loans of the Inter-American Development Bank have made private capital from the United States available to a wide variety of enterprises in Latin America. Among the larger participations have been those in loans totaling $16 million to two development banks in Venezuela, one for industry and the other for agriculture, which will re-loan the funds to a variety of private undertakings; and smaller participations have been taken in loans to a number of development banks in other Latin American countries, some public, some mixed, and at least one private. Substantial participations by U.S. private capital have also been taken in large loans to governments for "social overhead" investment, such as land settlement and irrigation projects in Mexico. Relatively few participations have been taken in loans made directly to private enterprise, and those that were taken were for rather small amounts. The largest, through the end of 1963, was for $500,000 in a $2 million loan to help establish an auto components plant in Argentina. Other loans with U.S. private capital participating have gone to help establish or expand such private undertakings as a pulp and paper plant in Colombia, a chemical plant in Honduras, auto component plants in Argentina and Brazil, a textile plant in Paraguay, and a cement plant in Peru.[37]

The sale of its own bonds and of participations in its loans represents the most clear-cut forms of foreign capital mobilization undertaken by the Inter-American Development Bank. But "the Bank has also promoted the mobilization of foreign resources through parallel financing, under which its own funds are supplemented with credits from external suppliers of capital goods and equipment."[38] In some cases these parallel or other concurrent private credits may represent only a small portion of the total cost of a project, in others, the IDB may simply supply the last piece of a nearly completed financing operation. Such concurrent financing operations are by nature elusive; there have doubtless been some which were never recorded by the Bank, and in others which have been identified, it is often

[37] IDB, *Annual Reports.*
[38] IDB, *Activities. . .* , p. 1. The term "parallel financing" is used by the IDB to denote private financing from sources other than the parent corporation or major shareholder. The term "concurrent financing" is broader, referring to any private financing which takes place in conjunction with a credit or guaranty from one of the risk-sharing agencies.

difficult to tell exactly what proportion of the private capital in a given enterprise is of U.S. origin.

The largest parallel financing operation to take place during the Bank's first three years of lending was in connection with the establishment of a petroleum refinery in Chile. The IDB authorized a loan of $11 million for this project, whose total cost was estimated at $34 million, and a private U.S. petroleum firm provided financing totaling an additional $8 million. Substantial investments from private U.S. sources were also made in connection with two loans to Brazil. One was a credit of $3.6 million to a $33 million government-sponsored synthetic rubber plant, which received loan financing from three major U.S. firms and a consortium of French banks as well as from local sources and the IDB. Seventy-five per cent of the stock of this corporation was scheduled to be turned over gradually to small local private shareholders. The other was a cellulose pulp mill in Brazil, for which the IDB had by early 1964 authorized loans totaling $8.7 million. The total cost of this project was estimated at more than $20 million, and the U.S. owner had provided a somewhat larger share of the total financing than had the Bank. In other instances, parent companies or major suppliers in the United States provided loan or equity funds for two automobile component plants in Argentina and one in Brazil, for a pulp mill in Colombia, and a heavy equipment plant in Mexico. The Phillips Petroleum Corporation purchased 10 per cent of the stock in a Mexican carbon black plant to which it also provided patent rights and technical assistance, and a large U.S. bank provided some of the loan financing for a sodium sulphate plant in Mexico, which also received funds from the IFC and its participants as well as from the IDB.[39]

The private U.S. investment capital made available for Latin American economic development through those

[39] IDB, *Annual Reports* and unpublished data.

concurrent financing operations we have been able to pin down has amounted in all to roughly $30 million; the IDB contribution to these same transactions was slightly less, perhaps $27 or $28 million. There are other instances in which U.S. private capital was obviously involved, but there is no way of knowing exactly how much. The sodium sulphate plant in Mexico, for example, received much of its equity capital from a subsidiary of another Mexican firm which is in turn owned 49 per cent by American Metal Climax, Inc. It would be impossible to trace through all these generations to arrive at an accurate estimate of the amount of U.S. capital invested in this particular project. Similarly, it is impossible to sort out the capital investment of U.S. origin in PERUINVEST, a private development investment firm founded by Peruvian, European, and United States stockholders, which received IDB loan funds. Omissions such as this obviously imply that the figure we have given for U.S. capital in concurrent financing operations is an underestimate, but it seems unlikely that they would change the general order of magnitude of the estimate.

When we compare the total of U.S. private participations with the net total of IDB commitments to those enterprises which involved participations, we find that the ratio is very low; the private funds of U.S. origin amounted to only about 6 per cent of the net IDB lending. When both the Bank's and the private components of concurrent financing operations are included in the calculation, the figure rises to about 15 per cent, still very low in comparison with the experience of the other international lending institutions, and reflecting the fact that in all of the participations and all but two of the concurrent financing operations, the private funds represented a small proportion of the net Bank commitment. Similarly, it is clear that, during the IDB's first three years of operations, the subscriptions of its members had provided the primary source of funds for loans from ordinary resources. Of the $335 million in loans of this category authorized as of the end of 1963, about $115 million, or 30 per cent, had been financed by private capital, $99.2 million through the sale of two bond issues in private capital markets, and another $15.1 million through participations. Lenders in the United States had purchased $75 million of the Bank's bonds, and had taken $13.5 million of the participations.

It would be wrong to assume that these low ratios imply the failure of the Inter-American Development Bank to fulfill its original purpose of mobilizing external capital for Latin American development. Rather, they reflect two things. One is the fact that the U.S. figures do not tell the whole story; local and other foreign private capital, as well as funds from other international lending institutions, have also provided financing for projects receiving IDB loans. When all these are taken into account, the picture looks quite different: "The total cost of the projects in whose financing the Bank participated with ordinary resource loans up to December 31, 1963 is estimated at $1,334 million. The Bank's loans represent 29 per cent of this amount."[40] This means that, for every dollar of development capital provided by the IDB, almost 3 additional dollars were provided by other sources.

The low ratios of private to public funds in IDB activities also reflect the extreme youth of the organization. The experience of the IBRD shows clearly that it takes time to establish firm relationships with private lenders, and three years is simply not enough time for the organization to have emerged from the pump-priming stage. The main purpose of the paid-in portions of the capital subscriptions was precisely to provide lending resources for the Bank's first few years of operations, until it has had time to acquaint investors with its structure and operations, create a market for its bonds, and establish a loan portfolio sub-

[40] IDB, *Activities. . .* , p. 2.

stantial enough to attract purchases as well as simultaneous participations by private lenders.

There are indications that, using the initial resources provided by capital subscriptions, the IDB has been laying the groundwork for new and expanded forms of capital mobilization which should begin to bear fruit in the near future. One of these is its cooperation with ADELA (Atlantic Community Development Group for Latin America) in creating a multinational private investment corporation for Latin America. The ADELA Investment Company, still in the formative stages during 1963, has as its immediate goal the raising of $40 million in equity capital from leading banks, corporations, and other investors in the United States, Japan, and Western Europe. The expectation is that the Inter-American Bank will not only provide loan capital for the new investment company, but that the two organizations will coordinate policies, pool knowledge, and cooperate in operations; that, in short, ADELA will serve as the equity affiliate or arm of the IDB.[41]

The Inter-American Bank is laying the groundwork within Latin America as well. As a result of its loan to the government investment corporation of Chile to develop an indigenous fishing industry, for example, a number of shipbuilding, commercial fishery, and other firms, both in the United States and elsewhere, are contemplating investment in Chile to take advantage of the new opportunities. Some of the results of this groundwork will eventually appear on the IDB records in the form of increased participations or concurrent financing, but the private funds mobilized indirectly—the private investments made in response to new opportunities created by infrastructure projects financed in part by the IDB, the broadened fi-

[41] U.S. Congress, Joint Economic Committee, Subcommittee on Inter-American Economic Relationships, *Private Investment in Latin America, Hearings*, 88th Cong., 2nd Sess., Washington, 1964, pp. 29-53.

nancial contacts created initially by participation in Bank loans, the private money, both local and foreign, mobilized by new development institutions established with IDB assistance—will never be formally recorded at all. Yet the strength of these influences, as much as the growth of actual participations and bond issues, will help to determine whether or not the Inter-American Development Bank fulfills its prophecy that "In the future, the ordinary capital operations will be more and more a bridge by which investment capital can find its way from private investors in developed countries to private borrowers in the developing economies of Latin America."[42]

RELATIONSHIP WITH THE BUSINESS WORLD

Several of the public risk-sharing institutions began to function effectively only after facing, and overcoming, a good deal of initial hostility on the part of the private business and financial community. But the Inter-American Development Bank, born into a world which had finally recognized the inability of private capital to shoulder the entire job of economic development unaided, and supported by the hard earned position of respect and confidence enjoyed by its elder sibling, the World Bank, received a warmer welcome. The statement of the U.S. Council of the International Chamber of Commerce during committee hearings on the Bank's establishment reflects the cautious enthusiasm which greeted the IDB. ". . . international financial agencies, such as the proposed Inter-American Bank, can serve as catalysts to private capital. . . . We believe that the proposed bank could serve to accelerate the process of economic development in a manner not being done by existing organizations."[43]

This receptiveness to the new organization was based

---

[42] National Advisory Council, *Special Report . . .* , p. 6.

[43] U.S. Congress, Senate, Committee on Foreign Relations, *Inter-American Development Bank*, *Hearings*, 86th Cong., 1st Sess., Washington, 1959, p. 57.

in part on faith in its sound operation, particularly since the major share of paid-in capital to be used for lending operations was to come from the borrowing nations themselves: "This financial participation by the Latin American Republics means that they will have a very real interest in making sure that the Bank is run on sound banking principles."[44] And in the Fund for Special Operations, where most of the capital would come from the United States, this country would also have the veto power over all proposed loans.

Most important of all, the members of the business and financial community in the United States favored the establishment of the IDB because they felt that it would do an important job which they themselves were not at the time equipped to do. The statement of the Executive Vice-President of the Bank of America reflects the position of many important members of the international banking community: "Loans in this [long] maturity range would help fill a need not directly being filled now by private sources of funds. . . . We have been asked increasingly to finance long-term projects for railway and highway development and similar purposes, but have been unable to commit funds for such long-term projects."[45] The case for complementary investment activities by public agencies was put even more strongly in the Report to the Joint Economic Committee by COMAP (Commerce Committee for the Alliance for Progress), a group of 25 businessmen chaired by the president of the W. R. Grace Company: "We have concluded that there is little hope for creating the kind of climate that U.S. investors want in Latin America without increasing substantially the amount of assistance which is being extended, and even then it is unlikely that normal conditions attractive to foreign capital

[44] *Ibid.*, p. 58.
[45] U.S. Congress, House, Committee on Banking and Currency, Subcommittee No. 1, *Inter-American Development Bank Act, Hearings*, 86th Cong., 1st Session, Washington, 1959, p. 47.

can be created for a number of years."[46] The business community's acceptance of the IDB was, and continues to be, based on the expectation that it can both help to fill the present gap in private development financing for Latin America and also serve to create the conditions which will ultimately eliminate it. The continued support of private lenders and investors is likely to depend on how well the Bank can fulfill these expectations, and at the same time maintain the conservative lending standards and low loss-ratios which the business and financial community regard as a *sine qua non* for their participation in its activities.

THE IDB: WHERE DOES IT FIT?

Because there were already a number of U.S. and international lending institutions engaged in making development loans to Latin America, some of them on terms and conditions very similar to those of the new organization, considerable concern was expressed at the time of the IDB's establishment that it should complement rather than compete with the activities of existing institutions. Its charter requires that it ". . . cooperate as far as possible with national and international institutions and with private sources supplying investment capital,"[47] and its annual reports reflect a conscientious effort "to avoid duplication of effort by coordinating the Bank's activities with those of other sources of external financing,"[48] through continuous consultation with other agencies engaged in Latin American lending.

At the highest policy level, the United States' views on the policies and operations of the various national and international lending institutions, including the IDB, are coordinated by the National Advisory Council. On the

[46] U.S. Congress, Joint Economic Committee, Subcommittee on Inter-American Economic Relationships, *Private Investment in Latin America, Hearings,* p. 62.

[47] IDB, *Agreement* . . . , Article I, Section 2(b).

[48] IDB, *Second Annual Report,* p. 12.

level of day-to-day operations and lending decisions, co-ordination is presumably carried out through informal consultations among loan officers of the various organizations, all of which have headquarters in Washington, D.C. It is impossible for an outsider to know just how often such consultation takes place, or how effective it is, but that some does take place is strongly suggested by the fact the IDB has on a number of occasions joined with one or another of its sister institutions in helping to finance a particular undertaking in Latin America. It has joined with the IFC and private investors, for example, in helping to finance the creation or expansion of several private manufacturing enterprises: a pulp mill in Chile, a heavy equipment plant and a sodium sulphate plant in Mexico. And as financial agent for the national development plans of a number of countries, it has taken on the role of coordinator of outside assistance provided by both public institutions and private investors. In 1962, for instance, it agreed with the U.S. Agency for International Development on a joint financing plan to provide more than $80 million toward projects forming a part of Bolivia's development plan. As the IDB expands its role as "financial agent" for its Latin American members in mobilizing external resources for their economic development, such "package deals" can be expected to become more and more common.

To say that there is considerable evidence that the Inter-American Bank cooperates with the other international lending institutions is not at all the same thing as saying that it does not, wittingly or unwittingly, compete with their activities. This last consideration comes down to the question: is there a role for the IDB which would not, in its absence, be filled equally well by one or another of the other international lending institutions, or by several of them together? In trying to answer this question, it is useful to compare the IDB with the organization it most resembles, the IBRD, in order to find out in what ways their functions and operating criteria differ.

Some of the ways in which the IDB differs from the World Bank are written into its charter. It is, as has already been pointed out, not only a strictly regional organization, but a "bank of borrowers rather than of lenders," in terms of financial and voting structure. Furthermore, it is specifically authorized to operate in the area of pre-investment financing—that is, technical assistance—whereas the IBRD has no such mandate, and performs these functions on a much more limited basis. By the end of 1963, the IDB had made technical assistance commitments of $23.5 million, $16.9 million from the Bank's own resources and $6.6 million from the Social Progress Trust Fund. About $15.6 million were authorized as loans and $7.9 million as non-reimbursable grants out of the net income of the Fund for Special Operations.[49] Such technical assistance activities can be of major importance in helping a developing country to mobilize increased amounts of capital, both local and foreign, and to make more effective use of the investment resources it has. They are particularly crucial in countries, like many of those in Latin America, which by all accounts are a long way from being able to attract substantial amounts of foreign private capital simply on the merits of their investment climate and investment opportunities. And, finally, the IDB is permitted, unlike the World Bank, to make loans to private entities without a government guaranty, giving it a good deal more flexibility in operations.

On the level of day-to-day operations, the IDB has sought to fulfill its role of supplementary financing by developing particular areas of expertise complementary to those of the other institutions. It has heavily emphasized loans to development institutions in Latin America, while the World Bank Group, coordinated by the Development Bank Services Department of the IFC, has generally focused on assistance to such institutions in other parts of the underdeveloped world. The Inter-American Bank

[49] IDB, *Activities* . . . , p. 2.

has also laid a good deal of stress on credits for financing basic water supply and sanitation works, "a type of financing hitherto generally neglected or inadequately served by other sources of external credit."[50] The IDB has also been more liberal than any other international lending institution in making ordinary loan funds available for financing local currency as well as foreign exchange costs of a project. The World Bank's general unwillingness to provide such financing has been the source of a good deal of criticism.

Finally, the Inter-American Development Bank has a unique political role to play. It is the bank for Latin America and, even more, it is "the bank of the Alliance," the financial agent, so to speak, of the Alliance for Progress. As such it has taken on major responsibilities in two areas of particular importance for the Latin American nations: support for regional integration and assistance in the financing of national development plans. During 1963, the Bank initiated a twofold program in support of the integration movement, consisting of technical assistance to encourage and coordinate the integration process, and the provision of financing initially up to $30 million from ordinary capital resources for intraregional exports of capital goods. The Bank is also committed to support development planning in Latin America by assisting in the mobilization of external capital resources required by these plans; it has already undertaken to act as the financial agent for Bolivia and Ecuador in the implementation of their plans, and expects to perform the same function for other Latin American nations in the near future.[51]

These various claims to uniqueness do not mean that the Inter-American Bank has carved a clearly delineated and undisputed place for itself in the panorama of international lending. The question of the order in which a

[50] IDB, *Second Annual Report*, p. 12.
[51] IDB, *Fourth Annual Report*, pp. 4-5.

prospective borrower in Latin America would approach the various lending organizations was raised during the Hearings on the IDB's establishment and the general impression was created that the new organization should serve as a "clearinghouse" for loans to Latin American countries, but no clear answer was forthcoming. Indeed, "the question as to whether the Inter-American Development Bank would be a lender of first or last resort has never been satisfactorily answered."[52]

This ambiguity can lead to frustrating and wasteful confusion for both would-be borrowers and potential lenders; more important, it increases the possibility that the various lending organizations may unwittingly undercut or interfere with each others activities. The IDB and its supporters point out that "Far from replacing other sources of external financing, the Bank's lending record has been established during a period when most other international as well as U.S. lending agencies have achieved unprecedentedly high commitment rates in Latin America."[53] But this argument, although persuasive, is not conclusive. The real question is whether the IDB's activities have increased the total of development lending commitments to Latin America over what they would have been in its absence, and to this admittedly difficult question the above statement does not afford an answer. Furthermore, the volume of lending is not alone a meaningful criterion of success; the question of quality is also crucial. The outcome of the highly competitive and insufficiently discriminating international private lending which took place during the interwar period is well known; it is important that the public lending institutions avoid any repetition of this catastrophe. The chief danger is not that officers of these institutions will be led through a desire to capture their "share" of the lending field to relax their standards in

[52] Raymond F. Mikesell, *U.S. Private and Government Investment Abroad*, Eugene, Oregon, 1962, p. 467.

[53] National Advisory Council, *Special Report . . .* , p. 15.

assessing the merits of a particular project, it is rather that uncoordinated lending activities can themselves jeopardize the creditworthiness of an enterprise by undermining the debt-servicing capacity of the country in which it is located. Careful coordination, not only of the over-all volume of loans to a given country, but also of their direction, their effect on production and exchange-earning capacity, and their repayment terms, is essential if this pitfall is to be avoided.

These strictures apply, of course, only to the "hard-loan" programs where low loss-ratios are for one reason or another important: the Export-Import Bank, the World Bank, the ordinary resources of the IDB. The "soft loans" provided by the International Development Association, the Agency for International Development, and the IDB's Fund for Special Operations and Social Progress Trust Fund are quite a different matter; they are financed from sources which are not intended to be self-supporting, and their credits are made according to a variety of special criteria, among which creditworthiness or probability of repayment rank relatively low. But this fact raises another problem which the IDB does not appear to have resolved completely as yet; the basis for distinguishing between loans from ordinary resources and those from the Fund for Special Operations—its hard-loan and soft-loan windows. The distinction is apparently not the type of project to be financed, since it has made loans for similar undertakings from both sources. The distinction appears to be the capacity to repay, determined by either the balance of payments position of the country as a whole or by the earning capacity of the particular project, which is affected by its location.[54] A case can be made for either of these criteria, but the underlying rationale should be made explicit. Only if it is clear which of these standards is being applied or, if both are used, under what conditions

[54] For a fuller discussion of these criteria, see Mikesell, pp. 568-569.

one or another is decisive, can "bargain-shopping" by a prospective borrower be minimized and most effective utilization of all the organization's lending resources be assured.

To keep things in proper perspective, we must remember that this discussion is more in the nature of caution than of criticism, a warning against possible pitfalls to be avoided more than an account of mistakes already made. During its first three years of operation, the Inter-American Development Bank set and maintained a brisk lending pace, it demonstrated that its structure and operational standards had profited from the experiences of its predecessors, and it developed some imaginative techniques for taking on new responsibilities in areas of crucial importance for Latin American development. The actual amounts of private capital mobilized by its activities are still small, but the relationships it has established with various private capital markets, the position it has assumed as over-all financial agent for a number of its developing member nations, and the leading role it is playing in the formation of a prototype multinational investment company all indicate that its effectiveness as a catalyst for the introduction of external capital into Latin American development should grow, and grow substantially, once it has had time to build up a substantial loan portfolio and a reputation based on it.

VIII · THE EXPORT-IMPORT BANK
OF WASHINGTON

Of the six American and international organizations which share the risks of foreign investment with private capital, the Investment Guaranty Program has concentrated solely on the issuance of guaranties to private investors, whereas the three international lending institutions have focused rather on various forms of joint direct commitment of public and private funds. Only two, the Export-Import Bank of Washington and the Agency for International Development, make extensive use of both loans and guaranties in their efforts to mobilize private funds for foreign development investment. And although the Export-Import Bank, the most venerable of the six risk-sharing institutions, has long possessed broad powers to offer both limited and full guaranties to private capital participating in its activities, it was not until late in 1961 that it began to use such guaranties, along with various types of direct financing, to attract medium or long-term private funds.[1]

PREWAR ORIGINS AND POSTWAR DEVELOPMENT

The Export-Import Bank of Washington has served varied and not always related objectives of United States domes-

[1] The only type of guaranty used before 1961 was the so-called "agency agreement," under which commercial banks disbursed their own funds to pay Eximbank loan commitments under the Bank's full repayment guaranty. By the end of 1960, some $450 million had been disbursed under such agreements since the Bank's beginnings, more than 90 per cent of it before the end of 1953. Outstanding balances under such agreements were less than $1 million, and it was obvious that these agreements were rapidly disappearing. Because the commercial banks bore no risk at all in these transactions, they were really acting as agents for the Eximbank rather than as private foreign lenders in any sense, and these agreements are therefore not considered in this discussion of private participation in foreign lending. The Eximbank, apparently sharing this view, has not included the amounts disbursed under agency agreements in its figures on private capital participation.

tic and foreign economic policy since its inception in 1934.[2] It was founded, as part of the New Deal employment expansion policy, to facilitate export trade, first with the Soviet Union and then, after debt negotiations with that country failed, with any part of the world but the Soviet Union. In 1935, George N. Peek, the Eximbank's first president, cited three reasons for its establishment: (1) commercial banks were unable to finance a large part of foreign trade, particularly capital goods transactions, because their policies did not permit them to make loans of more than six months' duration; (2) since other countries exercised a large measure of control over foreign trade, the United States needed some centralization of such trade in order to do business with them; and (3) American private banks were refusing to finance trade transactions for which they would have to accept blocked funds in payment. The Bank's announced policy was to make short-term credits available only relatively rarely, when such financing was not available commercially, but no such limitation was placed on credits of more than a year's duration.[3]

Although the Eximbank extended a few credits of the "development loan" type during 1938 and 1939, its sole

[2] Probably the best concise and readily available study of the operations of the Export-Import Bank from its beginning through 1956 is: Olin S. Pugh, *The Export-Import Bank of Washington* (University of South Carolina Essays in Economics, No. 5), Columbia, S.C., 1957. I have drawn heavily on this study, as well as on a reprint of: Hawthorne Arey, *History of the Operations and Policies of the Export-Import Bank of Washington*, U.S. Congress, Senate, Committee on Banking and Currency, *Study of the Export-Import Bank and the World Bank*, *Hearings*, 83rd Cong., 2nd Sess., 1954, Part I. The pages cited refer to the bound reprint in the Princeton University Library. For the more recent period, the most useful source has been: U.S. Congress, House, Committee on Banking and Currency, Subcommittee on Domestic Finance, *A Study of Federal Credit Programs*, 88th Cong., 2nd Sess., Washington, 1964, II, 351-389 (hereafter referred to as *FCP Study*).

[3] Gardner Patterson, "The Export-Import Bank," *Quarterly Journal of Economics*, LVIII (Nov. 1943), 65-69.

purpose during its first five years was to assist American exporters. In legislation passed in 1940, however, the Bank's maximum lending authority (for loans outstanding at any one time) was increased from $200 to $700 million, and it was given the authority to make loans which might give no direct and immediate aid to American exporters.[4] This authority was granted at the request of the President, who wished the Eximbank to serve as an instrument of U.S. foreign policy in aiding Latin American countries whose foreign markets had been cut off by the war. The Bank could now make loans to governments, or with a government guaranty, "to assist in the development of the resources, the stabilization of the economies and the orderly marketing of the products of the Western Hemisphere."[5]

One of the first such development loans was made in 1941, in the amount of $25 million, to help finance the construction of a $50 million steel mill in Brazil. Other such loans, often to development corporations, were made throughout the war to a number of Latin American countries, among them Haiti, Ecuador, Bolivia, and Chile. In 1942, on the recommendation of the State Department, the Eximbank established credits to help an American-owned enterprise, the International Telephone and Telegraph Company, fund obligations incurred in connection with the operation of radio and telephone systems in South America. Only a small part of this credit was utilized, however, and that was repaid before maturity.

With the cessation of hostilities in 1945, the lending authority of the Eximbank was again increased, from $700 million to $3.5 billion, and a third type of credit authorized. In recognition of the urgent need for financing to aid European reconstruction, the Bank began to make emer-

[4] *Ibid., passim.*
[5] U.S. Congress, House, Committee on Banking and Currency, *Increase the Lending Authority of the Export-Import Bank, Hearings,* 76th Cong., 3rd Sess., 1940, p. 1.

gency credits available to recipient governments to buy a wide variety of agricultural and industrial products in the United States. To permit the fullest utilization of such assistance, the 1945 legislation even included an explicit exception to the Johnson Act of 1934, allowing private participations in Eximbank loans to governments still in default on their debts to the United States Government. The Bank was now made an independent agency of the government, with its own Board of Directors and membership on the National Advisory Council on International Monetary and Financial Problems (NAC). All loan applications considered by the Eximbank have, since 1945, had to be passed on from a policy viewpoint by the NAC. Finally, this legislation formalized the relationship with private enterprise which had guided the Eximbank from its inception; the 1945 Act stated it to be the policy of Congress that the Bank "in the exercise of its functions should supplement and encourage and not compete with private capital."[6]

The program of emergency credits for general reconstruction and stabilization purposes dropped off to an occasional stabilization loan when the World Bank opened for business late in 1946, and the Eximbank returned to a program of selective credits designed to contribute, in the long run, to a better balance of two-way trade.[7] The Eximbank's involvement in development loan activity continued to grow, however, and was considerably accelerated by the 1949 announcement of the Point Four Program, one of whose four main "branches"[8] was the expansion

[6] *Export-Import Bank Act of 1945*, 59 *Stat.* 527 (1945).

[7] Export-Import Bank of Washington, *Fourth Semi-annual Report to the Congress for the Period January-June 1947*, Washington, 1947, pp. 4-5.

[8] The other three were: the development of a program of technical assistance for less-developed countries; an intensified effort to negotiate modernized "Friendship, Commerce and Navigation" treaties with an investment clause; and the increased use of foreign investment guaranties against political risks.

of just such loans by the Export-Import Bank. Because its resources were limited, the Bank continued to screen loan applications according to the criteria of need, urgency, the borrower's own resources, the possibility of finding other sources of funds, the borrower's ability to make effective use of the funds and to repay them, and the impact of the proposed loan on the U.S. economy.[9]

During the five-year period 1948-1953, sizable development credits were extended to countries around the world, among them Argentina, Brazil, Chile, Mexico, Canada, Indonesia, Italy, and Israel. Although a majority of these loans were to public authorities, a number of important credits were also extended to private interests, generally conditioned upon the simultaneous investment of private funds in an equal or larger amount. Among the more important of these transactions involving American parent companies were:

(a) Two loans, totaling approximately $50 million, to the Brazilian subsidiaries of the American and Foreign Power Company for the purchase of U.S. equipment for an electrical power expansion program. The total cost of the program was expected to be $98 million, with the remainder of the funds to come from retained earnings and the sale of equity securities in Brazil. In a similar arrangement, the Cuban subsidiary of the same firm received a $12 million Eximbank loan.

(b) A loan of $20.8 million to the Cerro de Pasco Copper Corporation in Peru to help finance the construction of a zinc refinery and related facilities. This loan was accompanied by a $9 million investment by the American parent company, which planned ultimately to finance the major share of the enterprise.

(c) A loan of $4 million to the Liberia Mining Company to develop rich iron ore deposits. An American

[9] William McC. Martin, Jr., "The Export-Import Bank and United States Foreign Loan Policy," *Proceedings of the Academy of Political Science*, xxii (Jan. 1947), 67-72.

steel company was among the stockholders who invested an additional $4 million simultaneously with the Eximbank credit.

The 1951 legislation had increased the Bank's lending authority by $1 billion to $4.5 billion, indicating Congress's apparent agreement with the view of the Bank's President that such an increase was necessary, despite $0.5 billion of uncommitted funds, because of the increased emphasis on loans to foreign business enterprises without government guaranty. In explaining the policy shift, the President pointed out that such loans ". . . approach more closely to the standards of private international financing than any other kind of financing done by the Export-Import Bank . . . it is our belief that they may well act as pilot loans toward the resumption of more normal financial relations between the United States and other nations. . . ."[10]

In 1953, however, the Bank, "reflecting the general attitude of the new Administration on the questions of public retrenchment and businesslike management,"[11] suffered a setback. New legislation replaced its five-man Board by a Managing Director and dropped it from membership on the NAC. One of the effects of this reorganization plan was to put the Bank more closely under the supervision of the Secretary of the Treasury who, in an effort to minimize the strain on the Treasury's cash position from the Bank's loan activities, attempted to steer it away from the financing of long-term development projects. As part of the same effort to conserve Treasury funds, the Bank announced that it would henceforth stress a more extensive use of guaranties (of credits extended by commercial banks) as a substitute for actual Eximbank loans. It also began to emphasize more strongly private participation in its lending, pointing out that, for every dollar loaned during the preceding five years directly or

[10] Arey, p. 100.
[11] Pugh, p. 12.

indirectly to private enterprise, more than $1.50 of private U.S. and private and public foreign capital had been invested as a direct result of the Bank's lending.[12]

In 1954, legislation representing a compromise between the views of the State and Treasury Departments restored the Eximbank's bipartisan Board of Directors and its membership on the NAC, as well as increasing its lending authority to $5 billion. The State Department's announcement that the Bank was "back in business" for economic development loans[13] was borne out by the announcement of the largest credit ever extended to a private borrower: a loan of $100 million to the Southern Peru Copper Company, an affiliate of the American Smelting and Refining Company and other U.S. mining companies, for the development of copper deposits in Southern Peru. The authorization was conditional upon the provision of the balance of the $205 million required for the project from private sources. During the same year, the Bank also noted a markedly increasing trend in exporter credit activity. This reflected the development, for the first time since the war, of a "buyers' market" in which foreign suppliers were offering increasing competition to American exporters, both in general and, specifically, in the credit terms extended to buyers.

By mid-1955 the Eximbank had authorized, since its inception, credits of $7.2 billion in 65 countries, of which $5 billion had actually been disbursed as loans and $2.7 billion of which was currently outstanding. In mid-1961, the corresponding figures were $12.1 billion, $7.8 billion, and $3.4 billion. During the intervening years, in 1958, the Bank's lending authority was increased from $5 to $7 billion "to meet increased demand for its activities"; otherwise, its basic program continued to function until mid-

[12] Export-Import Bank of Washington, *Sixteenth Semi-annual Report to the Congress for the Period January-June 1953*, Washington, 1953, p. 4.

[13] Pugh, p. 13.

1961 under the legislative mandate and general administrative patterns laid down in 1954.

NEW WAYS OF FINANCING EXPORTS

During the early 1960's, concern over the United States' worsening balance of payments and the stiffening competition encountered by U.S. exporters from their counterparts in other advanced countries, able to offer more favorable financing terms, led to a renewed emphasis on the original purpose of the Export-Import Bank: assistance to American exporters. Long-term development loans continued to be made at the request of overseas purchasers during the 1961-1963 period, and a number of them involved substantial concurrent investment of U.S. private capital. The largest of these was the $110 million Eximbank-AID credit to VALCO, a bauxite and alumina smelter project in Ghana which is expected to involve between $32 and $55 million of U.S. private investment.[14] Other important instances include loans of $34.5 million to the Liberian Mining Company mentioned earlier and $42 million to a Chilean electric power company, which together involved nearly $80 million of U.S. private equity, and balance of payments loans of $168 million to Brazil and $20 million to Argentina, plus a $90 million credit to the Mexican government development corporation, which together attracted concurrent loans from private U.S. sources totaling $106.5 million. But the major changes in the policies and activities of the Export-Import Bank during this period came in the form of new and expanded forms of direct and immediate aid to exporters of goods from the United States.

In his balance-of-payments message of early 1961, President Kennedy demanded "a new program under the Export-Import Bank to place our exporters on a basis of full equality with their competitors in other countries,"

---

[14] For a detailed description of this credit, and the private capital accompanying it see pp. 289-290.

along with "a study of methods through which private financial institutions can participate more broadly in providing export credit facilities."[15] The Eximbank's immediate response was simply to expand its existing facilities, broadening its medium-term loan program to include not only capital goods but also consumer durable goods, semi-finished products, and oil industry equipment as items eligible for financing.[16] But later in the year, after intensive study of the question and examination of several alternative proposals,[17] the Eximbank announced two new programs of exporter assistance: the commercial bank guaranty program and the exporter credit insurance (FCIA) program. A firm legislative mandate for these programs was provided by an amendment to the Export-Import Bank Act of 1945; although the original Act had contained a general guaranty authority, the amendment specifically authorized and empowered the Eximbank to "guarantee, insure, coinsure, and reinsure U.S. exporters and foreign exporters doing business in the United States in an aggregate amount not in excess of $1 billion outstanding at any one time against political and credit risks of loss arising in connection with U.S. exports; and to establish and maintain fractional reserves in connection therewith . . . [which] shall be not less than 25 per centum of the related contractional liability of the Bank."[18]

[15] U.S. National Advisory Council, *Report of the NAC for the period January 1-June 30, 1961*, Washington, 1962, p. 81.

[16] Export-Import Bank of Washington, *Report to the Congress for the twelve months ending June 30, 1961*, Washington, 1961, p. 14.

[17] For a description of the most important alternative proposal, for the creation of a private American Export Credit Guaranty Corporation with the right to borrow from the U.S. Treasury, see: U.S. Congress, Senate, Committee on Interstate and Foreign Commerce, *Foreign Commerce Study, Hearings*, 86th Cong., 2nd Sess., 1960, and U.S. Congress, House, Committee on Banking and Currency, Subcommittee No. 3, *Promotion of United States Exports, Hearings*, 87th Cong., 1st Sess., 1961.

[18] *FCP Study*, ii, 376.

One of the new forms of risk-sharing offered by the Eximbank to American exporters was an export credit insurance program, underwritten jointly by Eximbank and the Foreign Credit Insurance Association (FCIA), an association of more than 70 private insurance companies in the United States formed specifically for the purpose of writing such insurance in partnership with the Bank. Under this program, an exporter of goods or technical services can acquire 85 to 90 per cent coverage against nearly all the risks of export-financing. Among the insured risks are such commercial credit risks as insolvency of the buyer or protracted default (of more than six months' duration) and a broad group of political risks including: convertibility or transfer restrictions (but not devaluation); the cancellation or restriction of export or import licenses; war, revolution, civil commotion, "or other like disturbance"; expropriation, confiscation, or "intervention in the business of the buyer or guarantor by a governmental authority." Under the arrangements in force as of 1963, the Eximbank bore the entire liability for political risks and the commercial credit risk liability was shared equally between the Bank and the FCIA.[19] In mid-1964 a new arrangement was introduced, whereby the Eximbank carries all the political risk and the FCIA all the credit risk, with the bank re-insuring the latter for any individual losses over $150,000.

Export credit insurance is available to any exporter of products manufactured in the United States and sold for U.S. dollars. The chief criterion is that there be "reasonable assurance of repayment," determined with reference both to the credit position of the individual purchaser and the "prospects for availability in the buyer's country of foreign exchange."[20] The program is designed to be self-

[19] The equal sharing of commercial risk claims between the Eximbank and the FCIA was subject to the provision that the "Eximbank will cover any annual loss of more than $1 million in excess of net premium income." *FCP Study*, II, 385.

[20] *Ibid.*, p. 384.

supporting; premiums charged "are commensurate with the estimated risk involved" and, unlike the fixed premiums of the Investment Guaranty Program, are varied according to the riskiness of a particular transaction.[21]

Although the FCIA was created early in 1962, it did not issue its first comprehensive insurance policy for medium-term transactions (generally, of one to five years' duration) until July of that year.[22] A few months later, at the request of exporters, it made available to those who desired it a less expensive and less comprehensive form of insurance, covering political risks only. As of the end of 1963, $82.2 million of comprehensive policies and $10.7 million of policies covering political risks only had been written for medium-term export financing transactions under the FCIA insurance program.

The FCIA program offers exporters relief from nearly all the risks of foreign investment in the form of medium-term financing, but it does not solve their liquidity problem; most exporters are not in a position to tie up capital for the several years required by a medium-term transaction, even on an insured basis. In order to induce commercial banks to take over a larger share of this medium-term financing on a non-recourse basis, the Eximbank also introduced, in mid-1961, a plan for guaranties of commercial bank financing. Under this program, the Eximbank makes available to the banks guaranties against political risks, of the types described above for the export insurance program, on all maturities of their loans to exporters and against both political and commercial credit

[21] *Ibid.*, p. 387. Among the factors determining premium rates are: the term of sale, the market group (in terms of degree of risk) in which the sale is made, whether comprehensive or political-risk coverage is requested, and the percentage of the exporter's annual shipments made to "good" markets.

[22] Short-term political risk guaranties, for credits of 180 days or less, had been available from the Eximbank since May 1960. In October 1961, this program was turned over to the FCIA, under the same sort of risk-sharing agreement as has been described for the medium-term program.

risks on the later maturities, leaving the bank to carry the commercial risk on the earlier maturities.[23] The eligibility criteria for this program are roughly the same as those for the FCIA program, except of course that here it is commercial banks rather than the exporters who receive guaranty coverage, and the fee schedules for the two programs are also approximately the same.

The commercial bank guaranty program was greeted by a substantial demand for its services. Almost immediately, the Bank began writing such guaranties at a rate of more than $200 million a year and, by the end of 1963, the total face value of guaranties issued to commercial banks for medium-term export financing came to nearly $660 million. The greater share of Eximbank funds was still committed directly in the form of loans, mostly long-term trade development and project loans extended directly to a foreign borrower. But the new programs did, and indeed were designed to, cut sharply into the Eximbank's medium-term exporter credits; such credits dropped from $143 million in fiscal 1961 to $34 million and $40 million respectively in the two years that followed, after the guaranty and insurance programs were well under way.

In August 1963, the Eximbank's lending authority was increased by law from $7 to $9 billion; its guaranty and insurance authority was raised from $1 billion to $2 billion, subject to a 25 per cent reserve on all liabilities. As of the end of that year, the cumulative total of all credits, guaranties, and medium-term insurance issued by the Export-Import Bank since its inception in 1934 was $14.6 billion, of which $13.9 billion had been in the form of loans. Of the $14.6 billion total, $9.6 billion had been

[23] Under the administrative regulations in force at the time of this writing, the commercial bank is required to carry without guaranty "the first one-half of the commercial risk in transactions having maturities not longer than three years, and the commercial risk for the first 18 months in transactions with maturities of three to five years." *FCP Study*, ɪɪ, 377.

disbursed and $3.7 billion was outstanding. As indicated by the geographical breakdown shown in Table 16, slightly more than half the funds authorized had been designated to help finance exports to the less-developed areas of the world. Apparently this proportion has increased substantially in recent years; of the total of credits, guaranties, and insurance outstanding on December 31, 1963, approximately 75 per cent was directed toward less-developed areas.[24]

TABLE 16

Cumulative Statement of Eximbank Operations by Area:
Summary of Credits, Guaranties, and Insurance,
as of December 31, 1963[a]

(in millions of U.S. dollars)

Area	Autho-rizations	Cancel-lations, Lapses, Advances By Partici-pants	Disburse-ments	Repay-ments	Out-standing
Africa	538.7	122.3	312.6	154.6	157.9
Asia	3,421.0	628.3	2,278.4	1,282.9	995.5
Canada	776.2	592.6	183.3	183.2	0.1
Europe	4,489.0	811.3	3,073.5	2,501.8	571.7
Latin America	5,272.3	1,097.7	3,733.4	1,717.4	2,016.0
Oceania	63.4	36.2	23.9	17.6	6.4
Other Countries	13.1	8.7	4.4	4.4	—
Total	14,573.7	3,297.1	9,609.5	5,861.9	3,747.6

[a] Short-term insurance excluded. Disbursements under the short-term program totaled $465.5 million, and $127.8 million of such contracts were outstanding as of the end of 1963.

Source: Export-Import bank of Washington, *Report to the Congress for the Six Months Ended December 13, 1963*, pp. 136-142.

[24] Computed from figures given in: Export-Import Bank of Washington, *Report to the Congress for the six months ended December 31, 1963*, Washington, 1964, pp. 34-143.

RELATIONS WITH PRIVATE CAPITAL

Throughout the postwar period, the lending operations of the Export-Import Bank have been conducted under the legislative instruction, contained in the Export-Import Bank Act of 1945, that the Bank should "supplement and encourage and not compete with private capital." In general, the Bank has apparently found ample scope for loans which supplement rather than compete with private capital, and has concentrated on providing only types of financing that private commercial banks are not generally prepared to extend and for the handling of which appropriate institutions are only beginning to come into existence in the United States. The Bank considers the medium and long-term loans to foreign governments and firms which comprise the bulk of its lending to be of those types. When it extends other types of credits, such as those to American exporters, it does so only after assuring itself that financing cannot be obtained from private sources "because the risk is too large and because it is a type of business which the average bank does not engage in."[25] Private capital's confidence in the Eximbank's ability to avoid competing with it is attested to by the replies to an extensive survey of banks and other institutions engaged in foreign financing presented in hearings before the Senate Banking and Currency Committee in 1954. The numerous respondents were nearly unanimous in their opinion that the Bank's loan activities did not compete with, or in any way encroach upon, the province of private lending institutions.[26]

The positive side of the coin, the requirement that the Eximbank's activities should actively encourage private

[25] U.S. Congress, House, Committee on Banking and Currency, *Federal Reincorporation of the Export-Import Bank, Hearings*, 80th Cong., 1st Sess., 1947, p. 41.

[26] U.S. Congress, Senate, Committee on Banking and Currency, *Study of the Export-Import Bank and the World Bank, Hearings*, 83rd Cong., 2nd Sess., 1954, *passim*.

capital, is more complicated. Among the varied means which the Bank uses to accomplish this objective are its lending policies and operations, which are designed to stimulate private foreign investment indirectly, by affecting favorably the investment climate so important to potential lenders and investors abroad.

The Eximbank's program of development loans is predicated on the assumption that such assistance will, by improving the economic "background" of a country and contributing to economic and political stability, help to create a more profitable environment for private foreign investment. Many of its loans have been for the development of the "infrastructure" which is such an important prerequisite for profitable private enterprise, including electrical power, transportation, communication facilities, and the like. In this type of activity, the Bank sees itself as a pump-primer, concentrating on key improvements and key industries which will eliminate bottlenecks to progress and "get things going so that private enterprise can keep them going."[27]

The Eximbank's loan policies are designed in part to minimize defaults and thus prevent loss of U.S. Treasury funds, but also to encourage the development of "business-like" behavior and attitudes on the part of the borrowers and thus to pave the way for the growth of purely private lending relationships. While the Bank is "expected to incur risks beyond those which private capital and lending institutions are legally able and willing to assume, its loans must, in the management's judgment, offer reasonable assurance of repayment."[28] This implies that a loan must, directly or indirectly, increase the borrowing country's productive capacity in such a way that its ability to meet

[27] H. L. Gaston (Chairman, Eximbank), "Loans to Build Sounder Trade," *Commercial and Financial Chronicle*, Nov. 8, 1951, pp. 14-15.

[28] Arey, p. 120.

its foreign payments is also increased. In an effort to insure that its funds are actually used for productive purposes, the Bank states that it will generally make loans only for specific projects, and will make disbursements "only upon receipt of satisfactory evidence that the purposes of the loan have been or are being carried out."[29] Similarly, the Bank adheres to the widely held, and widely criticized,[30] rule-of-thumb which in general permits loans only to finance the dollar costs of a given project, on the assumption that loans repayable in dollars to cover local expenditures would place an unnecessary burden on the borrower's dollar-servicing capacity. In the case of the Eximbank, its primary purpose of aiding American export trade provides an additional rationale for the dollar-costs-only policy.[31]

On the books, this Bank exhibits a remarkably low loss-record, suggesting that its operating policies have been successful in assuring the soundness of its loans by banking standards. By its own accounting system, the Eximbank's total losses over all the years it has been in operation have been less than $4 million, or less than one-

[29] Export-Import Bank of Washington, *General Policies*, July, 1959. The Bank did, however, make a number of "general purpose" reconstruction loans immediately following World War II and has extended large "dollar exchange" stabilization credits to the United Kingdom and a number of Latin American countries in more recent years. These exceptions to the general rule, although few in number, totaled more than $3.5 billion, or more than 25 per cent of total credits authorized in the 1945-1963 period.

[30] The chief difficulty of the dollar-costs-only loan criterion is that it does not take into account the total effects, direct and indirect, of the project on the borrower's economy and thus on its balance-of-payments as a whole.

[31] The Bank's loans are not legally "tied" to purchases from the United States, and it has on occasion financed both local and third-country costs involved in the projects it was supporting. In practice, however, it will do so "only where this is clearly necessary to accomplishment of the basic purpose of facilitating U.S. trade." R. H. Rowntree, Chief, Economics Division, Export-Import Bank, letter dated Nov. 15, 1961.

twentieth of 1 per cent of loans disbursed.[32] This sum is covered many times over by the reserves, amounting to $885 million at the end of 1963, arising from profits on its lending operations. But for several reasons, the loss-figure given is deceptively low: the Bank is reluctant to declare in default past-due obligations, amounting to several times the figure given,[33] for which there is some expectation of eventual repayment; it has been willing to readjust the payment plan on certain of its loans, particularly large ones to governments;[34] and, most important, since many of its creditors are foreign governments, against whom the usual collection methods cannot be invoked, the Bank cannot always emulate the private banker's general policy of refusing to extend further loans to a borrower who appears in imminent danger of being unable to meet payments on present ones. Nonetheless, it is evident both from their public testimony and from opinions given privately in letters to the author that bankers find the Eximbank's lending record a satisfactory one.

The introduction during the 1960's of insurance and guaranty programs for medium-term export financing reflected an intensified emphasis on the encouragement of private capital. A major purpose in introducing these programs was to induce private banks and exporters themselves to undertake much of the lending for which the Bank had previously had to use its own funds. In both these programs the relationship between the Eximbank and the private financial institutions is a particularly close one, a partnership in which criteria and procedures are jointly determined.

[32] Bankers Trust Company, *Washington Agencies that Help to Finance Foreign Trade* (4th edn.), New York, 1964, p. 4.

[33] "Protracted defaults" on 11 loans, 5 of them to Cuba, aggregated $34.4 million ($19.8 million principal plus $14.6 million interest) as of December 31, 1963. The total outstanding principal on these 11 loans was $97.3 million. Export-Import Bank of Washington, *Report to the Congress for the six months ended December 31, 1963*, Washington, 1964, p. 7.

[34] Pugh, pp. 43-44.

The Foreign Credit Insurance Association, the private arm of the export credit insurance program, was designed to maximize the participation of the private insurance industry in a type of activity which it was obviously not prepared to undertake without Government support. The FCIA, which currently has more than 70 members, is open to all "responsible" private insurance companies. It acts as agent for the Eximbank in all insurance transactions, receiving and servicing applications and in general handling all contacts with exporters. It also makes the initial decisions concerning the issuance of policies, subject in the case of medium-term insurance to the approval of the Eximbank, which carries the major part of the risk. In order to provide a further stimulus to export financing by commercial banks, FCIA insurance policies are assignable to commercial banks which buy the exporter's paper.[35]

The commercial bank guaranty program is also designed to simulate as nearly as possible the normal commercial relationships of the private financial world, with only as much government activity as is required to induce private banks to undertake this type of lending. In establishing the program, the Eximbank consulted with commercial banks to ensure that the procedures used would be familiar and acceptable to them. The participation of more than 80 commercial banks in the program "has made it possible for exporters in most industrial areas in the country to apply to their own banks or through them to correspondent banks in larger cities for export credit financing on a non-recourse basis."[36] As in the FCIA program, exporters deal not with the Eximbank but with the private institutions, in this case the commercial banks, which handle loan applications and make the initial judgment as to whether they are eligible for an Eximbank

[35] As of July 1963, 33 per cent of the proceeds of medium-term policies had been so assigned. *FCP Study*, II, 388.

[36] *Ibid.*, p. 375.

guaranty. The final decision is up to the Eximbank, but it tends to confine itself to a determination of the political risks involved in a particular financing transaction, leaving the judgment of credit soundness to the commercial bank. Again, to make the program more attractive by increasing liquidity, the Eximbank guaranties are, with certain restrictions,[37] assignable to other private financial institutions.

Efforts to improve the climate for foreign investment abroad, the maintenance of sound, conservative lending standards in its own operations, the establishment of close working relationships with important segments of the private capital market—all these represent indirect but important ways of encouraging private capital participation in overseas lending. More directly, the Eximbank has over the years evolved a number of different patterns of private participation, designed to encourage the flow of private funds abroad either by increasing their participation in the Eximbank's own long-term loans or by making possible, through the provision of public loan funds or guaranties, private credit transactions which might not have taken place otherwise.

PATTERNS OF PARTICIPATION

Private foreign investment undertaken in conjunction with the long-term project or emergency trade development loans of the Export-Import Bank has been of two main types: voluntary purchases by commercial banks of portions, generally the early maturities, of Eximbank loans, and concurrent equity and loan investments in projects receiving Eximbank credits. Private participation in medium-term exporter credits takes quite a different form, generally consisting of credits extended by exporters or their

[37] "Banks may sell up to 50 per cent of the early maturities and all of the fully guarantied later maturities to other financial institutions on a non-recourse basis, or all maturities on a recourse basis." *Ibid.*, p. 379.

commercial banks which represent the minimum financing shares required by the Eximbank's eligibility rules for exporter loans, guaranties or insurance.

The oldest form of private capital participation in Eximbank activities is the purchase by commercial banks of early maturities of the Bank's credits, which dates back at least to the formation of the Private Capital Participation Division in 1946. The function of this Division, set up in furtherance of the mandate of the Export-Import Bank Act of 1945 that the Bank should supplement and encourage and not compete with private capital, was in part to act as "the representative of private capital" on committees considering loan applications, assuring the avoidance of competition by requiring the applicant to show that he had unsuccessfully attempted to borrow funds through private channels before coming to the Bank. Probably the more important aspect of its activity was, however, to stimulate the participation of institutional (portfolio) lenders in the Bank's loans through widespread personal contacts and a variety of informational and educational activities. Immediate evidence of what the Division could accomplish came in March 1946, when the Bank set up a $200 million reconstruction credit to the Netherlands on terms it believed to be acceptable to commercial banking institutions and invited them to participate in the loan. Fifty U.S. banks responded by taking participations totaling approximately $100 million at their own risk, without any guaranty from or recourse on the Eximbank.

During the five or six years following this initial achievement, the Private Capital Participation Division was hampered in its efforts by the fact that the U.S. Treasury discouraged the Eximbank from raising funds in the private capital market, fearing disturbances which might affect its own financings.[38] Because the Division was thus

[38] A. J. Redway, Chief, Private Capital Participation Division, Export-Import Bank, Interview of July 15, 1960.

discouraged from any vigorous campaign to overcome the commercial banks' reluctance to enter the field of foreign financing, there was extremely little participation by these institutions at their own risk before 1950. About 1952, however, the "tight money" situation and the desire to minimize the cash drain on Treasury funds by Eximbank loans prompted the Treasury to change its views, and the Division began intensive efforts to "educate" commercial banks on the attractions of foreign lending and the participation facilities offered by the Bank. In that same year, the Bank extended a $50 million "general purpose" loan to the kingdom of Belgium on the condition that U.S. commercial banks and trust companies be allowed to participate. In a heavily oversubscribed issue, 32 private banks bought $45 million of these notes at par (4 per cent), repayable over a five-year period, without recourse on the Eximbank.[39] In 1958, 11 private banks participated at their own risk to the extent of $54 million in a "package" Eximbank-IMF transaction with Argentina totaling $329 million. Commercial banks participated in numerous smaller loans and exporter credits as well, and by 1959 the Bank had a core of about 65 commercial banks which participated in its loans with "on-and-off regularity," depending chiefly upon the current domestic demand for money.[40] Toward the end of the 1950's, the Private Capital Participation Division concentrated on enlisting the participation of life insurance companies, which first began to show interest in this type of foreign lending in 1957,[41] and on stimulating equity as well as loan participation in its foreign credits.

[39] Export-Import Bank of Washington, *Fourteenth Semiannual Report of the Congress for the Period January-June 1952*, Washington, 1952, p. 12.

[40] Redway, Interview of July 15, 1960.

[41] Samuel C. Waugh, President of Eximbank, testimony in: U.S. Congress, Senate, Committee on Banking and Currency, *Increased Export-Import Bank Lending Authority*, *Hearings*, 85th Cong., 2nd Sess., 1958, p. 4.

The Export-Import Bank

Throughout its lifetime, the Private Capital Participation Division tried to get commercial banks to share *pari passu* with the Bank in all maturities of certain loans, and to find purchasers for some of the securities in the Eximbank's portfolio when offered for sale at par (with accrued interest) on the open market. In reality, however, the only form of participation in which institutional lenders evinced substantial interest was the purchase of early maturities of loans in which the Bank took the longer maturities. As a result, the Bank found itself giving up the most desirable (shortest-term) portions of loans at the same interest rate as it received on the longer maturities.

To restore balance to the term-structure of its own holdings, the Eximbank altered its policy radically in the early 1960's, abolishing the Private Capital Participation Division and no longer making the early maturities of particular loans available to private purchasers in the United States, except in a few special cases.[42] Instead, it introduced participation certificates, representing selected "baskets" of Eximbank paper of all maturities. But these certificates, unlike the earlier forms of participation they largely replaced, involve no element of private risk at all, since they are fully guarantied by Eximbank and can be converted into cash on semiannual dates after a two and one-half year waiting period.[43] What this means is simply that the Eximbank is borrowing from private banks rather than from the U.S. Treasury, thus conserving public funds but cutting down on the Bank's profits, since private money is more expensive.[44] These certificates, of

[42] For balance of payments reasons, sales of loans from portfolio, without recourse on the Eximbank, were offered abroad. About $80 million of such loans were sold to institutional buyers in Europe during 1962 and 1963. *FCP Study*, ii, 366 and information provided by G. E. McLaughlin, Vice-President, Eximbank.

[43] *Ibid.*, p. 363.

[44] The difference between the interest rate charged the Eximbank by the Treasury and the yield on the Eximbank's fully guarantied participation certificates has been in the range of ¼ to ½ of 1 per cent.

which $300 million were issued in fiscal 1962 and $250 million in fiscal 1963, do not represent true private participation in foreign investment, although the Bank attempts to use them to stimulate such participation indirectly, by making them available only to banks which participate in its operations in other ways, generally through the commercial bank guaranty or FCIA programs.[45]

The loan of Eximbank funds to American or American-owned enterprises operating abroad, in conjunction with simultaneous equity or loan investments by private interests, is a more recent form of joint activity, which began in the early 1950's. The Bank has repeatedly stated a preference for loans to private enterprise over those to governments and reserves the right to inquire into the availability of U.S. private funds before financing a foreign government or private firm in a given undertaking. Yet its loans have been preponderantly to foreign governments, and it was for some years reluctant to assist U.S. companies with U.S. public funds on the grounds that these firms have access to the American private capital market. In recent years, "with the evolution of our foreign assistance program and the increasing realization that it behooves the United States Government to do more to induce its nationals to play a greater role in the development of the less-developed countries, . . . the Bank has come more and more to the view that United States private enterprise should not be denied public funds for the very purposes that United States public funds are being loaned to foreign nationals."[46] Nonetheless, loans to U.S. controlled firms have probably totaled only about $600 million, or less than 5 per cent of the total value of Eximbank loan authorizations.[47]

[45] G. E. McLaughlin, Vice-President, Export-Import Bank, discussion in August, 1963.

[46] Walter Sauer, "The Export-Import Bank and Private Investment," *Federal Bar Journal*, XIX (Oct. 1959), 335.

[47] Raymond F. Mikesell, "The Export-Import Bank of Wash-

Development loans to private companies in foreign countries are made "to supplement private investment when necessary to assure that private funds will venture into the transaction or investment";[48] in general, the Eximbank requires that at least 25 to 50 per cent of the total cost of the project be in the form of private equity capital or subordinated assets. Such financing assistance extended to U.S. ventures abroad is of two main types: loans to existing United States enterprises abroad which would otherwise be unable to raise the capital necessary to fulfill the normal obligations of public utilities (e.g., the credits to the Latin American subsidiaries of the American and Foreign Power Company, cited above), and loans to new U.S. owned private enterprise abroad, intended to provide both a "psychological umbrella" for the investor and the necessary loan capital, often unavailable otherwise, against a private equity base.[49] Except for the $110 million dollar credit extended jointly by Eximbank and AID for the establishment of an aluminum smelter in Ghana, the bulk of these loans to U.S. controlled firms

---

ington," in Mikesell (ed.), *U.S. Private and Government Investment Abroad*, Eugene, Oregon, 1962, p. 470 and *Reports* of the Export-Import Bank for the period 1960-1963.

[48] Waugh, p. 4.

[49] Edward S. Lynch, "The Role of the Export-Import Bank in Fostering the Investment of United States Private Capital Abroad," *Study of the Export-Import Bank and the World Bank, Hearings*, pp. 830-831. The Eximbank makes also a third type of loan to foreign private enterprise, including subsidiaries or affiliates of U.S. firms. Under a 1951 amendment to the Defense Production Act of 1950, it can make loans to private business enterprises for the development or production of strategic materials, which it could not make under its regular legislative authority, when a certificate of essentiality has been issued by the State or Defense Department. (Section 302 of the Defense Production Act of 1950, as amended, 64 *Stat.* 932.) Mr. Rowntree estimates that only about $2.5 to $3.0 million of American private capital has gone abroad under this program, nearly all of it in connection with the 1952 credit to the Industria e Comercio de Minerios in Brazil for the production of manganese ore.

have been in Latin America; most have been in the fields of electric power and mining, although some have also been made for the manufacture of cement, chemicals, paper and pulp, and other industrial products. These loans represent a genuine risk-sharing by the Eximbank, since they are granted to foreign subsidiaries or affiliates without recourse on the parent companies. Although such loans to private enterprise in connection with development credits are small in number, they are generally for far larger amounts than the export credits, and therefore account for a much larger proportion of the dollar volume of Eximbank loans than their numbers alone would suggest.

During its first 20 years of operations, the Eximbank financed American exports chiefly through long-term project loans to foreign borrowers. Not until late 1954 were direct exporter credits introduced for medium-term transactions. In this type of operation the Eximbank, at the request of a U.S. exporter or financial institution, bought some of the purchaser's notes from the exporter without recourse on the latter. The size of such credits has varied enormously, ranging from $550 to aid the sale of a disc plow in Brazil to a number of credits in the $8-$13 million range to assist in the financing of aircraft exports, but on the average they have been small; although more than half of all Eximbank credit transactions have been of this type, they represent less than 1 per cent of the total value of its loans. A majority of the exporter credits have been for transactions with Latin American countries, but they have aided capital exports to all 6 of the inhabited continents and to both advanced and underdeveloped nations.

Since this form of financing was generally extended only for credit of more than a year's duration, it almost always assisted and encouraged the sales abroad of capital goods by making it possible for exporters to extend the long-term credit necessary to compete successfully with exporters in other industrial nations. It is doubtful that without Eximbank assistance such financing could take place on any significant scale; exporters themselves seldom have sufficient capital, commercial banks have generally regarded themselves as legally and practically unable to extend such credits for longer than the traditional 180 days, and specialized institutions for long-term financing have not been extensively developed in this country. And, although export-financing may not at first seem to qualify as foreign investment, the fact is that such credits are statistically indistinguishable from a loan to the receiving country of the same duration, and the effects on the recipient's economy are likewise the same as that of a "tied" loan.

In order to "insure the continued interest of the exporter in the effective operation of the equipment sold and to accustom him and his banks to foreign lending,"[50] the Bank always insisted that the exporter either assume himself or find private sources of financing for a certain minimum proportion of the total credit extended to the foreign supplier, to be carried on a *pari passu* basis with the Bank. The actual minima required have varied from time to time. In 1953, the Eximbank would provide a maximum of 56¼ per cent of the total purchase price, requiring at least 25 per cent in cash from the purchaser and the remaining 18¾ per cent as a credit extended by the exporter or his bank. In 1954 the required proportions were changed to 60-20-20 and in 1959 to 68-20-12 (the first figure representing a maximum and the last two, minima). In March 1960, an alternative formula was announced, designed to encourage commercial bank assistance to exporters granting long-term credits. The proportions were set at 55-20-15, with the remaining 10 per cent of a given purchase to be carried by a commercial bank.[51] If a commercial bank were willing to finance 10

[50] *Ibid.*, p. 832.
[51] Alternatively, the commercial bank could finance, without

per cent of a transaction without recourse on either the exporter or the Eximbank, the Bank would put up 55 per cent of the total without any independent investigation of the borrower's credit (although it might still examine the over-all exchange position of the country involved). This arrangement represented, according to a Bank official, "the first foreign financing without domestic recourse engaged in by U.S. commercial banks and the first time in the postwar years that such banks have entered into international banking with full responsibility."[52]

After the introduction of commercial bank guaranties and FCIA medium-term exporter insurance in 1961-1962, these new programs, with very few exceptions, took the place of exporter credits, substituting contingent commitments by the Eximbank in the form of guaranties[53] for direct loan commitments and thus cutting down sharply on the use of public funds.[54] In the case of the commercial bank guaranty program, a cash payment is required, usually 20 per cent but occasionally only 10 per cent, and the exporter must take 15 per cent of the financed portion of the transaction for his own account and risk, without guaranty. Then, if a commercial bank is willing to extend the remainder of the credit (usually 68 per cent of the invoice value of the transaction) without recourse on the exporter, the Eximbank will issue a guaranty to the commercial bank covering political risk on all maturities of its loan and commercial risk as well on the

---

recourse on the Eximbank, the first three semiannual installments of a credit with a maturity of three years or less, or the first four installments of a three-to-five year credit. Mikesell, p. 475.

[52] Interview with R. Henry Rowntree, Chief, Economics Division, Export-Import Bank, July 15, 1960.

[53] With respect to the Export-Import Bank programs, the terms "guaranty" and "insurance" appear to mean exactly the same thing.

[54] The commercial bank guaranty and FCIA insurance programs require only 25 per cent reserves against the Eximbank's liabilities.

later maturities, leaving the private institution to carry between 30 and 50 per cent of the commercial risk itself.

The rules governing eligibility for FCIA insurance on medium-term exporter credits are the same as for the commercial bank guaranty program, as far as the size of the down payment and the share of the credit which the exporter must carry at his own risk are concerned. But in this case the remainder of the financing, instead of being provided by a commercial bank, is put up by the exporter himself, generally under a comprehensive guaranty issued by the FCIA in partnership with Eximbank. When such a comprehensive guaranty is issued, all of the political risk and half the credit risk is carried by the Eximbank, the remainder of the credit risk jointly by the 70-odd private insurance companies which make up the FCIA.[55] In cases where the exporter wants insurance only against political risks, the entire liability is carried by the Eximbank, with the FCIA acting simply as its agent.

Both the commercial bank guaranty program and the FCIA insurance program involve two types of private financial participation. Both require a direct commitment by the exporter himself, who must carry a small portion of the credit entirely at his own risk. In addition, the bank guaranty program involves a larger direct commitment of funds by a private commercial bank, on a risk-sharing basis with the Eximbank. Finally, the insurance program requires a contingent commitment in the form of an insurance liability from a coalition of private insurance firms—the FCIA—again, on a risk-sharing basis whereby roughly half the commercial risk is carried by the private partners and the rest of the risk is borne by the Eximbank.

[55] Through 1963, the estimated risk to the insurer and consequently the premium on a comprehensive policy was split 70 to 30 per cent between the Eximbank and the FCIA. In mid-1964, when the FCIA took over 100 per cent of the commercial risk, with re-insurance provisions, the division was changed to 30 per cent Eximbank and 70 per cent FCIA.

AMOUNT OF PRIVATE PARTICIPATION

Precise figures on private participation in Eximbank activities do not exist for the years before 1952. For the period 1945-1948, the Bank estimated that "participation by private capital in current credits and allocations of the Bank have brought the total of American private investments abroad undertaken since mid-1945 in connection with the Bank's operations to well over $300 million."[56] For the years 1949-1951, even less information is available; all we have to go on is the statement of the Bank's Managing Director before the Senate Banking and Currency Committee that: "An analysis of all the credits which the Bank has authorized in the past five years (1949-1953) directly to private enterprises or to governments for relending to private enterprises, indicates that for every dollar which the Bank has loaned, more than $1.50 of private American capital or private or public foreign capital has been invested in the same enterprises . . . the amount of American capital per dollar of American public money that has gone in is a comparatively small proportion. Maybe it would be thirty cents."[57] Since the sum of the credits referred to during the years 1949-1951 is estimated at $350 million,[58] the multiplication of this figure by .3 yields $105 million as a rough estimate of the amount of private funds which flowed abroad in connection with Eximbank loans during those three years.

From 1952 through 1960, the Eximbank kept records, on an annual basis, of the amounts and types of private funds which were lent abroad in connection with all of its

[56] Export-Import Bank of Washington, *Seventh Semiannual Report to the Congress for the Period July-December 1948*, Washington, 1949, pp. 8-9.

[57] Glen E. Edgerton, Testimony in: *Study of the Export-Import Bank and the World Bank, Hearings*, pp. 62-63.

[58] Estimate provided by Mr. Rowntree.

activities. These figures, which total $1,147.6 million for those nine years, are reproduced in Table 17.[59] Column three represents "private participation" in the strict sense, that is, authorized Eximbank commitments taken over by others for their own account and risk. Column five, on the other hand, includes all the private funds, loan and equity, which have been lent abroad in connection with Eximbank credits, whether as actual participations in loans already undertaken by the Bank or simply in addition to, and simultaneous with, a Bank credit. The "Banks" heading refers to loans by commercial banks, while "Others" designates loans by insurance companies, trust funds, and U.S. industry and suppliers, and "Equity" signifies equity investments by U.S. companies and individuals.

Since 1960, the Eximbank has no longer made public complete estimates of the private foreign lending and investment which have taken place in connection with its activities. The semiannual reports of NAC continue to carry a paragraph entitled "private participation," but the categories of transactions included in these figures are constantly changing and shrinking, so that no consistent series can be derived from them. The figures given in Tables 18 and 19 for 1961-1963, compiled specifically for this study by the Eximbank, differ in two ways from the earlier data: they are on a fiscal year rather than on

[59] The figures reproduced in Tables 17, 18, and 19 are themselves based in part on estimates rather than on precise records. The figures for supplier participation, for example, are obtained by applying to the figure for total supplier credits (issued by the Eximbank and private participants together) in a given year the proportion the supplier is required to hold, on the assumption that virtually all suppliers take only the minimum required portion of any credit. The figures for equity participation are not based on such an across-the-board estimate, but probably involve a systematic downward bias, since they include only those equity participations which the Bank happens to learn about in the course of extending a loan and, in Mr. Rowntree's opinion, there are doubtless a number of such participations each year which fail to find their way into the Bank's records.

U.S. Private Funds Which Went Abroad in
Connection with Eximbank Credits,[a] 1952-1960

(in millions of U.S. dollars)

Calendar Year	Eximbank Credits in which there was Participation[a]		Private Participation in Eximbank Credits (without guaranty)		Private Financing Additional to and Concurrent with Eximbank Credits (without guaranty)			Total Private Participation (without guaranty)		
	Gross	Net	Banks	Others	Banks	Others	Equity	Banks	Others	Total
1952	172.7	120.9	47.2	4.6	—	.7	29.5	47.2	34.8	82.0
1953	10.0	10.0	—	—	—	1.6	13.7	—	15.3	15.3
1954	138.5	134.7	3.8	—	.3	23.1	95.4	4.1	118.5	122.6
1955	135.6	129.1	6.5	—	2.1	43.0	14.8	8.6	57.8	66.4
1956	180.9	169.6	10.8	.5	1.4	39.4	11.2	12.2	51.1	63.3
1957	473.5	354.8	118.7	—	50.8	64.9	80.1	169.5	145.0	314.5
1958	422.1	409.6	12.5	—	137.6	25.0	44.8	150.1	69.8	219.9
1959	300.0	242.4	57.6	—	84.8	56.3	20.3	142.4	76.6	219.0
1960 (to June 30)	150.0	144.1	5.9	—	5.9	15.1	17.7	11.8	32.8	44.6
Total	1,983.3	1,715.2	263.0	5.1	282.9	269.1	327.5	545.9	601.7	1,147.6

[a] Includes project loans, emergency foreign trade loans, commodity credits, and exporter credits. Does not include activities under the Defense Production Act of 1950 (see note 29), the short-term political-risk guaranty program, the local currency "Cooley" loan program (see Chapter IX), or the Bank's operations as agent for other U.S. Government programs.

Source: Export-Import Bank of Washington, Economics Division.

TABLE 18

U.S. Private Funds Which Went Abroad in
Connection with Eximbank Long-Term Credits, 1961-1963
(in millions of U.S. dollars)

Fiscal Year	Eximbank Credits in which There Was Participation[a]		Private Participation in Eximbank Credits (without guaranty)		Private Financing Additional to and Concurrent With Eximbank Credits (without guaranty)			Total Private Participation (without guaranty)		
	Gross	Net	Banks	Others	Debt	Equity	Total	Banks	Others	Total
1961	450.0	425.7	23.3	1.0	100.0	95.0	195.0	123.3	96.0	219.3
1962	325.0	276.8	36.2[b]	12.0	80.0	25.0	105.0	116.2[b]	37.0	153.2[b]
1963	275.0	211.3	45.7[c]	18.0	50.0	7.0	57.0	95.7[c]	25.0	120.7[c]
Total	1050.0	913.8	105.2	31.0	230.0	127.0	357.0	335.2	158.0	493.2

[a] Includes project loans, emergency foreign trade loans, and commodity credits
[b] Does not include $300.0 of portfolio sales with recourse on Eximbank
[c] Does not include $250.0 of portfolio sales with recourse on Eximbank
Source: Export-Import Bank of Washington.

TABLE 19

U.S. Private Financing Made Available in
Connection with Eximbank Medium-Term Credits and Insurance, 1961-1963

(in millions of U.S. dollars)

Fiscal Year	Exporter Loans	Authorizations of Medium-Term Credits			Total Medium-Term Credits	U.S. Private Lending Associated with Medium-Term Credits
		Commercial Bank Guaranties	FCIA Insurance			
			Compre-hensive	Political Risk Only		
1961	208.5	9.1	—	—	217.6	47.6
1962	38.0	236.9	—	—	274.9	285.5
1963	51.4	219.1	27.2	2.7	300.4	302.0
Total	297.9	465.1	27.2	2.7	792.9	635.1[a]

[a] This total includes approximately $140 million of unguarantied private funds; the remainder received some form of partial guaranty coverage under either the commercial bank guaranty or the FCIA insurance program.

Source: Export-Import Bank of Washington.

a calendar year basis, and the figures for private financing made available in connection with medium-term transactions, which were combined with the data on participations in long-term credits for the 1952-1960 period, are shown separately. This separation was dictated by the introduction of the two new medium-term export financing programs, commercial bank guaranties and FCIA insurance, which involve entirely new types of concurrent private financing. Whereas the traditional forms of Eximbank financing involved only direct commitments by the Bank and unguarantied loans and investments from the private sector, the new programs involve in addition contingent commitments, in the form of guaranties or insurance, by the Eximbank and the FCIA and guarantied as well as unguarantied private credits. Thus, for comparability with earlier years, the $493 million of private participation in long-term Eximbank credits during 1961-1963 should be combined with the $635 million of U.S. private lending associated with the Bank's medium-term financing transactions during the same period. Of this latter sum, all but about $140 million was lent under some form of guaranty against all political risks and a portion of the commercial risks.

In all, between the beginning of 1952 and mid-1963, an estimated $2.3 billion of U.S. private funds went abroad in conjunction with the activities of the Export-Import Bank, more than $1.8 billion of it without any type of guaranty from or recourse on the Eximbank, the rest under the protection of the commercial bank guaranty or FCIA insurance programs. The amount of private capital exported per dollar of net Eximbank commitments to the same transactions is approximately sixty cents when the direct loan operations alone are considered, and about the same when the new guaranty and insurance programs are included in the calculation.

Although private participation in the broad sense has increased markedly over the period represented in Tables

17 through 19, its outstanding characteristic is an extremely erratic year to year fluctuation, both in the individual components and in the over-all total. The reasons for this erratic behavior are numerous and hard to pin down. Only occasionally is a Bank officer able to point to some specific circumstance, such as the "slow down" directive from the Treasury under which the Bank operated during 1953 or the 1962 policy decision to switch from unguarantied participations by banks in the early maturities of Eximbank loans to fully guarantied participations certificates, as the cause of a sharp change in the volume of participations. But there can be little doubt that one of the most important factors, at least where the "Banks" component is concerned, is the year-to-year variation in commercial bank liquidity due to fluctuation in the domestic demand for loan funds. Thus, in the first half of 1957, the NAC Report on the Eximbank pointed out that "A continuation of the unprecedented demands upon the private capital market in the United States for credit curtailed the participation by commercial banks and other financial institutions in Export-Import Bank loans during the period under review."[60] A banker's statement explains why this is the case: ". . . let me first point out some of the factors which must be weighed *prior* to a consideration of the merits of individual loan applications. First: funds must be readily available. If the bank loan portfolio is a relatively substantial percentage of deposits (upwards of sixty-five per cent) and if the needs of long established domestic customers evidence strong credit demand, the possibilities of obtaining approval on a foreign loan are substantially reduced."[61] As long as commercial banks continue to practice this type of capital rationing in favor

[60] U.S. National Advisory Council, *Report to the President and the Congress on the activities of the NAC for the period January 1-June 30, 1957*, Washington, 1958, p. 27.

[61] Letter from officer of large commercial bank which participates in Eximbank and World Bank loans, November 23, 1960.

of domestic borrowers, the Eximbank's efforts to secure participations will be at the mercy of the American capital market's current situation.

BUSINESS VIEWS: ENTHUSIASM AND CONFLICT

As is true of all the risk-sharing organizations, any predictions about the future success of the Eximbank in stimulating private foreign investment must be made on the basis not only of its past record but also of the attitude toward it voiced by the groups possessing the funds for overseas investment. But, unlike some of the others, the Eximbank has not had to face, at least in the postwar period, any deep-seated hostility from major segments of the foreign investing population. Whenever private groups have criticized the Bank, either in Congressional hearings or in trade journals, it has been on the grounds that the Bank should do more to assist them or should perform its present functions more efficiently, not because they feel that its existence and functions are an improper use of public funds or an unwarranted encroachment on the free-enterprise system. On the contrary, representatives of the American Bankers' Association, the National Foreign Trade Council, and other powerful business groups have "consistently testified in support of the Bank's operations before Congressional Committees."[62]

In preparation for hearings before the Senate Banking and Currency Committee in 1953[63] on the respective roles of the World Bank and the Export-Import Bank, the Eximbank questioned over a hundred commercial and investment banks, American exporters, and American and

[62] Arey, p. 120. The only significant exceptions to this generalization were some of the criticisms voiced in the 1960 and 1961 hearings cited in note 17, by proponents of a rival plan for export credit guaranties. Their objections received little support from the business community.

[63] U.S. Congress, Senate, Committee on Banking and Currency, *Study of the Export-Import Bank and the World Bank, Hearings,* 83rd Cong., 2nd Sess., 1954.

foreign firms, all of whom had participated in some way in the Bank's loans, on their opinion of the Bank's success in carrying out its legislative mandate to supplement and encourage and not compete with private capital. The banks were almost unanimous in saying that the Eximbank did not compete with them but rather served an essential function in providing medium and long-term foreign financing inappropriate for them to handle because of considerations of risk, marketability, and domestic demand. Of all those interviewed, only one or two felt that the Bank was an unnecessary government subsidy which prevented trade from staying on a "sound" basis.

There is something basically paradoxical in the requirement that the Bank avoid competing with commercial banks and, at the same time, encourage their participation in its activities, for presumably it can avoid competition only by making a type of loan which is not attractive to the commercial institutions. This is reflected in the bankers' insistence, in the same hearings, on their willingness to participate in Eximbank activities chiefly on a guarantied basis, which is not true private investment at all. But despite the limitations placed on it, the Eximbank clearly did stimulate commercial bank lending at their own risk in some cases, as evidenced by the following statement by a vice-president of the Bankers Trust Company: "I am fairly sure that the credits extended by the Export-Import Bank in which Bankers Trust participated would not have been obtainable from private sources without the facilities of the Export-Import Bank at the time the loans were made."[64]

In their comments on the Eximbank, bankers have repeatedly stressed their respect for its "low loss record"

[64] *Ibid.*, p. 233. Among the important credits referred to were the $200 million credit to the Netherlands in 1946, of which private banks took 50 per cent, and the 1952 loan of $50 million to Belgium, of which private banks took 90 per cent.

and "adherence to strict banking criteria."[65] The comment
of a vice-president of the Central National Bank of Cleveland, which has participated at its own risk in several
Eximbank loans, is typical: "I am confident that these
fine records can be attributed to a strict adherence to
sound banking principles by the management of these organizations [the Eximbank and the World Bank] as well
as extremely thorough investigations of all loan applications and a complete knowledge of economic conditions
in all the countries of the free world."[66]

The apparent acceptance by private bankers of the
Eximbank's stated loss-record at its face value is somewhat surprising, in view of the qualifications cited above
which surely cannot have escaped the notice of men highly
experienced in such matters. Their stress on its adherence
to "sound" banking principles is even more puzzling, in
view of the fact that 10 large private American banks
participated in the Bank's "bailout" loan to Colombia
in 1957, when that country was near financial collapse.
This behavior could be interpreted as an indication that,
their statements for public consumption notwithstanding,
the lending rules which private bankers set for themselves
and to which they expect a public agency in whose activities they participate to adhere may not be so rigid and
inflexible as the widespread use of the term "strict banking standards" might indicate. On the other hand, such
lending activities may not be as inconsistent with conservative banking behavior as they seem on the surface.
For commercial bank participations in Eximbank loans
have almost always been in the early maturities which,
even without any formal guaranty, are protected by the

[65] The replies to a query directed by this author to about twenty
commercial banks which have participated in Eximbank loans
commented repeatedly on the "truly remarkable record" of the
Eximbank. Since nearly all the respondents wished to remain
anonymous, I am not citing exact sources here.

[66] Flemming Kolby, Vice-President, Central National Bank of
Cleveland, letter dated November 11, 1960.

longer maturities of the same credit held by the Eximbank itself.

American business firms operating abroad (generally through subsidiaries or affiliates) have also voiced the general opinion that the Eximbank performs a vital function well and efficiently, particularly since the World Bank's requirement of a government guaranty virtually rules out direct loans to private enterprise. A vice-president of the American and Foreign Power Company, whose subsidiaries are collectively one of the Eximbank's largest private debtors, pointed out in both the 1953 and 1954 Banking and Currency Committee Hearings that the Bank's aid came at a time when demand outstripped the companies' ability to finance expansion and "was a decisive factor in enabling this American private enterprise to maintain its position and stay in business."[67] Other testimony has indicated that private firms are favorably impressed by the Bank's status as an independent agency, its ability to mobilize private funds through loans and guaranties instead of relying entirely on tax appropriations, to keep its funds revolving on a self-liquidating basis, and to earn a profit on its operations.[68]

Of the three private groups in American enterprise affected by the Eximbank's activities, the exporters have been perhaps the most emphatic defenders of its functions and operations. Their testimony has stressed repeatedly the absolute necessity of long-term credit facilities, available almost exclusively from the Bank, to enable them to compete with the exporters of other countries in third markets. Many have expressed the opinion that the Bank has made possible heavy equipment sales abroad which could not otherwise have taken place; the representative of a large firm exporting tractors declared

[67] U.S. Congress, Senate, Banking and Currency Committee, *Export-Import Bank Act Amendments of 1954, Hearings*, 83rd Cong., 2nd Sess., 1954, p. 44.

[68] *Ibid.*, p. 56.

that ". . . it is not uncommon for members of this industry to lose sales in old established markets on the basis of terms alone . . . we are faced with a total vacuum insofar as commercial bank assistance is concerned."[69] The existence of such a vacuum filled only by the Eximbank was emphasized even more strongly in 1960 hearings on the establishment of export credit guaranties. The representative of a major manufacturers' group emphasized that ". . . there has been only one major contribution in export credit facilities availability made in the United States, and that has been by the Export-Import bank . . . we have not had a major contribution in this area from private institutions of any character. . . ."[70]

The various hearings and surveys of business opinion have also, of course, elicited frequent criticism of the Eximbank from the business community, but it has generally been on the grounds that the Bank's services were fine as far as they went but that they did not go far enough. Many exporters have expressed the desire for broader export-credit facilities to give them a more favorable competitive position. Apparently few who requested Eximbank services have been denied them, but complaints about slow processing, inability to elicit advance commitments from the Eximbank, and a distinct bias against or at least lack of interest in small loans have been registered with some persistence, as have protests against the Bank's allegedly excessive caution and conservatism in lending. Among suggestions made, all with a critical edge, have been: an end to the red tape, confusion, and delays characterizing the lending agencies in general and consoli-

[69] *Ibid.*, p. 42. Just previously, the president of the Washington Board of Trade had asserted that "Business now finds it almost impossible to get long-term financing for foreign trade from private sources in the United States. . . ."

[70] Testimony of Charles W. Stewart, President, Machinery and Allied Products Institute, in: U.S. Congress, Senate, Committee on Interstate and Foreign Commerce, *Foreign Commerce Study, Hearings*, p. 145.

dation of their activities; the provision of "soft loans" (variously interpreted as long-term, low-interest loans or dollar loans repayable in foreign currencies); a more flexible source for small loans in the $25-100 thousand range; and an increased utilization of private funds on a fully guarantied basis.[71]

All these criticisms were registered before 1961; since then the Eximbank has introduced new programs specifically designed to meet all of them except the demand for soft loans. This last, which is essentially a request for more subsidy, would involve the Eximbank in activities which would severely distort its present operating criteria and its position in the hierarchy of U.S. and international lending institutions. The Eximbank's sale of $550 million of participation certificates in 1962 and 1963 represented the utilization of guarantied private funds on an unprecedented scale, while the new commercial bank guaranty and FCIA exporter insurance programs also involve private funds under various degrees of guaranty coverage. In addition, the two new export-financing programs have already done much to streamline the processing of applications for credit assistance and have created conditions far more receptive to small applicants than the older direct-loan programs could possibly be. Most important of all, these new programs permit exporters to deal not directly with a public agency but through traditional, familiar channels, either with their own commercial banks or, in the case of the FCIA program, with a coalition of private insurance companies. The very existence of these programs, and the fact that more than 70 private insurance companies and an even larger number of commercial

[71] U.S. Congress, Senate, Banking and Currency Committee, *Export-Import Bank Act Amendments of 1954, Hearings,* p. 42; U.S. Department of Commerce, *Reportorial Review: Responses to Business Questionnaire Regarding Private Investment Abroad,* Washington, 1959, p. 1; U.S. Congress, Senate, Committee on Interstate and Foreign Commerce, *Foreign Commerce Study, Hearings,* pp. 163-178; Mikesell, pp. 193-194.

banks willingly participate in them, testifies to important progress in "the creation of a feeling of partnership between U.S. companies and the U.S. government," an attitude which is of such crucial importance in maximizing the contribution of American private enterprise to development abroad.[72]

The most severe criticism of the Eximbank's policies has come from the other side, from those concerned less with its services to the American business community than with its contribution to foreign economic development. One of the Eximbank's greatest shortcomings, say these critics, is its application of the "harsh standards of bankability"[73] to loan applications. Its extreme caution, insistence on self-liquidating loans, high interest rates, and credits repayable in dollars and for dollar purchases only—all severely restrict, they say, the Bank's usefulness in assisting foreign economic development. It is often said, further, that the reasons for these strict standards and high interest rates, the one due to Congressional insistence that the Bank refrain from undercutting private finance, the other both to this prohibition and to the fact that the Bank must pay for the funds it lends the same rate of interest as the Treasury pays on our national debt, are due simply to an outmoded structure and could easily be changed by suitable legislative modifications. At the same time, the Bank is frequently charged (though generally not by the same critics) with lack of success in mobilizing private participation.[74] In view of the stress placed by the private financial community on adherence to strict standards of bankability, it would on the face of things appear that the Bank could satisfy one group of critics only by increasing the displeasure of the other.

Such a view would, however, be based on several over-

[72] Mikesell, p. 192.

[73] Peter B. Kenen, *Giant Among Nations*, New York, 1960, p. 144.

[74] Pugh, p. 35.

simplifications. The first relates to the Bank's actual behavior with respect to the "strict bankability" criterion. While the general run of its loans have indeed been of the cautious, self-liquidating variety, a number of the largest ones, motivated strictly by political considerations, have been to bail friendly governments out of payments crises under conditions which, in several instances, were far too risky to merit approval by pure banking standards.[75] The effectiveness of the Eximbank as an aid to economic development can be more trenchantly criticized on the grounds of erratic behavior and unpredictability[76] than because of consistent adherence to cautious commercial lending standards.

Secondly, the Bank's record in attracting private financing into its activities has not been insignificant; an estimated $2.8 billion of private funds have accompanied Eximbank credits abroad in the postwar period, about $2.1 billion of it entirely at its own risk, the rest under a risk-sharing guaranty or insurance agreement with the Bank. Since Eximbank disbursements of its own funds over the same period totaled approximately $9.1 billion, the private funds increased by nearly one-third the medium and long-term foreign financing generated by Eximbank activities. And, over the period 1952-1963, such private capital flows were roughly half the size of the net authorized Eximbank credits in which there was some private participation.[77]

[75] For example, the "bail out" loans to Argentina in 1950 and Brazil in 1953; both these credits, one for $125 million and the other for $300 million, were extended to enable the settlement of commercial indebtedness to the United States. Pugh, p. 26.

[76] Kenen, who uses the phrase "harsh standards of bankability" in connection with the Eximbank, also indicts it on these grounds, p. 143.

[77] The latter figure, although it covers a more limited period, is perhaps a more meaningful one, since many of the Eximbank credits, particularly those granted immediately after World War II, were not intended to be of a type attractive to private capital. "Funds disbursed" represents authorizations minus private capital

Finally, the behavior of private lenders themselves, as opposed to their generalizations for public consumption, indicates that there is no hard and fast division in their minds between "sound" projects and "soft" development assistance, but rather a gradual shading over from one into the other. The participation of 10 large private American banks in the Eximbank's general stabilization loan to Colombia in 1957, for example, seems to suggest the willingness of private finance to participate in a type of loan not traditionally regarded as "bankable," that is, attractive to commercial lending institutions. Certainly such institutions, which control the bulk of private funds available for lending, will remain committed to the exercise of caution with other people's money and will doubtless always be highly selective in their participation in foreign development lending. But clearly the Eximbank's success in avoiding loss (even though it is often through refinancing) has attracted private lenders into areas which they would not enter alone.

Because the policies and programs of the Eximbank were undergoing such far-reaching changes during the early 1960's, it is difficult to predict its effect in the future on the basis of past performance. Clearly its future success in stimulating long-term private foreign lending and investment will depend heavily on how high a priority it places on this particular function, as compared with a variety of other goals, including its primary one of financing U.S. exports. In recent years, the Bank's marked shift in emphasis from long-term to short and medium-term financing, and from the attraction of unguarantied to partially or fully guarantied private funds, suggests that such considerations as the competitive needs of U.S. ex-

participation, credits which expired unused, and portions of outstanding credits as yet undisbursed. Figures for "authorized credits (net)" are net of private participations, but still contain unused and undisbursed funds, and so are somewhat larger for any given period than the "funds disbursed" figure.

porters, the exigencies of the U.S. balance of payments, the intent to conserve Treasury funds, and the desire to restore balance to the term-structure of the Eximbank's own loan portfolio have taken precedence over the aim of maximizing the participation of private funds in foreign lending and investment on a genuine risk-sharing basis.

Although the architects of the Eximbank's new programs probably did not intend and perhaps did not foresee any conflict between them and the mobilization of private capital for foreign lending and investment, there are at least two reasons why the shifts in emphasis just described can be expected to cut down on the participation of such capital in Eximbank activities. For one thing, private funds are not likely to go abroad at their own risk if they have the option of obtaining a full or partial guaranty, and the Bank's current stress on its various guaranty programs is bound to reduce its efforts to attract private capital on an unguarantied basis. In addition, the exporting countries' competition to make short and medium-term financing for their own exports easily available to the less-developed nations must eventually cut into the ability of these countries to service longer-term debt and therefore into the willingness of the national and international lending agencies to extend it.[78]

The figures in Tables 17, 18, and 19 indicate that, while the participation of private funds in the Eximbank's medium-term credits, on a guarantied basis, increased markedly during fiscal years 1962 and 1963, after the introduction of the new financing programs, both the participation and the concurrent investment of such funds on an unguarantied basis in connection with the Bank's long-term credits dropped off noticeably from the levels they seemed to be establishing in the late 1950's. The evi-

[78] On this problem, see: Raymond F. Mikesell, "Some Conclusions for Public Policy in the Light of Current Developments," in Mikesell (ed.), pp. 556-557.

dence of two years is hardly sufficient to establish a trend, but the above reasoning suggests that this shift is a natural result of the Eximbank's own shifts in emphasis. The Export-Import Bank has over the years amassed a considerable battery of instruments for stimulating the flow of private capital into development lending and investment abroad. Its future effectiveness in performing this function will depend in large part on how closely it shapes its activities to fit this particular end.

IX · THE DEVELOPMENT LOAN FUND—AGENCY FOR INTERNATIONAL DEVELOPMENT

THE "SOFT LOAN" COMPROMISE

The Development Loan Fund was created as a result of severe criticism of our Mutual Security Program as it operated during the first five years of the 1950's, leveled by a Special Committee of the Senate set up to study the program.[1] The new fund represented ". . . a compromise between new grants for development and an end to economic aid." The DLF's proponents argued that it would meet the chief criticisms of the Special Committee in that it ". . . would disentangle the goal of economic development from other policy aims . . . ," would put such aid in long-term rather than short-term and loan rather than grant form, and would extend it on an individual project or program basis with clearly defined criteria rather than an over-all country basis.[2] It seems to have been largely on these grounds that the creation of the DLF was finally accepted by the many factions in the Senate and House, each of which had its own views as to the form, if any, that economic aid to less-developed nations should take.

The Development Loan Fund legally came into being in 1957 as Title II of the Mutual Security Act of 1954, as amended. The opening section concludes its *Declaration of Purpose* as follows: ". . . The Congress accordingly reaffirms that it is the policy of the United States, and declares it to be the purpose of this title, to strengthen friendly foreign countries by encouraging the develop-

[1] U.S. Congress, Senate, Special Committee to Study the Foreign Aid Program, *The Foreign Aid Program, Hearings*, 85th Cong., 1st Sess., 1957.

[2] Testimony of John B. Hollister, Director, ICA, in: U.S. Congress, House, Committee on Foreign Affairs, *Mutual Security Act of 1957, Hearings*, 85th Cong., 1st Sess., 1957, Section VI, pp. 1217, 1230.

ment of their economies through a competitive free enterprise system; to minimize or eliminate barriers to the flow of investment capital and international trade; to facilitate the creation of a climate favorable to the investment of private capital; and to assist, on a basis of self-help and mutual cooperation, the efforts of free peoples to develop their economic resources and to increase their productive capabilities."[3] To carry out these purposes, ". . . the President is hereby authorized to make loans, credits, or guaranties, or to engage in other financing operations or transactions (not to include grants or direct purchases of equity securities . . ." or guaranties of equity investment against normal business-type risks). The criteria for loan decisions were set forth as follows in the 1957 legislation:

"(1) Whether financing could be obtained in whole or in part from other free world sources on reasonable terms,

"(2) the economic and technical soundness of the activity to be financed, and

"(3) whether the activity gives reasonable promise of contributing to the development of economic resources or to the increase of productive capacities in furtherance of the purposes of this title."

Finally, "the Fund shall be administered so as to support and encourage private investment and other private participation furthering the purpose of this title, and it shall be administered so as not to compete with private investment capital, the Export-Import Bank or the International Bank for Reconstruction and Development."[4]

The 1958 Mutual Security legislation changed the status of the DLF from a component of the ICA to an autonomous Government corporation. The Fund remained, however, under the foreign policy guidance of the Secretary of State, and the Deputy Under-Secretary of State for Economic Affairs was made Chairman of its Board of

[3] *Mutual Security Act of 1957*, 71 *Stat.* 357.
[4] *Ibid.*, pp. 357-358.

Directors, which also included the Director of the ICA, the Chairman of the Board of Directors of the Eximbank, the Fund's own Managing Director and the U.S. Executive Director of the IBRD. Indeed, this subordination to State Department objectives was stressed by the *Report* of the Committee on Foreign Relations: "The Fund is an instrument of American foreign policy, and is intended to be under the foreign policy direction of the Secretary of State, whether incorporated or unincorporated."[5] The 1958 legislation also added to the three loan criteria a fourth, which was designed to insure consideration of the possible domestic economic implications of the Fund's operation:

"The possible adverse effects upon the economy of the United States, with special reference to areas of substantial labor surplus, of the activity and the financing operation or transaction involved."[6]

Another addition to the "General Authority" section made explicit the requirement that "loans shall be made by the Fund only on the basis of firm commitments by the borrowers to make repayment and upon a finding that there are reasonable prospects of such repayment."[7]

Yet another criterion for DLF financing transactions was added to the Mutual Security legislation the following year, linking such aid to the behavior of the potential borrower's government:

"The Fund in its operations shall recognize that development loan assistance will be most effective in those countries which show a responsiveness to the vital long-term economic, political, and social concerns of the people, demonstrate a clear willingness to take

[5] U.S. Congress, Senate, Committee on Foreign Relations, *The Mutual Security Act of 1958*, *Report*, 85th Cong., 2nd Sess., 1958, p. 113.

[6] *Mutual Security Act of 1958*, 72 *Stat.* 263.

[7] *Ibid.*

effective self-help measures, and effectively demonstrate that such assistance is consistent with, and makes a contribution to, workable long-term economic development objectives."[8]

The Foreign Assistance Act of 1961 brought a number of radical changes in the United States' program of development loans. It abolished the DLF as a separate agency, transferring its operations to the new, all-encompassing foreign aid agency, the Agency for International Development in the Department of State; the term "Development Loan Fund" remained in the legislation, but it referred now to one of several sources or types of foreign aid funds rather than to a separate administering agency. AID absorbed not only the long-term dollar lending program of the DLF, but also the local-currency "Cooley" lending program previously administered by the Export-Import Bank and the Investment Guaranty Program, as well as a number of other grant, loan, and technical assistance programs formerly the province of ICA.

Along with this change in administration came some definite shifts in emphasis. One of these was an increased stress on long-range development programming; such programming by the less-developed countries was now regarded as a pre-condition to receiving assistance and, in addition, the requirement that U.S. financing be in general confined to specific projects was softened to permit "program" as well as "project" lending. Greater emphasis was also placed on the importance of self-help among the recipients of aid, "the demand for a more substantial commitment on the part of the recipient countries."[9]

These changes were reflected in the legislative criteria for development loans. Most of the criteria were carried over more or less intact from the DLF legislation, but

[8] *Mutual Security Act of 1959*, 73 *Stat.* 248.
[9] Ross D. Davis, "Capital, Credit and Growth," *AID Digest* (June 1962), 20.

the language of the self-help requirement was sharpened, and a new standard was added: "the consistency of the activity with, and its relationship to, other development activities being undertaken or planned, and its contribution to realizable long-range objectives."[10] Two years later a clause was added to the self-help provision stating specifically that the signing of agreements instituting the Investment Guaranty Program would be regarded as "a significant measure of self-help . . . improving the climate for private investment both domestic and foreign."[11] When the Alliance for Progress section was added to the Foreign Assistance Act of 1962, authorizing a special program of grant and loan assistance to Latin America, substantially the same loan criteria applied, plus specific consideration of "the efforts made by recipient nations to repatriate capital invested in other countries by their own citizens."[12]

The AID era also brought a renewed stress on the importance of the protection and participation of private enterprise, both local and foreign, reflected in a variety of provisions and programs to be discussed in detail in a later section. And, finally, the new program brought substantial changes in the repayment terms and conditions of development loans. The loans made by the DLF were "soft" in that they could be repaid in the currency of the borrowing country rather than in dollars, although they were "dollar-denominated"—that is, in the event of depreciation of the borrower's currency vis-à-vis the dollar, he was required to repay an amount sufficient to equal the sum of dollars originally lent. Interest rates varied from 3½ per cent on "economic overhead" projects to the current Eximbank rate, generally between 5¼ and 5¾ per cent, on profit-making projects. Repayment periods averaged approximately 15 years, and generally

[10] *Foreign Assistance Act of 1961*, 75 *Stat.* 426.
[11] *Foreign Assistance Act of 1963*, 77 *Stat.* 380, 388.
[12] *Foreign Assistance Act of 1962*, 76 *Stat.* 258.

began one year from the date of the loan or, in the case of private enterprise, one year after the project went into operation.

Dollar loans made by AID, in contrast, are repayable in dollars, largely to avoid the problems and embarrassment caused by large accumulations of foreign currencies. But, to avoid placing unrealistic demands on the foreign debt-servicing capacity of borrowing countries, "softer" or more liberal loan terms were established, based on "the individual country's capacity to repay foreign debt, rather than on the character of the activity to be financed, as had been the practice previously."[13] Loan maturities up to 40 or 50 years were authorized, with grace periods as long as 10 years, and interest rates varying between ¾ per cent and 5¾ per cent. In the Foreign Assistance Act of 1963, minimum interest rates were set of ¾ per cent during the grace period and 2 per cent thereafter.[14]

The emphasis on long-range planning which accompanied the transfer of development lending responsibility from the DLF to AID also revived an old battle concerning the funding of these programs. At the time of the DLF's establishment, its supporters stressed the importance of making it independent of annual Congressional appropriations, feeling that this alone would make long-range planning possible and give potential borrowers and investment partners alike the necessary confidence in its stability. On the basis of suggestions contained in a number of reports by government and business groups,[15] the Executive Branch recommended and Congress legislated a two-year authorization for the Fund without fiscal year limitations on spending, a compromise intended to

[13] Davis, p. 20.

[14] *Foreign Assistance Act of 1963*, 77 *Stat.* 380.

[15] The Presidential reports were by the President's Citizen Advisors on the Mutual Security Program (Fairless) and the International Development Advisory Board (Johnston). The private organizations reporting were the Committee for Economic Development and the National Planning Association.

provide both ". . . continuing Congressional control of the fund's resources and . . . adequate assurance of continuity."[16] But the full amounts, totaling $1,125 million, authorized for fiscal years 1958 and 1959 were not appropriated; only $300 million was appropriated for the first year and $400 million for the second.

When a shortage of funds forced a supplemental appropriation of $150 million to keep DLF alive, a battle royal was set off in the 1959 Mutual Security Act hearings on the form of its capitalization.[17] The Senate Foreign Relations Committee favored a form of financing similar to that of the Eximbank or the U.S. contributions to the IBRD, with Congressional authorization of a five-year authority to borrow from the Treasury at the rate of $1 billion per year. But its House counterpart and the Executive Branch opposed such a borrowing authority independent of the appropriations procedure, although the President had originally favored it. In the end the Senate had to be satisfied with a two-year authorization of $700 million for fiscal year 1960 and $1.1 billion for 1961, of which only $550 million was actually appropriated for each year, leaving DLF once again out of funds and in need of a supplemental appropriation to keep going by mid-January 1961.[18]

When DLF was absorbed into AID in November 1961, this problem of having to make long-range plans on the basis of single-year appropriations was one of its legacies. Although the original proposal for AID would have provided its development loan funds through a long-term borrowing authority, the final legislation of 1961 made it

[16] U.S. Congress, House, Committee on Foreign Affairs, *Mutual Security Act of 1957, Hearings*, 85th Cong., 1st Sess., 1957, Part VI, pp. 1218, 1221.

[17] U.S. Congress, Senate, Committee on Foreign Relations, *Mutual Security Act of 1959, Hearings*, 86th Cong., 1st Sess., 1959, pp. 1245-1249.

[18] Letter from George A. Wyeth, Jr., Assistant Deputy Managing Director for Private Enterprise, DLF, dated November 4, 1960.

once again subject to annual Congressional appropriations, authorizing it to lend up to $1.2 billion in fiscal year 1962 and $1.5 billion in each of the fiscal years 1963-1966. The amounts actually appropriated for fiscal 1962 and 1963 were somewhat less. But the program's continuity and self-sufficiency were nevertheless increased in a number of ways. Appropriations were placed on an "available until expended" basis, that is, funds not utilized during one fiscal year could be carried over into the next without affecting the size of new appropriations. In addition, AID was given authority to make advance commitments (subject to appropriation) "in the interest of orderly and effective execution of long-term plans and programs of development assistance,"[19] an authority which, it was hoped, would put Congress under some moral obligation to appropriate funds to meet such commitments. Finally, with the requirement that all dollar loans be repaid in dollars, the "revolving fund" provision carried over from the original DLF legislation, permitting payments on loans to revert to the lending agency, should have acquired new importance. As long as the bulk of repayments were made in inconvertible currencies of severely limited usefulness, these funds were likely to prove more of an embarrassment than a help. In dollar form, repayments can be expected eventually to add to AID's effective supply of working capital, but only if they are freed from the restrictions imposed by the Foreign Aid Appropriations Act of 1964, which at present prevent the re-use of such funds.[20] In any case, in view of the long grace and repayment periods and low interest rates of most AID dollar loans, repayments are not likely to be-

[19] Davis, p. 20.

[20] Section 116 of this law forbids the use of AID funds, and therefore of AID personnel, to administer the use of monies accruing to the DLF and AID revolving funds. Section 117 specifies that such monies may be used only when specifically authorized in future Appropriations Acts. *Foreign Aids and Related Agencies Appropriations Act, 1964, 77 Stat.* 860.

come a significant source of additional lending funds in the near future.

THE ENCOURAGEMENT OF PRIVATE ENTERPRISE

AID and its predecessor, DLF, have employed two major types of activity to encourage private enterprise. The first is, of course, the extension of loans and guaranties directly or indirectly to private borrowers. The second comprises a wide variety of measures to improve the climate for private investment abroad, including assistance to public investment in the basic economic infrastructure so important for profitable private investment, and to increase interest in and information about such investment among businessmen at home. Included in the second group are the steps taken to assure that loan applicants make "the maximum reasonable effort" to obtain capital in whole or in part from private sources.[21] In checking on the "effort" actually made, aid agency representatives have on occasion approached banking institutions to find out whether they could be induced to provide the capital requested or some part of it. These measures also include the widespread and increasing use of management, engineering, construction, and other technical services provided by private U.S. firms under AID contracts. Although services connected with contracts are not in themselves private investments, they can be expected, in the long run, to stimulate new or increased foreign investment by the firms providing them.

In November 1959 responsibility for stimulating private capital participation in DLF loans was consolidated in a newly created Office of Private Enterprise. The three major responsibilities of this office were described as:

"(1) To secure the maximum feasible participation by U.S. and foreign private enterprise in DLF activities . . .

[21] DLF, *Mutual Security Program-DLF, Fiscal Year 1961 Estimates* . . . , p. 24.

by informing the business community of the broad authority and great flexibility the DLF possesses under its statute and . . . by working actively with representatives of private enterprise on specific proposals.

"(2) To foster, encourage and support the development of private enterprise systems in developing countries . . . [particularly by] making loans to intermediate financial institutions such as Industrial and Agricultural Development Banks, Small Industries Corporations, Savings and Loan Associations, etc., which in turn make credits available to local private individuals, partnerships and corporations. The Office of Private Enterprise is responsible for recommending DLF policies for loans to these institutions and . . . for providing specific advice on particular applications and on the monitoring of the operations of such institutions.

"(3) To explore, develop and recommend general policies for and specific uses of DLF guaranty authority."[22]

Speeches and visits to business groups, consultations with potential private investors, the arrangement, often under Commerce Department auspices, of executive "seminars" on investment opportunities in less-developed areas were among the methods used by this office to spur the interest of private enterprise in participation in DLF investments. The Office also served as a liaison with other agencies having similar broad objectives, such as ICA's Office of Private Enterprise and Investment Guaranties Division, the Department of Commerce, and the International Finance Corporation.

DLF intended originally that its stimulation of private investment should take two main forms: first, the provision of loan capital to enable private enterprise to embark on projects it might otherwise be unable to undertake and, second, the purchase of convertible debentures suitable for later re-sale to private investors. This second

[22] DLF Manual Order MA-3.5 (Aug. 30, 1960), pp. 1-2.

method never actually functioned; DLF did make a few of its investments partially in the form of convertible debentures, but none of these was turned over to private hands during its four years of operation. In fact, none of DLF's methods of mobilizing private capital functioned very effectively; under a section headed "Accomplishment of Purposes," the *Terminal Report of the Development Loan Fund* confessed that "DLF's effort to encourage activity by U.S. private enterprise in less-developed countries was its least successful endeavor. Although some American private enterprise was involved, this was relatively small."[23]

The Foreign Assistance Act of 1961, which established AID, included an intensified emphasis on the participation of private enterprise in economic development, and an enlarged arsenal of instruments to encourage such participation. It not only gathered in one place all the existing instruments for mobilizing private capital—dollar loans directly to private enterprise or to development banks for relending to private enterprise, local-currency Cooley loans, the specific-risk investment guaranty program—but added two new ones: extended or all-risk guaranties for certain special classes of investments, and government cost-sharing for investment surveys conducted by U.S. owned business firms. The so-called Hickenlooper amendment added the following year pointed out explicitly the relationship between a country's eligibility for aid and its behavior toward U.S. owned private investments: it provided for the suspension of assistance to any country which nationalized or expropriated U.S. owned property and failed to take appropriate steps to discharge its obligations to the owner, including full and prompt compensation in convertible foreign exchange.[24]

[23] AID, *Terminal Report of the Development Loan Fund*, Washington, January 1962, p. 2.
[24] *Foreign Assistance Act of 1962*, 76 *Stat.* 261.

The Congressional mandate to mobilize private capital for development was further strengthened in the Foreign Assistance Act of 1963, where the encouragement and protection of U.S. private foreign investment became a major theme. References to the maximum utilization of private enterprise in AID operations and to the importance of the creation of a favorable climate for foreign investment by aid-recipient nations are scattered through almost every section of this law. The development loan criterion relating to the availability of financing from other sources was amended to include specifically "private sources within the United States," and an addition to the list of criteria required that any project receiving assistance must "provide for appropriate participation by private enterprise." The authorization section required that not less than 50 per cent of the funds to be appropriated for development and Alliance for Progress loans in fiscal years 1965 and 1966 should be available for loans made to encourage economic development through private enterprise.

The expectation that aid-recipient countries will take positive steps to encourage private foreign investment, including the institution of the full Investment Guaranty Program, was specifically stated in the 1963 law. The Hickenlooper amendment was expanded to include among the grounds for suspension of assistance the repudiation or nullification by a foreign government or government agency of existing contracts or agreements with U.S. citizens or U.S. owned entities, and any actions, including but not limited to discriminatory taxes or regulatory measures "which have the effect of nationalizing, expropriating, or otherwise seizing ownership or control of property so owned." And finally, in addition to continuing all the existing programs for mobilizing private enterprise, the 1963 Act provided for the establishment of an "Advisory Committee on Private Enterprise in Foreign Aid," to make recommendations, before the end of

1964, on how to achieve most effective use of the private enterprise provisions of the Act.[25]

Under the aegis of its legislative mandate, AID embarked on a wide variety of activities, centered in its Office of Development Finance and Private Enterprise, designed to improve the climate for foreign investment in development countries on the one hand and, on the other, to encourage businessmen and other potential investors in the United States to take up investment opportunities in these countries. To those countries which request it, AID has furnished consulting services to assist in the formulation of laws and regulations to encourage private enterprise, the creation of industrial development programs, the establishment of development banks and centers, and the identification of specific investment opportunities. But these activities have been limited responses to specific requests, rather than all-out efforts to promote local and U.S. investment, and particularly joint ventures between them, utilizing all the available instruments. Obviously, it was not practically possible to launch such efforts simultaneously in the 80 countries which receive U.S. aid, so the Office of Development Finance and Private Enterprise decided to concentrate on 4 countries—Colombia, Thailand, Pakistan, and Nigeria—one in each of the 4 key regions in which the U.S. has major commitments.

In each of these 4 countries, a pilot program has been initiated to develop the most effective utilization of all the programs available to stimulate local and U.S. investment. In these countries AID is actually taking the initiative, in collaboration with the Department of Commerce, in seeking out U.S. firms interested in exploring specific investment opportunities identified by AID survey missions in such high-priority industries as food processing, lumber and paper products, and machine tools. AID hopes that the fruits of these activities will demonstrate

[25] *Foreign Assistance Act of 1963, passim.*

to the host countries the possibilities, and the advantages, of creating a climate favorable to the rapid development of the private sector. In mid-1963 it was able to report that a number of investment plans were under way in these countries as a direct result of its efforts.[26] To provide expert advice on the specific problems arising in such a growth process, AID has more recently sponsored the formation of an Executive Service Corps, through which successful U.S. businessmen, "at liberty" because of retirement or other reasons, can make their managerial and technical skills available to private firms in developing countries.

In its efforts to acquaint U.S. businessmen with the investment opportunities existing in developing countries, and with the types of financial and other assistance available to them from both U.S. Government and international agencies, AID has gone somewhat beyond the usual mimeographed circulars and speeches to business groups. During 1963, it printed and distributed more than 35,000 copies of *Aids to Business (Overseas Investment)*, a brochure containing concise descriptions of the various AID programs available to aid present or prospective foreign investors, as well as of the other international financial agencies and private financial institutions that provide various types of financing assistance for such investment. At about the same time, it established its own Businessmen's Information Center, a clearinghouse "which provides information on doing business or investing in connection with AID programs and guides businessmen to the appropriate offices and officials in AID to answer their questions."[27] In addition, AID is setting up a catalog of investment opportunities, consisting of card-

[26] U.S. Congress, House, Committee on Foreign Affairs, *Foreign Assistance Act of 1963, Hearings*, 88th Cong., 1st Sess., Washington, 1963, pp. 459-460.

[27] U.S. Congress, House, Committee on Foreign Affairs, *Foreign Assistance Act of 1964, Hearings*, 88th Cong., 2nd Sess., Washington, 1964, p. 48.

sized abstracts which bring together in one place, for the first time, some 2,000 feasibility studies and surveys of particular investment opportunities in developing countries, prepared by a wide variety of public and private organizations. Plans are under way to keep the catalog current by automatically adding new studies and surveys as they are made.

Of the various types of informational assistance offered by AID to prospective foreign investors, only one is specifically provided for in legislation: the financing of investment surveys. Funds had long been available, under the Technical Cooperation Program of ICA, for investment feasibility studies, and such activity has continued under AID auspices, but these studies must be made by outside experts—organizations that would not benefit directly from the study. This limitation meant that the Government would not respond to the initiative of a private firm which wanted to explore the feasibility of a possible investment, and besides, U.S. business firms clearly prefer to make their investment decisions on the basis of their own surveys rather than someone else's. Recognizing these facts, the Foreign Assistance Act of 1961 established a program whereby AID would provide up to half the financing for surveys of investment opportunities by U.S. firms which wished to explore such opportunities but did not feel justified in making the expenditure. Under such an arrangement, AID pays half of the costs of an approved investment survey, with the agreement that if the firm decides to go ahead with the investment, it will reimburse AID for the funds expended. If the potential investor decides, within an agreed period of time, *not* to go ahead with the investment, AID will have borne half the cost. In such cases, the survey becomes the property of the U.S. Government, which "may then utilize the survey for any appropriate purpose." Any prospective investment which will further the economic development of a less-developed, friendly nation and which is consistent with the host country's development program is eligible for survey assistance, except that surveys of mineral extraction opportunities are ineligible for AID participation.[28]

The investment survey program did not really get under way until mid-1962, so the initial appropriation of $1.5 million was carried over into fiscal 1963. By mid-1963, however, the new program had definitely begun to gather steam; more survey agreements were signed during the first half of that year than in the previous 13 months. By the end of the first quarter of 1964, 74 applications for investment surveys in more than 20 underdeveloped countries had been approved and granted, representing a maximum AID participation of less than $1 million and anticipated total capital investments of more than $200 million. The low average cost of AID participation in a survey—about $12,000—indicates that the program is reaching, as AID intended that it should, small and medium-sized firms which are likely to have little overseas contact or experience, and would be less likely than larger firms to incur alone the costs of investigating a possible foreign venture.

AID emphasizes the "seed capital" nature of the investment survey program, where government expenditures of a few thousands of dollars may result in investments of several million. It points out that, in the three cases where maximum AID participation exceeds $40,000, "the total anticipated capitalization of each investment is in excess of $15 million."[29] But just how much leverage these AID expenditures actually exert depends, of course, on how many of the surveys result in a positive decision to invest. Of the 12 surveys completed at the end of 1963, 2 had resulted in positive decisions to invest, one by the McGraw-Hill Publishing Company to start a book dis-

[28] AID, *Aids to Business (Overseas Investment)*, Washington, 1963, pp. 7-8.

[29] U.S. Congress, House, Committee on Foreign Affairs, *Foreign Assistance Act of 1964, Hearings*, p. 48.

tribution venture in Nigeria and the other by the Livingstone Coating Corporation to establish a plastic coating factory in Mexico. By April 1, 1964, 3 more firms had made positive investment decisions, pending the final negotiation of financing arrangements, 2 for investments in housing components and prefabricated housing in Colombia and 1 for a cement factory in British Honduras. The combined anticipated total capital investment of these 5 firms was about $17 million, while the corresponding figure for the 13 firms which had arrived at negative investment decisions was between $35 and $40 million, about three-quarters of which was accounted for by a single firm.[30] But these figures are no more than straws in the wind and probably not very reliable ones at that; the vast majority of the firms undertaking the 74 approved investment surveys had not made up their minds as yet, and it will be some time before sufficient information is available to evaluate the effects of the new investment survey program.

All the activities so far described operate only indirectly on the risks of foreign investment, either by helping to improve the climate for such investment in developing countries or by providing services to prospective investors in the United States aimed at increasing their knowledge and confidence concerning overseas ventures. But AID has also inherited from its predecessors several programs which use Government funds to share directly in the risks of foreign investment itself, either by making loans, in dollars or in local currencies, to help finance foreign undertakings, or by offering various types of investment guaranties. It is only with these programs that substantial measurable flows of private funds into economic development can be associated.

[30] AID, "Monthly Investment Survey Report," April 1, 1964 and information provided by the Investment Survey Section, Office of Development Finance and Private Enterprise.

DOLLAR LOANS

The operations of the Development Loan Fund were confined almost exclusively to dollar loans to finance the foreign exchange costs of economic development projects. During its first year of operations it made commitments for 77 loans in 36 countries, totaling $698 million, which almost exactly exhausted the Fund's initial capital resources. Fifteen months later, at the end of fiscal 1960, the DLF had approved a total of 151 loans in 44 countries, for a total of $1,356 million.[31] When it terminated operations on November 3, 1961, the DLF had during its four years of operation approved more than 200 dollar loans in 50 less-developed countries, with a total value of $2,160 million, most of which was repayable in local currencies. Geographically, this total broke down as follows: South Asia (chiefly India and Pakistan), $843 million; Near East, $427 million; Latin America, $327 million; Far East, $274 million; Africa, $152 million; and Europe, $137 million. Disbursements, which are generally a rather small proportion of total loan approvals since they are made not in a lump sum but as payments are actually made for work in progress, totaled $632 million. Finally, cumulative interest earnings and loan repayments as of the DLF's termination date came to $65 million, again, most of it in local currencies.[32]

Because the advent of AID coincided with an increased emphasis on aid in the form of long-term development loans, as opposed to both development grants and short-term supporting assistance, the new agency's rate of development lending was a good deal brisker than that of its predecessor. By the end of fiscal year 1962, when it had been in operation for eight months, it had authorized 59 dollar loans totaling $1,089 million to cover the for-

[31] DLF, "Development Loan Fund Activities in Fiscal Year 1960," Washington, 1960 (Mimeo.).

[32] AID, *Terminal Report of the Development Loan Fund.*

eign exchange costs of development projects and programs; during the year that followed 112 such loans were authorized (including those authorized under the Alliance for Progress legislation), with a total value of $1,279 million. All in all, between the time DLF began operations early in 1958 and the end of 1963, the U.S. aid agencies had authorized a total of nearly $4.5 billion in development loans, less than $2 billion of which had actually been disbursed. Of these authorizations, $2,738 million were for loans to countries in the Near East-South Asia region, $832 million for Latin America, $384 million for the Far East, $333 million for Africa, and $137 million for Europe, indicating that no development loans had been authorized in Europe since AID began operations.[33]

Although the elimination of barriers to the flow of investment capital and the creation of a climate favorable to such investment in less-developed countries were among the stated purposes of the Development Loan Fund, the very creation of this organization represented a recognition by the United States Government of the fact that private capital could not be expected to provide the major share of development assistance, and that the provision of government-to-government loans to speed the process of development might be the most effective way of readying less-developed countries for mutually profitable private investment. It was clear from the outset that, despite the somewhat rhetorical commitment to the encouragement of private investment contained in its authorizing legislation, the bulk of DLF's loans would be to governmental bodies. And, in fact, loans made directly to private enterprise always represented a rather small part of DLF's operations, despite its expressed desire that they should come to occupy an increasingly important share of its commitments. The Fund's *Terminal Report*

[33] AID, *Operations Reports* for fiscal years 1962 and 1963, Washington 1962 and 1963, and information provided by the Office of Development Finance and Private Enterprise.

showed that, of its 220 dollar loans, 42 had been made directly to the private sector; their dollar value of $246.9 million represented about 12 per cent of the organization's dollar loan authorizations. All but 7 of these loans, with a combined value of about $10 million, had been made in the area of industrial development, in keeping with DLF's position that "in every case where we have an application from a government for an industrial undertaking, we look into the possibility of private enterprise handling it instead of the government."[34]

Loans made directly to private enterprise, both U.S. and foreign, have been an even smaller proportion of total development lending under AID than they were under DLF; of the nearly $2.5 billion in dollar development loans authorized by AID by the end of 1963, less than $170 million was in the form of direct credits to private enterprise.[35] In terms of numbers, 16 of AID's nearly 200 authorizations were designated for the private sector, 7 of them for a variety of enterprises located in India. This low ratio is not surprising, in view of the terms and conditions AID has set for loans to private enterprise. In its *Aids to Business* pamphlet, the agency cites the various legislative criteria, described earlier, which its dollar loans must meet, and stresses in addition that it "is limited to financing only those activities which occupy a relatively high priority position in the country's development program," and that it will in general help to finance only the dollar costs of a project. Most important, it emphasizes even more heavily than did DLF the fact that it is a

[34] Testimony of Dempster McIntosh, Managing Director, DLF, in: U.S. Congress, Senate, Committee on Appropriations, *Second Supplemental Appropriations Bill, 1959, Hearings*, 86th Cong., 1st Sess., 1959, p. 653.

[35] U.S. Congress, House, Committee on Foreign Affairs, *Foreign Assistance Act of 1963, Hearings*, p. 500, and "Statement" of Seymour M. Peyser, Assistant Administrator for Development Finance and Private Enterprise, AID, before the House Foreign Affairs Committee, April 13, 1964, p. 10.

lender of last resort, to be approached only when all other possible sources of financing in the free world have been exhausted. To drive the point home, it lists many of these sources, including not only private banking and other long-term lending institutions but also the Eximbank, World Bank, IFC, IDB and, for relatively small loans, development banks. Only after it has been ascertained that none of these institutions are interested in making a particular loan, can AID consider it. And, "since our [AID's] rate of interest to private borrowers is the same as that of the Export-Import Bank, the need for direct dollar loans to U.S. private firms will probably continue to be relatively limited."[36]

About half the dollar loans to the private sector have been made, not directly, but to intermediate credit institutions, themselves both public and private, for relending to local or joint private ventures. DLF and AID have favored these development banks and related institutions, which are often the only available source of medium and long-term industrial investment in developing countries, because they provide a means of assisting the small enterprises which are the mainstay of a private-enterprise economy and yet with which, for administrative reasons, the U.S. aid agency cannot deal directly.

During its lifetime, DLF made 40 dollar loans totaling $220 million to intermediate credit institutions, mostly industrial development banks. By the end of fiscal year 1963, AID had authorized a total of $166 million more.

---

[36] *Ibid.* The AID's loan terms to private enterprise are more stringent than those described earlier for development loans in general. Under a recently worked-out "two step" procedure, the private borrower repays the loan in local currency to the host government, at an interest rate identical to that charged for project loans by the Eximbank (currently 5¾ per cent) and over a period determined by the commercial life of the goods and services being financed. The host government then makes repayment in dollars over a longer period determined by its capacity to service dollar debt.

All in all, as of mid-1963, 58 dollar development loans totaling $386 million had been authorized for 49 intermediate credit institutions in 32 developing countries, $199 million for industrial development banks and the rest for housing or agricultural credit institutions. Institutions in Latin America received $208 million of this total; the Near East-South Asia region, $137 million; the Far East, $23 million, and Africa, $18 million.[37] Although most of the loans made by these institutions are to locally owned enterprises and will therefore probably only rarely involve the American funds which are the direct object of consideration here, they show every sign of becoming crucial factors in the emergence of the free-enterprise sector in newly developing countries.

LOCAL CURRENCY LOANS

Most loans extended by U.S. lending institutions to foreign investors are made and repayable in dollars, and are almost always extended only for purchases of goods and services in the United States. Even if dollar loans to cover local costs were available, American businessmen would be extremely reluctant to contract them, since the danger that currency depreciation or convertibility difficulties might make repayment difficult or impossible creates a strong desire to hold the dollar investment in foreign enterprises to a minimum. To help fill the gap created by the shortage of local-currency funds for medium or long-term borrowing in many countries, Congress passed, in August 1957, the so-called "Cooley Amendment"[38] to the Agricultural Trade Development and Assistance Act of 1954 (P.L. 480). This amendment provides that a part of the foreign currencies received in payment for

[37] AID, "AID Assistance to Intermediate Credit Institutions," Washington, 1963.

[38] The amendment, which forms Section 104 (e) of Public Law 480, is so called after the man who proposed it, Congressman Harold D. Cooley, then Chairman of the House Committee on Agriculture.

the sale of American surplus agricultural products under the Act referred to should be made available for loans to American private business enterprises operating in the country concerned. Senator Hubert Humphrey, one of the chief supporters of the amendment, pointed out that "The inability of American companies (or their subsidiaries) to borrow local currencies for normal operational needs is an important deterrent to foreign investment. The loans are either not available or the interest rates prohibitive."[39]

The Cooley Amendment provides that: ". . . not more than 25 percentum of the currencies received pursuant to each such [P.L. 480 sales] agreement shall be available through and under the procedures established by the Export-Import Bank for loans mutually agreeable to said bank and the country with which the agreement is made to United States business firms and branches, subsidiaries, or affiliates of such firms for business development and trade expansion in such countries and for loans to domestic or foreign firms for the establishment of facilities for aiding in the utilization, distribution, or otherwise increasing the consumption of and markets for, United States agricultural products. . . ."[40] In accordance with the authority contained in this paragraph, the President issued, on December 12, 1957, an Executive Order vesting in the Eximbank the full authority to administer the loan program.

Beyond prohibiting loans ". . . for the manufacture of any products to be exported to the United States in competition with products produced in the United States or for the manufacture or production of any commodity to be marketed in competition with United States agricultural products or the products thereof," and providing

[39] U.S. Congress, Senate, Committee on Agriculture and Forestry, *Policies and Operations under Public Law 480, Hearings,* 85th Cong., 1st Sess., 1957, p. 373.

[40] Cited in: Edmund Pendleton, Jr., "Foreign Currency Loans to Private Business," *The Commercial and Financial Chronicle,* March 20, 1958.

that "foreign currencies may be accepted in repayment of such loans," the legislation itself gave the Eximbank no detailed directives regarding the administration of the Program. Soon after the first funds became available for loans, the Bank itself announced the operating rules under which the program would be conducted. After listing the provisions of the legislation itself, the Bank stated that "While the loans may be made for any purpose consistent with these general objectives, in countries where the amount of the eligible applications exceeds the funds available the Bank may limit the purposes for which it will lend by such devices as giving priority to the financing of fixed assets.[41] It added that affiliation with a U.S. firm, required by the law, would be determined by "share of ownership or degree of control of the applicant by a U.S. firm; common ownership of the applicant and its U.S. parent by a third firm; or general commercial and operating ties."[42]

The Eximbank's decision concerning interest rates on Cooley loans was simply that "interest rates are similar to those charged for comparable loans in the country concerned."[43] The interest rates referred to are those charged by a development bank or similar institution in the country concerned (generally between 5 and 12 per cent), rather than those of the commercial banks, which are usually much higher. These rates are, however, a good deal higher than those customarily levied on similar loans in the United States. They were intended in part as a substitute for a maintenance-of-value clause which would protect the lender if the foreign currency were depreciated, but chiefly to avoid unfair competition with the host country's

[41] Export-Import Bank of Washington, *Foreign Currency Lending*, Washington, 1958.

[42] *Ibid*. Prospective borrowers must have at least 25 per cent U.S. equity participation, or 15 per cent if a management contract or similar ties with a U.S. firm exist.

[43] Export-Import Bank of Washington, *Foreign Currency Lending*.

own financial institutions and the granting of a competitive advantage to U.S. firms and their affiliates.[44] This latter consideration is particularly important, since the approval of each Cooley loan must be negotiated separately with the host government.

At the beginning of 1962, the administration of the Cooley loan program was transferred from the Eximbank to the new Agency for International Development. But the criteria and conditions of these loans remained essentially the same as before. AID has, however, taken steps to simplify the processing of Cooley loan applications, to publicize the availability of these funds to the business community through press releases and its *Aids to Business* pamphlet, and to make the program "more attractive to potential American investors by not requiring a guaranty from the U.S. investor or a local bank."[45] The requirement of such a guaranty in all loans not made directly to a U.S. firm was fairly standard procedure under the Eximbank's administration. In addition, AID has laid down some ground rules of its own: for an enterprise to qualify as U.S. affiliated, at least 20 per cent of its equity must be held by a U.S. firm, and AID will not generally authorize a loan in instances where the total debt of an enterprise, including the Cooley loan, would exceed 150 per cent of the equity.[46] The range of interest rates remained about the same as under Eximbank, the repayment terms tended to become somewhat longer.

Although the statute itself permits rather than requires that 25 per cent of the proceeds of commodity sales agreements be set aside for Cooley loan purposes, the Conference Report on the bill made clear the legislators' intent:

---

[44] U.S. Congress, House, Committee on Agriculture, *Extension of Public Law 480, Hearings,* 86th Cong., 1st Sess., 1959, p. 293.

[45] AID, "Report on Local Currency Loan Activities (Cooley Loans)," Jan. 1, 1962 through Dec. 31, 1963.

[46] Information provided by Mr. Michael F. Speers, Loan Officer, Office of Capital Development and Finance, Bureau for Near East and South Asia.

"This provision expresses a firm but general policy of the Congress that a substantial portion (25 per cent unless there are compelling reasons for using a less amount) should be used for loans. . . ."[47] The policy, therefore, was to press vigorously for this maximum proportion, "except in cases of overriding considerations of foreign policy, United States budgetary needs, or refusal by a foreign government to accept a sales agreement under such terms."[48] In practice, however, this policy seems to have turned out to be more general than firm: the average amount allocated to Section 104(e), or Cooley loans, loans in all sales agreements signed between August 1957 and July 1963 was less than 10 per cent. Of the 40 countries which signed such agreements during this period, less than half provided for the full 25 per cent, and 7 failed to make any provision at all for Cooley loans.[49]

Since the Cooley Amendment applied only to sales agreements negotiated after August 1957, and since loans could not be made until the bank deposits actually became available to the Bank through sales under the agreement, the first funds for this program did not become available until June 1958. A year later, 330 applications had been received and 72 credits authorized in 13 countries for a foreign currency equivalent of $34.1 million, while 10 more totaling $3.6 million awaited the approval of 5 host governments. Sixty-seven of the 72 credits granted were to United States firms; the others were to foreign firms "which will expand the home market for

[47] U.S. Congress, Conference Report No. 683, 85th Cong., 1st Sess., 1957.

[48] U.S. Congress, House, Committee on Agriculture, *Extension of Public Law 480*, pp. 290-291.

[49] AID, *Operations Reports* for fiscal years 1962 and 1963, pp. 70-71, 86-87. The seven countries whose agreements made no provision for Cooley loans were Brazil, Burma, Congo (Leopoldville), Poland, Spain, United Kingdom, Yugoslavia.

U.S. agricultural commodities."[50] In certain countries, such as Mexico, Colombia, France, and Israel, acceptable applications far exceeded the funds available, and the Bank had to ration funds by restricting financing to fixed assets rather than working capital. In India and Pakistan, on the contrary, American firms showed little interest in borrowing the sums available, and the Bank adopted a policy of "pushing" these funds by advising bankers in U.S. financial centers of their availability.[51]

When the Eximbank turned the Cooley loan program over to AID at the end of 1961, after four and one-half years of operation, it had approved a total of 162 credits for a total equivalent to $95.1 million. Under AID, the lending pace was somewhat brisker; by the end of 1963, it had approved 85 credits for a total of $90.9 million. All in all, by that date, 247 Cooley loans had been authorized in some 25 different currencies totaling $186.0 million. These funds had helped to finance a wide variety of private industrial, retail, and service enterprises, as well as several private development banks. The largest loan to date, for the equivalent of $17.5 million, went to help finance a joint venture of two U.S. and one Indian firm in the construction of a $68 million fertilizer plant, to which a loan of $27 million was simultaneously authorized by the Eximbank. The average Cooley loan is much smaller; most have been under $1 million and only two over $5 million. More than 90 per cent of the credits have been made to U.S. firms or their affiliates.[52]

Geographically, the Cooley loans have been concentrated in the few countries where heavy demand coincided with the availability of substantial amounts of Public

[50] U.S. Congress, House, Committee on Agriculture, *Extension of Public Law 480* . . . , p. 289.

[51] *Ibid.*, p. 295.

[52] AID, "Report on Local Currency Lending Activities (Cooley Loans)."

Law 480 funds for such loans: Colombia, India, Israel, Pakistan, the Philippines, and Turkey. By region, the distribution of credits made between mid-1958 and the end of 1963 was as follows:

Near East—South Asia	$143.5 million
Latin America	21.1 million
Europe	11.8 million
Far East	9.2 million
Africa	0.4 million

The geographical concentration has been increasing with time. During the last two years of the period, no loans were made in Europe at all, and nearly 90 per cent of the credits were in the Near East-South Asia region.[53]

As of March 31, 1964, roughly $90 million of Cooley funds were available for loans in the 23 developing countries indicated in Table 20. In 10 other countries, available Cooley funds had been exhausted. The list of countries in which local-currency loans are available varies from month to month, as currency supplies are created by new sales agreements or exhausted through lending. Some countries, such as Peru and the Philippines, have been off the list and then on again, when new sales agreements replenished the supply of funds. But the total amount of money available for such loans has been dropping in recent years, from around $200 million in mid-1962 to less than $100 million at the end of 1963. This decrease reflects both the accelerated pace of lending activity and some drop-off in the amount of funds being made available for Cooley loan purposes.[54]

[53] *Ibid.*

[54] Cooley funds which remain unutilized three years after the signing of a sales agreement are deobligated, that is, transferred to another Treasury account. Apparently more than $200 million of Cooley funds have been withdrawn from the program, either because they were deobligated after remaining unused or because, in a few cases, they were taken over for emergency disaster relief.

TABLE 20
Cooley Loan Funds Available,
as of March 1964

Country	Currency Available (in thousands of U.S. dollar— equivalents)
Funds Available	
Bolivia	$ 1,203
China (Taiwan)	5,360
Colombia[a]	875
Ethiopia	41
Finland	332
Greece	2,373
Guinea	537
India	17,815
Indonesia	1,335
Israel	9,085
Korea	3,260
Morocco	1,946
Pakistan	7,698
Paraguay	209
Peru	876
Philippines	1,300
Sudan	1,011
Syria	1,144
Tunisia	3,512
Turkey	7,785
UAR (Egypt)	21,632
Uruguay	20
Vietnam	483
Total	$89,832
Funds No Longer Available	
Argentina	—
Ceylon	—
Chile	—
Cyprus	—
Ecuador	—
France	—
Iceland	—
Iran	—
Italy	—
Mexico	—

[a] New applications were no longer being accepted in Colombia, as applications on hand already exceeded available funds.

Sources: Agency for International Development, Information Staff, Press Release of March 24, 1964, and AID, *Operations Reports,* fiscal years 1962 and 1963.

Probably the chief difficulty under which the Cooley loan program has operated is the irrelevant criteria under which funds are made available to it. Whether or not loans are available in a given country, and in what amount, depends neither upon the demand of American private business for such funds nor on the advantages, from the foreign policy viewpoint, of encouraging U.S. private investment there. Funds are available only in countries with which the United States has negotiated sales agreements for American surplus agricultural commodities, in amounts determined jointly by the size of the sales agreement and the proportion the country is willing to release for Cooley loan purposes. In an effort to break this rigid link between surplus food and private-enterprise loans, AID has recently been "exploring new techniques to generate local currencies for lending to private firms where Cooley funds are not available."[55] The mechanism for this expansion will almost certainly be local development banks: in 1962, AID made it known that several million dollars in local currency was available to qualified U.S. firms from the National Development Bank in Brazil, and in 1963 it cooperated with the World Bank in setting up the Private Investment Fund in Colombia, which is designed to make local currency loans to both local and jointly owned private ventures.

THE FLOW OF PRIVATE FUNDS THROUGH GOVERNMENT LOANS

Relatively few of the dollar development loans extended by DLF—AID have been extended directly to private enterprise; even fewer have been to U.S. owned or affiliated firms. During its lifetime, DLF made 9 loans involving the participation of private American funds. Eight of these, some for less than $1 million and none for more than $10 million, provided financial assistance to a shipbuilding company and a coke-oven plant in Taiwan, a

[55] AID, "Statement" of Seymour M. Peyser . . . , p. 11.

joint public-private paper plant in Tunisia, a pulp and paper firm in the Philippines, a textile manufacturer in the Sudan, a forestry development project in Ethiopia, a saw-mill in Liberia, and a Guatemalan firm which makes coffee-bags out of locally available kenaf fibres.[56] All of these are joint enterprises, involving local as well as American investment; two, in fact, are entirely under local ownership, with American funds involved only in the form of loan capital.

In January 1961, DLF signed a loan agreement which, it was hoped, would serve as the prototype for the ideal joint venture "package," consisting of joint activity by the U.S. Government, American industry, and American private finance, combining with local industry and private finance in the sponsorship of development projects. The agreement provided for a $129.6 million loan (the largest single loan made by the U.S. Government for an industrial project abroad) for the construction of a $245 million integrated steel plant in Turkey. Koppers Associates, an organization formed by three U.S. firms, Koppers Company, Inc., Westinghouse Electric International Corporation, and the Blaw-Knox Company, undertook the design, engineering, and construction supervision of the Eregli Iron and Steel Works, as well as joining with Turkish industrialists and the Turkish Government in providing loan financing. In all, by the end of 1963, $19 million had been invested in the project by U.S. investors under convertibility and expropriation guaranties, and another $86 million by Turkish private investors.[57]

During the first two years of AID's operation, 6 more loans were made to joint enterprises involving U.S. private participation. These included a rubber plant in Brazil, a hydroelectric project in Peru, a pulp and paper

[56] Compiled from information furnished by the Office of the Deputy Managing Director for Private Enterprise, DLF and the Office of Development Finance and Private Enterprise, AID.

[57] *Ibid.*, and DLF Press Release No. 129, Jan. 5, 1961.

plant and a machine-tool plant in India, and private development banks in Costa Rica and Panama. All in all,
as Table 21 shows, by the end of 1963 $46.3 million of
U.S. private equity and loan capital had participated with
DLF—AID in dollar loans for industrial enterprise in the
less-developed areas. The total Government funds lent
to these same 16 enterprises was $176.7 million, repre-
senting a ratio of approximately 25 cents of American
private money for every dollar of public funds invested
in the same enterprise.[58] When *all* private funds invested
in DLF-AID projects are considered, including local
capital and funds from other capital-exporting countries
as well as capital originating in the United States, the
amount of private money invested reaches about $300
million, and the figure for private money invested per
dollar of U.S. public funds rises to about 90 cents.[59]

In sharp contrast with the dollar loan program, local-
currency Cooley loans are made exclusively to private enterprise, and almost entirely to U.S. owned or affiliated
firms. Complete data on the amount of U.S. capital invested in connection with Cooley loans are not available,
but enough information is available to piece together a
fairly reliable estimate of the total magnitude of these
funds.

The Eximbank estimated that by mid-1960 "the Bank
had helped finance projects representing an investment of
$202.4 million, of which $66.1 million was in Cooley
loans, $65.7 million in additional dollar investment, and

[58] Neither these figures nor those in Table 18 include the $110
million AID-Eximbank loan to the VALCO project in Ghana; if
they did, the commitment of public funds would rise to $286.7
million, the figure for private U.S. funds to $100.3 million, and
the amount of private money per dollar of private funds to roughly
35 cents. The details of this transaction, and the reasons for
leaving it out here, are given on pp. 289-290 below.

[59] Calculated from data provided by the Office of the Deputy
Managing Director for Private Enterprise, DLF and the Office
of Development Finance and Private Enterprise, AID.

TABLE 21

U.S. Private Funds Which Have Gone Abroad
in Connection with DLF—AID Loans
(in millions of U.S. dollars)

| | Dollar Loan Program | |
Fiscal Year	*DLF—AID Commitment*	*U.S. Private Funds*
1959	18.8	12.9
1960	6.3	4.7
1961	129.6	19.2
1962	3.4	2.3
1963	8.6	3.8
1964 (first half)	10.0	3.4
Total	176.7	46.3

Local-Currency "Cooley" Loan Program[a]

Period	*AID Commitment*	*U.S. Private Funds*
June 1958-June 30, 1960[b]	66.1	136.3
July 1, 1960-Dec. 31, 1961[b]	29.0	58.0[c]
Jan. 1, 1961-Dec. 31, 1963	90.9	172.5[d]
Total	186.0	366.8

[a] In dollar—equivalents

[b] Cooley Loan Program administered by Export-Import Bank

[c] Estimate based on ratio of public-to-private capital in preceding and succeeding periods

[d] Estimate based on extrapolation of public-to-private funds ratio in Near East-South Asia loans. Loans to this region represented 92 per cent of the dollar volume of all Cooley loans in this period.

Sources: Compiled from data provided by: Export-Import Bank of Washington, Economics Division; Development Loan Fund, Office of the Deputy Managing Director for Private Enterprise; and Agency for International Development, Office of Development Finance and Private Enterprise and Office of Capital Development and Finance, Bureau for Near East and South Asia.

$70.6 million in additional foreign currency investment," nearly half of the total in India alone.[60] For the period after AID took over administration of the Cooley Program, 1962 and 1963, quite detailed information is available on the Near East-South Asia loans which represent roughly 90 per cent of the dollar value of Cooley loans made during this period. AID figures indicate that dollar equity and dollar loan investments in these projects, together with reinvested earnings, totaled $158.6 million.[61] If we assume that the ratio of private capital to Cooley funds was roughly the same in the loans made to all other areas, it appears that more than $170 million in private capital was invested in Cooley loan projects during these two years.

For the intervening 18 months, July 1960 through December 1961, we have no information. But, since the ratio of private to public funds was almost exactly 2 to 1 in both the earlier and the later periods, it seems reasonable to assume it was the same during the intervening years. Cooley loans totaling $29.0 million were extended during this period,[62] implying private investment of about

[60] These figures are obtained from a "Memorandum to the Files" dated July 20, 1960, provided by R. H. Rowntree of the Eximbank. The memorandum notes: "The following estimate is based on several broad assumptions: (1) that 'additional investment' means equity or loan funds, which the applicant planned to put into the project in question in addition to the Cooley loan, but excluding all funds already invested in the project or enterprise, (2) that all additional funds, whether or not intended for financing dollar costs, were obtained in foreign currencies unless the applicant specifically mentioned a dollar investment, and (3) that whenever the applicant failed to obtain from the Export-Import Bank the full amount requested, the difference was obtained elsewhere."

[61] Unpublished data provided by Office of Capital Development and Finance, Bureau for Near East and South Asia, AID.

[62] There is some discrepancy in the figures reported for this period; the Eximbank *Reports* cite total loans of $36.0 million, while AID data indicate a total of $29.0 million. The discrepancy can probably be accounted for by the difference between "authorizations" and "approvals" in a given time period; in any case, the

$58 million. Putting all these estimates together in Table 21, it appears that the loan commitments totaling $186 million which were made under the Cooley program through the end of 1963 were accompanied by U.S. private capital amounting to approximately twice as much.

EXTENDED-RISK GUARANTIES

DLF possessed a broad guaranty authority, limited only by a legislative prohibition against the guaranty of equity investments against normal business-type risks, and the DLF staff had high hopes for the all-risk guaranty as a means of bringing institutional loan capital into development activities. But in reality, the DLF's guaranty authority remained little utilized; it issued only three such guaranties during its four years of operation. Two of these were full-repayment guaranties to institutional lenders. One, a guaranty agreement with the Bank of Monrovia in Liberia, a wholly owned subsidiary of the First National City Bank of New York, committed DLF to a maximum liability of 50 per cent of a projected total of $1 million of medium and long-term loans to a variety of small industrial enterprises. The agreement required the approval of the DLF for all loans over $100 thousand. The other covered a projected $4.5 million loan by two U.S. commercial banks to the Ingalls-Taiwan Shipbuilding Company, an enterprise into which U.S. and local investors had each put an equal share of equity capital. This guaranty, which was later reduced to $650 thousand along with the loans it covered, became the largest loss to date under any guaranty contract; the Government had to pay out the full $650 thousand when the shipbuilding firm went bankrupt.

The only guaranty of an equity investment issued by DLF was one covering the $54 million investment of the

figure used is the one which is consistent with the data for later years and for the Cooley program as a whole.

Kaiser Aluminum and Chemicals Corporation and the
Reynolds Metal Company in VALCO, a huge bauxite
and aluminum smelter project in Ghana.[63] Under this
agreement, the U.S. Government agreed to buy the investors' interest in the project if a specified dollar amount
of loss (approximately $5 million) resulted from various
causes—not including "normal" business risks.[64] Although
this guaranty was authorized in 1961, the contractual
agreement provided that the investment would not be
made nor the guaranty go into effect until some six years
after the authorization date, since it would require at least
that long for the necessary electric power generating facilities to be completed.

DLF's guaranty authority was carried over into AID
by the Mutual Security Act of 1961, and broadened to
permit the guarantying of equity investments against business risks as well. In fact, the only types of risk now excluded from coverage were losses due to fraud or misconduct on the part of the investor himself and risk covered
by normal insurance, such as fire or theft. The intention
here was to provide, rather than full protection against

[63] This guaranty was authorized early in 1961; a year later, a
loan totaling $110 million was authorized to the same firm, to be
made half by the AID and half by the Eximbank, and to be
administered by the latter organization. All these figures are
maxima, to be reached only if the project ultimately turns out to
cost as much as the highest estimate of $164 million. In the event
that lowest cost estimate of $122 million turns out to be correct,
the private investment will be only $32 million, the AID-Eximbank
share $90 million.

Since this transaction involves an Eximbank loan, an AID loan,
and an extended-risk guaranty, it could have been listed in any of
the three categories. It was decided to include it in the last category, since private funds which go abroad with the very limited
risk-exposure remaining under an extended-risk guaranty do not
represent private investment in quite the same sense as the private funds which have accompanied public loans under conditions
where all or most of the risk is taken by the investor himself.

[64] Bruce E. Chubb and Verne W. Vance, Jr., "Incentives to
Private U.S. Investment Abroad under the Foreign Assistance
Program," 72 *Yale Law Journal* 3 (1963), 500.

some risks, "some protection against substantially the full range of risks"[65] in special, high-priority situations where the risk of loss appeared high. These guaranties are based on a share-the-loss approach; the legislation provides that not more than 75 per cent of an investor's stake in any project can be covered. The new law limited the issuance of such guaranties to projects located in countries which had agreed to institute the Investment Guaranty Program, and further restricted the amount of any individual guaranty to $25 million in the case of loans and $10 million in the case of any other type of investment. The maximum authorization for extended risk guaranties was set at $90 million in the 1961 legislation and raised to $180 million the following year.

The intent of Congress was clearly that extended-risk guaranties should be issued only in special, high-priority cases, but the exact eligibility criteria have never been very clear. The legislation stated simply that such guaranties might be issued "where the President determines such action to be important to the furtherance of the purposes of this title . . . *Provided*, that guaranties issued . . . shall emphasize economic development projects furthering social progress and the development of small independent business enterprises. . . ."[66] An AID press release gave examples of the type of investments which might be considered: agricultural credit institutions, credit unions, cooperatives, low-cost housing projects, food-processing plants and those producing farm machinery and equipment, building materials, water supply and sanitation equipment.[67] The *Aids to Businessmen* handbook points out that "the rules governing eligibility for specific-risk

[65] U.S. Congress, House, Committee on Foreign Affairs, *The International Development and Security Act, Hearings*, 87th Cong., 1st Sess., Washington, 1961, p. 406.

[66] *Foreign Assistance Act of 1961*, 75 Stat. 430.

[67] "AID Ready to Receive Applications Under Investment Guaranty Program," *U.S. Department of State Bulletin*, XLV (Nov. 27, 1961), 899.

guaranties also apply to the extended-risk 'general' guaranties." It adds, further, that such guaranties "will be considered only for projects where it can be clearly demonstrated that the private investment would not otherwise be made," and only for "investments in industries, or other areas of economic activity, which have been identified by A.I.D. as being of sufficient importance to qualify for a development loan."[68]

Whatever the precise criteria for eligibility for extended-risk guaranties, it is clear that AID has so far found very few applications which meet them. As of the end of 1963, AID had issued only two such guaranties. One was a guaranty of $618,750 covering 75 per cent of an $825,000 loan to a subsidiary of the Cabot Corporation of America for the construction of a carbon black plant in Colombia. The guarantied loan funds represented a minority component of the project's total financing, which was estimated at $3.85 million, about two-thirds of it to come from U.S. sources. The second was a guaranty, not to exceed $7 million, covering an average of 50 per cent of the holdings by U.S. citizens or corporations of Class B debentures of PASA, an integrated petrochemical project in Argentina sponsored by 5 U.S. companies. The total cost of the project was estimated at $72 million, most of it to come from U.S. sources. In both these cases guaranty coverage was limited to the loss of principal only, and the PASA contract provided in addition that losses covered by specific-risk guaranties were not included. Because PASA investors were expected to (and did) purchase specific-risk guaranty coverage, the fee for the extended-risk guaranty was only 2 per cent, while in the Cabot contract it was set at 6 per cent. At the end of 1963, AID reported that it had on file more than 60 inquiries about this type of guaranty, 15 of which "have passed beyond the explanatory stage and represent poten-

68 AID, *Aids to Business* (*Overseas Investment*), p. 26.

tial guaranties of approximately $70 million in 11 countries."[69]

The most complete repayment guaranties of all are offered by AID to private United States loan investments in self-liquidating demonstration housing projects in Latin America. In the Mutual Security legislation of 1960, Congress had urged special consideration of loans and guaranties to stimulate private investment in the housing field,[70] and in 1961 a paragraph was added to the Investment Guaranties section of the Foreign Assistance Act which provided specifically for extended-risk guaranties "of investments made by United States citizens, or corporations, partnerships, or other associations created under the law of the United States or of any State or territory and substantially beneficially owned by United States citizens in pilot or demonstration housing projects in Latin America of types similar to those insured by the Federal Housing Administration and suitable for conditions in Latin America."[71] The total face value of such guaranties was limited to $10 million in the 1961 law, but was raised to $60 million in 1962 and to $150 million the following year. Guaranty coverage for any single investment is limited to $5 million, and only applications for the construction of new, owner-occupied housing projects will be considered.

The Latin American housing guaranty "provides full protection in U.S. dollars against loss, for any reason, of the guarantied portion of the investment,"[72] excepting, of course, losses due to fraud or misconduct for which the investor is responsible. The legislation requires "appropriate participation by the investor in the loan risk,"[73] and AID initially limited the maximum guaranty coverage

[69] AID, "Statement" of Seymour M. Peyser . . . , p. 7.
[70] *Mutual Security Act of 1960*, 74 *Stat.* 135.
[71] *Foreign Assistance Act of 1961*, 75 *Stat.* 432.
[72] AID, "Housing Guaranties," information sheet dated April 13, 1964.
[73] *Foreign Assistance Act of 1962*, 76 *Stat.* 256.

to 90 per cent of the investor's interest. But the policy was soon changed to permit guaranties covering 100 per cent of the investment, leaving the possible loss of a few months' interest, for the period between the occurrence of default and the payment of a claim, as the only risk borne by the private investor.

As of the end of 1963, housing guaranties totaling $61.0 million had been authorized to cover the long-term financing for projects in 8 Latin American countries: Argentina, Chile, Colombia, El Salvador, Honduras, Mexico, Panama, and Peru. In two cases guaranty agreements had been signed and construction started; in the others, agreements were in the process of review or negotiation. The two earliest contracts, totaling $9.5 million, were for 90 per cent coverage; all the rest provided 100 per cent coverage. This means that the total U.S. investment in these projects was $62 million, all but $1 million of it made under a full-repayment guaranty. AID estimated the number of houses represented by the 11 authorizations at about 15,000. At the same time, 42 additional applications for 14 countries were under review, representing a total of approximately $235 million.[74]

THE PROBLEMS OF ACHIEVING EFFECTIVENESS

With the exception of the specific-risk Investment Guaranty Program, which has been dealt with in a separate chapter because it had been operating for many years before either DLF or AID came into existence and even today remains an administratively self-contained unit within the larger agency, the various techniques used by the aid agencies to mobilize private capital for development investment were introduced during the era of "receding horizons," when the emphasis on the primacy of private investment had yielded to the urgency of the capital needs of the developing countries in the free world.

[74] AID, "Housing Guaranty Applications," memorandum dated Jan. 17, 1964.

Perhaps partly for this reason, each of these risk-sharing techniques—dollar loans, local-currency loans, and extended-risk investment guaranties—have encountered serious obstacles to their effectiveness as stimulants to the export of long-term U.S. private capital to the developing nations.

Whereas several of the other public risk-sharing institutions had to face considerable suspicion and hostility from the private business and financial community at the time of their inception, the chief opposition to the idea of dollar loans by DLF seemed to come, not from this source, by from another lending agency of the United States Government. In the hearings held in 1957 in the House Foreign Affairs Committee on the Title II (DLF) amendment to the Mutual Security Act, Eximbank President Samuel Waugh expressed the fear that soft DLF loans, if made in areas which were currently servicing hard loans and appeared capable of continuing to do so, would drive out not only Eximbank financing but private foreign investment as well.[75] The reaction of the private business community, if one can judge by the absence of testimony by its representatives in appropriate legislative hearings was, at first, largely one of indifference.

There is little evidence that private investors shared the Eximbank's views concerning DLF's encroachment upon their territory. In a speech before the House in April 1959, Congressman Frank Coffin[76] of Maine said that: "In my own investigation, I made a particular point of inquiring if private banks had been critical of DLF from the point of view of taking opportunities where they could have done the job. I found only one case where a private financial institution initially raised an objection. On further investigation, it appeared that the terms of the

[75] U.S. Congress, House, Committee on Foreign Affairs, *Mutual Security Act of 1957, Hearings*, p. 330.

[76] In February 1961, Mr. Coffin, who had played an important role in the drafting of the original DLF legislation and subsequent amendments, was appointed Managing Director of the DLF.

proposed private loan were these: first, a loan at 10 per cent interest; second, a 10 per cent equity in the enterprise; and third, repayment in 13 months . . . the private corporation which made the offer has since admitted that DLF made a proper judgment in this particular case."[77]

Mere lack of hostility on the part of the business community is hardly adequate, however, to insure the success of a program in attracting American private funds into development investment. The list of private participations by American investors in DLF projects is short and the individual participations generally small. Only in one instance—the Eregli steel plant in Turkey—did large equity investors and institutional lenders evince a substantial interest in DLF activities. But the promise of this one impressive "package" venture has not so far been fulfilled under AID administration. Only 6 out of nearly 200 AID dollar credits have involved U.S. private capital, and in each case the U.S. private investment has been less than $3 million. It would appear that the DLF—AID dollar loan program has managed to avoid encroaching on areas which might be of interest to private capital but that, on the other hand, it has not yet succeeded in attracting the attention and interest of the business and financial community on a large scale.

The major barrier to the large-scale mobilization of private funds through the dollar lending program appears to be its ill-defined scope of operations in this sphere. Such loans are expected to be economically "sound" and yet not sufficiently "bankable" to be acceptable either to private sources or to any of the other international lending agencies. The distinction between these two criteria is often far from clear in actual practice, and the narrow line DLF was expected to tread often brought it criticism from both directions at once. On the one hand, Eximbank officials maintained that, by making loans to areas

[77] *Congressional Record, House,* 86th Cong., 1st Sess., 1959, cv, 6538.

perfectly able to repay in hard currency (e.g., for housing in Australia), the DLF brought into operation a variety of Gresham's Law, whereby "soft" loans drive out "hard" ones and thus offer unfair competition to those lending on traditional terms.[78] At the other extreme, the 1959 *Report* of the Boeschenstein Committee on World Economic Practices recommended that the Fund significantly broaden its sphere of lending operations. It argued that: "While loans should not be extended when funds are available on reasonable commercial terms, they should not be denied simply because the applicant may have ample credit. It is a matter of willingness to risk—not merely of ability to borrow."[79]

There is little doubt that such a policy, particularly if combined with the Committee's further recommendations for the relaxation of the maintenance-of-value repayment rule and of the requirement that at least 50 per cent of the capital in an enterprise receiving DLF funds come from private sources,[80] would have brought forth a surge of private U.S. equity capital eager to participate in DLF loan transactions, or rather, to secure DLF funds for their own operations. But whether such a policy would have increased the total amount of United States funds flowing into productive investment abroad is another question, and a more doubtful one. It seems more likely that the availability of such terms would simply have provided a windfall for equity funds which would often have gone abroad in any case, and might even have reduced the total outflow of private funds by serving as a substitute for the private loan funds—or else for the "hard" loans of other agencies to which the equity investor might other-

[78] Interview with Eximbank official, March 31, 1960.

[79] Committee on World Economic Practices, *Report*, Washington, 1959, p. 3.

[80] These same suggestions were made by business firms replying to the Commerce Department's questionnaire, published at about the same time as the Boeschenstein Report. See: U.S. Department of Commerce, *Reportorial Review* . . . , p. 1.

wise have turned. The decision of DLF's successor, AID, was to maintain the same terms and conditions for loans to private enterprise as its predecessor, and at the same time to make very clear its position as lender of last resort, to be consulted only after all other possible sources of financing have been exhausted. The result has been to banish concern about Gresham's law, since its loan terms to private enterprise are about the same as the Eximbank's, but for this very reason, to limit severely the scope for direct dollar loans by AID to U.S. private investors.

The local-currency Cooley loan program, with a specific legislative mandate to address itself exclusively to the needs of private enterprise which precludes any uncertainty about its sphere of operations, has been far more successful in mobilizing U.S. private funds. The U.S. Government's commitment of funds under the Cooley program through 1963 was approximately the same as the total commitments it made to projects involving U.S. private capital under the dollar development loan program during the same period, but the amount of private American money invested was more than eight times larger.

The major difficulty facing this program stems from the fact that the criteria governing the administration of Cooley loan funds do not necessarily coincide at all with those determining either the desirability or the effectiveness of encouraging the flow of American private funds to a particular area. At present, it is not clear whether the program is designed primarily to give selective encouragement to private foreign investment or simply to dispose of surplus and sometimes embarrassing holdings of foreign currencies. Direct investors abroad seem to agree that government provision of local-currency funds to private business might be one of the most effective measures to stimulate investment in underdeveloped areas.[81] The Cooley loan program is a first step in this

[81] Jack N. Behrman, "Promoting Free World Economic De-

direction, but much more will have to be done to break the present rigid link between surplus food sales agreements and the availability of funds before the program can fill the existing need with maximum effectiveness.

At first glance, it would appear that the ineffectiveness of the extended-risk guaranty program, even more than that of the dollar loan program, stems from the failure of DLF—AID to utilize its broad powers in this respect. But actually the problem lies deeper, and there are good reasons for this non-utilization. For an investment in which the private investor carries no risk is not truly private investment at all; in this sense an extended-risk guaranty can be said to mobilize private investment only to the extent that it attracts into a project unguarantied capital which would not otherwise have gone abroad. It is this absence of the essential ingredient of private investment—the bearing by the investor of some of the risk—that doubtless underlay the opinion of the Clay Committee in its report to the President on foreign assistance, that ". . . the Committee has serious doubts as to the wisdom of guaranties against commercial risk. . . ."[82] It is also the consideration which lies behind the oft-expressed concern that, unless all-risk guaranties were limited to substantially less than 100 per cent of a loan investment, the guarantied paper might compete in the U.S. market with the Treasury's own paper bearing lower interest rates.[83] In giving a full-repayment guaranty, the Government is not so much mobilizing private capital as

velopment through Direct Investment," *American Economic Review*, L (May 1960), 271-281.

[82] U.S. Department of State, *Report to the President of the United States from the Committee to Strengthen the Security of the Free World: The Scope and Distribution of United States Military and Economic Assistance Programs*, Washington, 1963, p. 19.

[83] U.S. Congress, House, Committee on Foreign Affairs, *The International Development and Security Act, Hearings*, 87th Cong., 1st Sess., Washington, 1961, p. 916.

borrowing private funds to make government loans. It would seem, therefore, that it should confine the use of such guaranties to cases which would justify a direct government loan, and where it seems likely that the long-run cost, both direct and indirect, to the Government will be less in the case of a guaranty than it would be in the case of a public loan. The exception to this stricture might be instances where the important thing to mobilize is not so much money as technical or managerial know-how. This seems to be the thinking underlying the Latin American housing guaranty program, where the U.S. capital provided is far less important than the external economies which are expected to accrue to the Latin American housing market from the demonstration effect of North American construction and financing methods.

"Perhaps the most interesting aspect of the DLF is that there is gathered in one institution all of the techniques which are presently available to promote private investment abroad."[84] So spoke the Fund's General Counsel during the first year of its operations. And, while the DLF did not in truth command all the available means of getting private funds to move abroad, it did possess a broad spectrum of them. It could lend in hard or soft currencies and demand repayment in either; it could make straight loans or investments with equity type features, such as convertible debentures; it had a broad authority to offer both limited insurance and full repayment guaranties to private investors. Yet in more than four years it issued only three guaranties,[85] wrote no insurance con-

[84] Ralph W. Golby, Address before the Second International Investment Law Conference of the American Society of International Law, Washington, 1958, p. 22.

[85] Until legislation authorizing fractional (50 per cent) reserves for guaranty commitments was passed in 1959, guaranties were actually more expensive to the DLF than direct loans, since they involved the commitment of funds equal to their face value and earned a fee of only 2 per cent rather than interest of more than 5 per cent (on loans to private enterprise).

tracts against specific risks, and failed to turn over any of its convertible debentures to private investors.

Part of DLF's failure to make full use of its broad powers can be attributed to the lack of an effective administrative organization for dealing with private capital. A 1958 staff study by the ICA's Office of Management Planning reported that DLF had apparently decided to act simply as banker rather than as a partner in the development of investment projects, and concluded that "The DLF does not have a private enterprise program of any size, and its guaranty program is for all practical purposes a dead issue."[86] The establishment in late 1959 of the Office of Private Enterprise—which was carried over into AID as the Office of Development Finance and Private Enterprise—to concentrate specifically on the stimulation of the private sector represented one answer to these criticisms; the placing of the guaranty authority on a fractional reserve basis was another. Clearly this wave of interest in the attraction of private funds bore some fruit; the 1961 package financing of the Eregli steel mill in Turkey could not have been completed without considerable initiative and active planning on the part of the Fund's staff.

But subsequent experience suggests that the failure of DLF to become an important force in the mobilization of private capital for economic development went deeper than administrative fragmentation or staff disinterest. Both the legislative mandate and the administrative structure of AID indicated an increased stress on the participation of U.S. private enterprise in development programs. And in two cases—the specific-risk Investment Guaranty Program and the Cooley local-currency lending program—the new organization has met with success; both these programs have clearly been strengthened by the

[86] ICA, Office of Management Planning, *Staff Study: An Analysis of ICA Responsibilities and Activities for the Stimulation of Private Enterprise*, Washington, 1958, pp. 58-60.

elimination of the overlapping and often conflicting authorities which existed before all U.S. programs to encourage long-term private investment in developing countries were put under the jurisdiction of a single agency.[87] But, as we have seen, the programs carried over from DLF itself—dollar development lending and extended-risk investment guaranties—have yet to attract large-scale private investment into development projects abroad.

The very limited success of these two programs in attracting private funds probably stems from the very nature of the authorizations under which they operate. The broad powers for private capital mobilization granted DLF in its authorizing legislation tended to obscure the fact that this function played a very small role in the rationale underlying the organization's creation. The DLF came into being in 1957 as part of the acknowledgment of receding horizons regarding the transition from public to private capital exports, the recognition that United States development assistance was too urgent to await the provision of private funds which were not likely to be forthcoming in adequate amounts in the foreseeable future. At that time, the legislative provisions regarding the promotion of private investment were largely window-dressing to help secure Congressional approval of the enabling legislation; the main emphasis was on the provision of public funds for development on easier terms than those offered by the Eximbank. And this emphasis was carried over into the legislation which created AID; despite the frequent references to private capital and private enterprise in the foreign assistance legislation of the 1960's, it seems clear that the interest is less in the mobilization of private capital per se than in utilizing private funds in cases where the interests of private investors

[87] The Export-Import Bank, which remained a separate organization, is specifically oriented towards export financing. Therefore, both its sphere of operations and the techniques it uses are somewhat different from those of the development assistance programs.

happen to fit in with the over-all country development plans encouraged and sponsored by AID. This viewpoint is clearly dominant in the administration of the dollar loan and extended-risk guaranty programs; and it is not surprising that few projects have appeared at once sufficiently profitable to interest private investors and sufficiently crucial to a country's over-all economic development to justify AID's use of these "last resort" instruments to encourage private investment—instruments it feels it can use only in cases where it is certain the private financing would not otherwise be forthcoming.

The conclusion which emerges from the DLF—AID experience is an obvious one. In programs where the emphasis is solely and specifically on the mobilization of U.S. private capital for development investment abroad, the Government's efforts have met with considerable and growing success. In instances, on the other hand, where this mobilization is regarded simply as a byproduct of the primary effort to provide assistance in meeting the goals of a jointly determined over-all economic development plan, the ratio of private to public funds has remained low. This is not so much a matter of fault or failure as of the fact that, under the present interpretation of dollar loans to private enterprise as a strictly last resort measure and of extended-risk guaranties as an extraordinary form of assistance to be used only in carefully selected cases of unusual importance, there is not, nor is there expected to be, much scope for the mobilization of private funds.

X · SUBSTITUTE OR COMPLEMENT?— THE ROLE OF RISK-SHARING AGENCIES IN MOBILIZING PRIVATE FUNDS

During the 18-year period from 1946 through 1963 the export of long-term private capital from the United States increased substantially, as did the outflow of private funds exported specifically in conjunction with the activities of one or another of the risk-sharing agencies. Both the general outflow of private funds and its agency-related component give every indication of continuing their expansion during the mid-1960's. But in judging the effectiveness of the risk-sharing agencies in mobilizing private American funds for development investment abroad, these facts alone are not enough. Much more important are changes in the relationship between the two magnitudes. Do the long-term investments made in conjunction with the activities of the six agencies form a significant proportion of the total annual outflow of such funds? Has there been any noticeable trend toward an increasingly important role for agency-related investments, or have their movements in relation to the outflow of private funds as a whole been so erratic as to make prediction pointless? In judging the efficacy of the risk-sharing agencies we must have some idea, too, of how large an expenditure, or at least commitment, of public funds was required over the 18-year period to set in motion the accompanying flow of private capital.

THE GROWTH OF U.S. INVESTMENT ABROAD

Over the period 1946-1963 as a whole, as column (2) of Table 23 shows, the net outflow of long-term private capital from the United States—in both direct and portfolio form—increased from an average annual rate of $0.6 billion in 1946-1948 to an average of $3.0 billion in 1961-1963.[1] When the reinvested earnings of subsidiaries are added to the net figures for direct investment,[2] as in the "Private" columns of Table 27, the rates become $1.0 billion and $3.6 billion respectively—again, a more than three-fold increase.

Of the two major forms of long-term private investment abroad, direct investment revived most rapidly after World War II. This investment increased gradually during the first five years following the cessation of hostilities at a rate of slightly more than $1 billion per year, about half of which represented the reinvestment of foreign earnings. During the years 1951-1955, the annual rate of direct investment rose to about $1.5 billion, and in 1956-1957 reached an all-time record rate of more than $3 billion annually. Total direct foreign investment dropped sharply to $1.8 billion during the domestic recession of 1958; during the four years that followed it returned to annual outflow levels between $2.5 and $3.0 billion, and in 1963 reached a rate of $3.4 billion, slightly below the 1957 peak. Over the 18-year period as a whole, the book value of American direct investment abroad increased by some $32 billion, a little more than half of which came from new dollar outflows and the rest from reinvested earnings of subsidiaries.[3]

[1] U.S. Department of Commerce, Office of Business Economics, *Balance of Payments, Statistical Supplements* (to Survey of Current Business), Washington, 1952, 1958, 1963, and *Survey of Current Business*, June and Aug., 1964. All figures for U.S. private investment abroad, unless otherwise noted, come from these publications.

[2] In discussing direct investment, I am following the definition of the Department of Commerce: "Foreign investments in which American investors or parent companies have a controlling interest, consisting of an ownership of 25 per cent or more of the voting stock of the foreign subsidiary companies, or unincorporated foreign branches." U.S. Department of Commerce, Bureau of Foreign and Domestic Commerce, *Factors Limiting United States Investment Abroad*, Washington, 1953, I, 2.

[3] Net outflow of capital plus undistributed earnings of subsidiaries together equal, with minor adjustments, the change in book

With the important exception of Latin America, the less-developed areas of the world have always received a small proportion of American direct investment abroad. And their share grew even smaller during the period under discussion; investment in the relatively high income areas—Western Europe, Canada, Japan, Oceania, and the Union of South Africa—has risen more rapidly during the postwar years than has direct investment in the relatively low-income areas of Latin America, Asia, and Africa.[4] At the end of 1963, as Table 22 shows, a little less than 25 per cent of U.S. direct investment abroad was located in South America and about 10 per cent in Asia and Africa, or 8 per cent if the advanced countries of Japan and the Union of South Africa are omitted from the reckoning. A cross-classification of the area and industry categories would show that American business investment in the less-developed areas is far more heavily concentrated in the extractive industries—mining, smelting, and petroleum—than it is in advanced countries; nearly 40 per cent of the direct investment in the underdeveloped parts of Asia and Africa, for example, is accounted for by the petroleum investments in the Middle East. In developed countries, in contrast, manufacturing enterprises have attracted the largest and fastest-growing shares of direct investment from the United States.

The markets of Western Europe attracted an increasing proportion of American direct investment during the five-year period ending in 1963; during these years, the proportion of such investment located in Western Europe grew from 16 to 26 per cent. Latin America's share dropped off markedly during the same period, from 32 to

---

value of direct foreign investments. It is this total figure which is generally implied when reference is made to "the amount" of direct investment abroad in a given year.

[4] Raymond F. Mikesell, "U.S. Postwar Investment Abroad: A Statistical Analysis," in Mikesell (ed.), *U.S. Private and Government Investment Abroad*, Eugene, Oregon, 1962, p. 58, and *Survey of Current Business*, 1961-1964 (Aug. issues).

24 per cent, as the flow of U.S. funds into the area fell from the peak caused by huge petroleum investments in Venezuela in 1957. The flow of U.S. funds to Asia and Africa accelerated noticeably in 1958 and has continued to grow, at a more modest rate, since then; the share of the world total received by these areas increased slightly, from 8 to 10 per cent, between 1958 and 1963. There is little question that, barring unforeseen political developments, direct investment in the underdeveloped world will continue to increase, but it shows a persistent tendency

TABLE 22

U.S. Direct Foreign Investment
by Area and Industry, December 31, 1963
(Total Book Value: $40.6 billion)
(in percentages)

By Area		By Industry	
Canada	32	Manufacturing	37
Western Europe	26	Petroleum	34
Latin America[a]	24	Mining and Smelting	8
Asia and Africa	10	Trade	8
Other[b]	8	Public Utilities	5
		Other Industries	8

[a] Including European dependencies
[b] Oceania and International
Source: *Survey of Current Business* (Aug. 1964), 10-11.

to concentrate in a few countries, and the opportunities offered investors by the European Common Market make it doubtful that the less-developed areas will soon be able to attract an increased share of U.S. business investments abroad.

During the first decade following World War II, the general feeling in the United States was that memories of the losses sustained by portfolio investors during the financial debacle of the 1930's—by 1938 $2.5 billion of foreign dollar bonds, or 40 per cent of the total then outstanding, were in default on interest payments, while losses due to the collapse of market values were also counted in the billions[5]—would prevent the revival of large-scale portfolio investment in basic development projects. The fact that investors were indeed wary, despite the fact that all but 15 per cent of the bonds floated by underdeveloped countries during 1920-1931 either had never been in default or had resumed servicing after adjustment,[6] seemed clear from the persistently small outflow of portfolio funds during this period. During the five years 1946-1950, such private lending totaled only $1.6 billion, of which $1.0 billion represented purchases of new public issues, chiefly those of Canada and the World Bank, and the rest loans by U.S. banks, mostly to Western European countries, and purchases of existing securities. Since $1.1 billion of old security issues were redeemed during that period, the net outflow of portfolio funds from the United States totaled only $0.5 billion over those five years.

The average annual net outflow of portfolio investment increased considerably during the 1950's, as indicated in the last three columns of Table 23. It reached a peak of $1,440 million per annum during 1958, even while the domestic recession was causing a marked drop in direct investment abroad. Although Canadian and World Bank issues continued to account for the bulk of new security issues, Israel had emerged by the beginning of the 1950's decade as a small but steady contender for such funds. And by 1956 Belgium, Norway, Australia, the Union of South Africa, and Cuba had also floated issues successfully on the New York market, all but the last in conjunction with a simultaneous loan by the World Bank. Now, too, American interest in foreign equity securities, particularly those of leading companies in Canada, West-

[5] Cleona Lewis, *The United States and Foreign Investment Problems*, Washington, 1948, p. 142.

[6] Gordon Gray, *Report to the President on Foreign Economic Policies*, Washington, 1950, p. 62.

TABLE 23

U.S. Net Private Long-Term Capital Outflow, 1946-1963
(in millions of U.S. dollars)

(1)	(2)	(3)	(4)	(5)	(6)
Calendar Year	Total	Direct Invest- ment, net	New Security issues	Redemp- tion of old issues	Other long-[a] term, net
1946	103	230	85	−308	96
1947	798	749	396	−295	− 52
1948	790	721	150	− 62	− 19
1949	740	660	118	−103	65
1950	1,116	621	254	−301	542
1951	945	508	491	−113	59
1952	1,066	852	286	− 66	− 6
1953	550	735	270	−138	−317
1954	987	667	309	−124	135
1955	1,064	823	128	−190	303
1956	2,554	1,951	453	−174	324
1957	3,301	2,442	597	−179	441
1958	2,625	1,181	955	− 85	574
1959	2,274	1,372	624	− 94	372
1960	2,537	1,674	555	−201	509
1961	2,624	1,599	523	−148	650
1962	2,881	1,654	1,076	−203	354
1963	3,506	1,862	1,269	−195	570

[a] Chiefly loans by U.S. banks and purchases of existing securities
Source: *Balance of Payments, Statistical Supplement* (revised edition-1963) and *Survey of Current Business* (June 1964).

ern Europe, and the Commonwealth countries,[7] was reviving; by the end of 1958, U.S. holdings of foreign-currency securities, chiefly in equity form, nearly equaled holdings of dollar bonds. Although less-developed countries were in general still unable to raise funds by issuing securities in the United States market, a large proportion of the long-term loans made abroad by U.S. banks went

[7] Edward M. Bernstein, *International Effects of U.S. Economic Policy* (Study Paper No. 16 for the Joint Economic Committee, 86th Cong., 2nd Sess.), Washington, 1960, p. 60.

to such borrowers, many of them originating "in projects undertaken by U.S. companies and largely financed through the Export-Import Bank."[8] Such lending increased from 1953 onward, particularly in 1957.

By the end of 1958 the number of "new" borrowers (i.e. countries other than Canada, Israel, and the IBRD) which had floated public issues in the United States totaled 11. The flotations of such borrowers, as well as the sales of securities of foreign corporations, continued to rise during the next few years, and in 1960 a $100 million issue sold privately by a Mexican institution marked the first time since the 1930 debacle that a major Latin American republic was able to raise substantial funds in the United States market. In the middle of 1959, the Government's chief analysts of foreign investment statistics predicted a return to "normalcy": "It now appears that with the relaxation of exchange controls in Europe at the end of 1958 and the emergence in several countries of a better balance between savings and local demands for investment funds, the international movement of private capital for portfolio investment is likely to expand significantly. Changes in relative interest rates among countries assume an added importance under these circumstances."[9] These words were written despite the fact that it was then obvious that portfolio investment in 1959 would fall below the 1958 peak. Indeed, the outflow of capital into long-term portfolio investment was under $1 billion in both 1959 and 1960, and only a little more in 1961. Most of the drop in new issues was caused, however, by a deliberate shift by IBRD toward greater borrowing in European markets, while the rest of the reduction was due to a general narrowing of interest rate differentials, thus bearing out rather than contradicting the analysis quoted above. Long-term portfolio investment

[8] *Ibid.*

[9] Samuel Pizer and Frederick Cutler, "Capital Flow to Foreign Countries Slackens," *Survey of Current Business*, Aug. 1959, p. 28.

spurted again in 1962 and 1963, reaching an all-time high of more than $1.6 billion in the last year of the period. New issues of Canadian securities dominated portfolio lending during these years, and new issues of Western European countries and Japan also increased. But the sale of securities of less-developed nations in the U.S. market remained a rarity.

At the end of 1963, private long-term foreign investments held by U.S. citizens or corporations totaled more than $17.6 billion. The sale of new security issues in the United States dropped off sharply during the second half of 1963 after the President asked Congress to enact an Interest Equalization Tax on such issues retroactive to the middle of that year, and there was little indication that such sales would revive during 1964, when such a tax was enacted into law. But, although the indications were that the new tax would have its intended effect of checking the increase in long-term portfolio investment abroad, the opportunities for less-developed countries to borrow portfolio funds from the United States appeared to brighten rather than darken. For one thing, the security issues of such countries and corporations located in them are specifically exempt from the tax, and the reduced profitability to American investors of lending to advanced countries may make them look more favorably at the lower-rated issues of the developing nations. For another, "while the capital outflow through purchases of foreign securities was diminishing, there was an offsetting upsurge in [medium and long-] term loans by banks," which were in part also exempt from the new tax.[10] And such bank loans, unlike security issues, have generally been available to borrowers in a wide variety of less-developed countries, particularly in Latin America. In general, by the end of 1963, there were a number of indications that

[10] *Survey of Current Business*, Aug. 1964, p. 8. Bank loans with a term of less than three years are exempt from the Interest Equalization Tax.

private long-term portfolio investment was returning to the scene as a limited but gradually expanding technique for making American capital available for the task of economic development.

THE IMPORTANCE OF AGENCY-RELATED INVESTMENT

Over the first 15 years of the postwar era, the average annual outflow of long-term capital from the United States more than tripled. But how much of this multiple expansion can we associate with the operations of the six risk-sharing agencies which attempt to mobilize private funds for investment abroad? Did the agency-related component of American private investment abroad, in other words, grow more or less important as time went on?

Two slightly different approaches to this last question are shown in Table 24. In the top half of Table 24, American long-term funds invested abroad in conjunction with the activities of the six risk-sharing agencies are compared with the total net outflow of long-term private capital from the United States, for each of the six three-year periods (because sufficient data on agency-related capital outflows for comparisons on an annual basis were not available). These ratios yield no discernible trend or pattern; the effect of the six agencies appears to have been strongest in the earliest period when, although only two of them were in operation, their activities seem to have accounted for a third of the entire net outflow of long-term private capital. Their effect dropped sharply, according to these figures, in the next three periods, and then rose markedly in the last to a position slightly less than it had enjoyed a decade before. Even taking into account that the high ratio of the first period is due to the fact that 40 per cent of the very small total outflow of portfolio funds came from a single public issue of IBRD bonds, the over-all impression remains one of erratic movement, with no consistent trend toward greater effectiveness despite a proliferation of the number of institutions engaged in risk-sharing activities and a fairly steady increase in the absolute amount of funds channeled abroad by these agencies.

In the lower half of Table 24, essentially the same comparison is made, but with two major additions to the capital-outflow figures which represent the denominators of the ratios. The first is that gross rather than net figures are used for portfolio investment, to provide comparability with the figures for agency-related investment, which are gross of redemptions. The other is the inclusion of reinvested earnings as well as dollar outflows in the figures for direct investment; it is these two components which together determine changes in the book value of direct investment abroad, and the direct investments made in conjunction with the six agencies represent both types of funds.

These additions not only make the two sets of figures being compared more consistent, but also bring to light something more closely resembling an upward trend in the ratio of agency-related to total private investment abroad. The sharp drop from a high ratio in the earliest period, due chiefly to fluctuations in public issues of World Bank bonds, remains, although it is somewhat less pronounced than before. But with the exception of this first drop, the picture is now one of a general, although not wholly consistent, upward movement in the influence of these risk-sharing institutions on the export of long-term private capital from the United States, terminating in an over-all peak for the final segment of the 18-year postwar period.

The comparisons made here between American private investment abroad and its agency-related component are at best very rough ones. Lack of data on agency-related investment made estimation for each three-year period difficult and occasionally arbitrary. Three of the agencies compile their statistics by the calendar year, two by the fiscal year, and one changed from the first basis to the

TABLE 24

U.S. Private Capital Invested Abroad in Conjunction
with the Risk-Sharing Agencies in Relation to Total Long-
Term Private Capital Investment, 1946-1963

(in millions of U.S. dollars)

(A) Ratio of agency-related U.S. foreign investment to net long-
term private capital outflow from the United States

(1)	(2)	(3)	(4)
Period	*Total outflow, net*	*Agency-related Private Investment*	*(3) as percentage of (2)*
1946-1948	1,691	566	33
1949-1951	2,801	266	9
1952-1954	2,603	556	21
1955-1957	6,919	915	13
1958-1960	7,436	1,840	25
1961-1963	9,011	2,529	28
Total	30,461	6,672	22

(B) Ratio of agency-related U.S. foreign investment to total long-
term private foreign investment, including portfolio investment *gross* of redemptions, and the reinvested earnings of
subsidiaries

(1)	(2)	(3)	(4)
Period	*Total Investment*	*Agency-related Private Investment*	*(3) as percentage of (2)*
1946-1948	3,627	566	16
1949-1951	4,981	266	5
1952-1954	5,382	556	10
1955-1957	10,962	915	8
1958-1960	11,104	1,840	17
1961-1963	13,374	2,529	19
Total	49,430	6,672	13

second in mid-1960. Since it was impossible to put them all on a uniform basis, the use of three-year periods rather than annual figures for comparison is designed to lessen the distorting effect of this discrepancy. An even more important reason for the use of three-year periods is that the figures for "commitments" of funds, from which the statistics relating to the six agencies are compiled, do not exactly correspond, for any given year, to the data on actual outflows of funds which make up the balance of payments statistics. The actual flow of money to a given enterprise may take place at the same time as, or even slightly before, the date of commitment by a lending agency and the accompanying private investors, but in many cases it tends to stretch out one, two, or as much as four years beyond the commitment date. No general pattern for the flow-of-funds has been determined by any of the agencies; we know only that many commitments of funds will not be reflected completely in the balance of payments statistics on capital outflows for that same year, but will be distributed in some way over that year and the ones immediately following. But, while all these qualifications make precise comparison impossible, the general picture indicated in the lower half of Table 24 re-

---

Table 24 continued

Sources:
　Column 2:
　　Balance of Payments-Statistical Supplement (1952 and 1963 edns.) and *Survey of Current Business* (June 1964, Aug. 1964).
　Column 3:
　　Investment Guaranty Program: Table 6
　　　IBRD: Tables 9, 10, 11. The $28.7 of participations grouped as "prior to 1952" in Table 10 was divided equally over the 1946-48 and 1949-51 periods.
　　　International Finance Corporation: Table 13
　　　Inter-American Development Bank: Table 15 and p. 197
　　　Export-Import Bank of Washington: p. 237 and Tables 17, 18, 19
　　　Development Loan Fund—Agency for International Development: Table 21

mains: that private loans and investments made in conjunction with the operations of the risk-sharing agencies became, on the whole, an increasingly important part of gross United States private investment abroad over the 18 years 1946-1963. During the final three years of this period, at any rate, roughly one out of every five private U.S. dollars which went into long-term investment abroad did so in connection with the lending or guarantying activities of one of the six institutions whose function, in whole or in part, is to channel private funds into development investment abroad.

PRIVATE CAPITAL AND PUBLIC FUNDS: TWO COMPARISONS

The proportion of U.S. private funds invested abroad which has been channeled through the operations of the six risk-sharing institutions represents one aspect of these agencies' effectiveness as mobilizers of private capital; the amount of American public money which has been required to do the channeling represents another. In chapters 5 through 9 it was noted that the average ratio between U.S. private funds and public monies which moved abroad together in the same transactions varied widely among, as well as within, the five lending organizations. The ratios summarized in Table 25 range from $2.90 of U.S. private capital which flowed abroad for each dollar the IFC invested in enterprises which also attracted private funds from the United States, down to the fifteen cents of American private money which accompanied every dollar of funds committed to loans involving private participations by the fledgling Inter-American Development Bank. The Cooley loan program administered since 1962 by AID also attracted a high proportion of private money, two private dollars for every dollar of public funds. But the dollar lending program of the DLF—AID attracted only about twenty-five cents for every dollar it committed to such joint enterprises, putting it near the lower end of this particular scale, along with the

TABLE 25

Dollars of U.S. Private Capital Committed per
Dollar of Public Funds Committed[a] in Agency Investments
in Which There Was U.S. Private Participation

Agency	*Private Funds per Public Dollar*
World Bank	$ .20
International Finance Corporation	2.90
Inter-American Development Bank	.15
Export-Import Bank[b]	.60
DLF—AID	
Dollar Loan Program	.25
Cooley Loan Program	2.00
Total (Average)	$ .40

[a] The figures for commitments of public funds used in the comparisons are net of private participations but not of reductions and cancellations.

[b] Direct credits only; guaranty and insurance programs excluded from calculation.

Sources:

World Bank: See Chapter V, Note 54
International Finance Corp.: Table 13
Inter-American Development Bank: Table 15 and p. 197
Export-Import Bank: Tables 17, 18, 19 and p. 237
Development Loan Fund—Agency for International Development: Table 21

World Bank, whose loan commitments involving private participations or joint operations were accompanied by about twenty cents of American private funds for every IBRD dollar committed. In the middle is the Export-Import Bank, which since 1952 attracted about sixty cents of private money for every loan dollar it committed to joint public-private undertakings. Because the organizations with low private-public dollar ratios together account for a far larger volume of joint operations than do those with higher ratios, the average figure for the five lending institutions combined is only forty cents of private funds from the United States for each public dollar committed to joint undertakings—or 2.5 public dollars for every private one.

In Table 26, the quantitative relationship between private and public funds involved in the operations of the six risk-sharing agencies is approached somewhat differently. Now *all* the activities of the six institutions are taken into account, rather than only those representing joint public-private investment in the same undertaking and, at the same time, only the United States' share of the public monies committed to these agencies is considered. The results are the two sets of percentages shown on the right hand side of the Table. The first reflects the relationship between *unguarantied* private funds which have moved into foreign investment and the public funds *directly* committed in loan operations; the second indicates ratios between the *total* amounts of private funds involved, both unguarantied and guarantied, and the sum of public monies committed *directly* for disbursement as loans plus several alternative estimates of the funds committed *contingently*, as backing for guaranties and insurance.

The general conclusion of this analysis is the same as that gleaned from the earlier one: that the private American capital which has been invested abroad in conjunction with the activities of the six risk-sharing agencies is only a fraction of the public funds tied up in their operations. But, for individual organizations, the two approaches yield sometimes startlingly different results. True, whatever approach is used, the IFC remains at the top of the list with a ratio of private to public funds in the vicinity of three to one; this consistently high ratio reflects both its insistence that at least half the capital for any undertaking in which it invests must come from private sources and the attractiveness to American investors of its profit-oriented policies. But, concentrating first on the set of ratios involving direct loan and investment transactions only, we see that the World Bank, which averaged the next to the lowest proportion of private U.S. money in the earlier comparison, now displays a ratio topped only by those of the IFC and the Cooley loan program. This shift is due to the fact that in the present comparison only the United States' share of the IBRD's paid-in capital is considered, giving a figure for public funds which is much smaller than the total amount of IBRD money loaned in transactions in which private U.S. capital was also involved. For the same reason, the IDB's public-private ratio is nearly twice as large in this comparison as it was in the earlier one.

Of the two American lending institutions which held intermediate positions in the earlier analysis, the DLF—AID's dollar loan program displays by far the lowest proportion in this one, amounting to less than 1 per cent of the public funds committed. And yet, in joint enterprises, private U.S. funds averaged 25 per cent of the DLF—AID commitment; these two facts make sense only if transactions involving private capital are a very small proportion of the credits extended under the DLF—AID dollar lending program. And this is indeed the case: of the several hundred dollar development loans authorized as of the end of 1963, less than 20 involved any form of participation by U.S. investors. The private U.S. equity and loan funds channeled abroad through Eximbank loans equaled about 60 per cent of the net Eximbank credits in which there was private participation during the first 18 postwar years, but less than 25 per cent of net total Eximbank credit authorizations during the same period. Again, this discrepancy can be traced to the fact that American private funds have participated in only a fraction of Eximbank credits; less than two-fifths of these credits—by dollar volume—were accompanied by private funds.

When one tries to make comparisons of the private and public funds involved in the various guaranty and

TABLE 26

U.S. Private Capital Invested Abroad
in Conjunction with the Risk-Sharing Agencies
in Relation to U.S. Public Funds Committed to
These Agencies, 1963

(in millions of U.S. dollars)

	Private Funds		Public Funds		Percentages	
	Unguarantied Investment (1)	Guarantied Investment (2)	Direct Commitment (3)	Contingent Commitment (4)	Unguarantied Private Investment as Per cent of Direct Public Commitments (1) ÷ (3)	Total Private Investment as Per cent of Total Public Commitments (1 + 2) ÷ (3 + 4)
Agency						
Investment Guaranty Program	—	766.3	—	a) 1,434.5 b) 358.6 c) 0	—	a) 53.4 b) 213.6 c) —
World Bank	880.5	1,560.0[a]	635.0	a) 5,715.0 b) 1,360.3 c) 0	138.7	a) 38.4 b) 122.3 c) 384.3

International Finance Corporation	119.0		35.2		338.1	338.1
Inter-American Development Bank	44.0	75.0[a]	150.0	a) 200.0[b] b) 34.5 c) 0	29.0	a) 34.0 b) 64.5 c) 79.3
Export-Import Bank of Washington	2,185.9	495.0	9,393.4	a) 495.0 b) 123.7 c) 0	23.3	a) 27.1 b) 28.2 c) 384.3
DLF-AID Regular Programs	42.9	135.8	4,634.2	a) 127.6 b) 63.8 c) 0.6	0.9	a) 3.8 b) 3.8 c) 3.9
Cooley Program	366.8		186.0		197.2	197.2
Total[c]	3,639.1	3,032.1	15,033.8	a) 7,972.1 b) 1,940.9 c) 0.6	24.2	a) 28.9 b) 39.2 c) 44.3

Table 26 continued

ᵃ Includes $1,515 million of IBRD bond issues and $75 million of IDB bond issues which are not directly guaranteed, but which are "covered" by the callable portions of the United States' capital subscriptions, as explained.

ᵇ Increase in callable capital did not become effective until after December 31, 1963.

ᶜ This total is not adjusted for "overlapping" cases where a single private investment involved the activities of more than one risk-sharing institution. This double-counting, which probably amounts to somewhere between $50 and $100 million, gives the over-all percentage estimates a slight upward bias. On the other hand, these same figures are biased downward because of the omission of untraceable instances of concurrent private investment.

Sources:

Investment Guaranty Program: Column (2), Table 6; column (4), Table 3, note a.

World Bank: Col. (1), Tables 10 and 11; col. (2), Table 9; col. (3), *Eighteenth Annual Report*, p. 42. Col. (4), *Ibid., Annual Reports*, and data provided by the IBRD, Treasurer's Office, Securities Division.

International Finance Corporation: Col. (1), Table 13; col. (2), *Seventh Annual Report*, p. 37.

Inter-American Development Bank: Col. (1), Table 15 and p. 197; col. (2), p. 191; col. (3), *Fourth Annual Report*, pp. 36-37; col. (4), *Ibid.*

Export-Import Bank: Cols. (1), (2), and (4), Tables 17, 18, and 19; col. (3), Export-Import Bank of Washington, *Report to the Congress for the six months ended December 31, 1963*, p. 142 and *Report to the Congress for the period July-December, 1956*, p. 82.

Development Loan Fund—Agency for International Development: Col. (1), Table 21; col. (2), pp. 289-294; col. (3), *Terminal Report of the DLF*, "AID Dollar Lending-Fiscal Years 1962 and 1963—Summary" (AID, office of Development Finance and Private Enterprise memorandum, Aug. 1963), and information provided by the Office of Development Finance and Private Enterprise.

insurance programs operated by the American and international risk-sharing organizations, the situation becomes much more complicated. This is because the concept of a "contingent commitment" of funds is by its very nature a fuzzy one. Exactly how much U.S. public money is actually committed to the operations of these programs? In the broadest sense, the full faith and credit of the United States Government stands explicitly behind the guaranties issued by its own agencies and, up to the amount of its callable capital subscriptions, behind those of the international institutions as well, implying that the size of the reserves specifically set aside for the payment of claims is not a critical factor. In the narrowest sense, one could argue that only those sums actually disbursed in the payment of claims should be counted, but this would render meaningless the whole concept of contingent commitment, as well as being unknowable until all of the programs have terminated. An operational basis of contingent commitment must lie somewhere between these extremes, but there is no actuarial basis for defining it. Some information is available about the past experience of the U.S. Government as lender and insurer: losses sustained over the lifetimes of all the direct and insured loan programs of the Federal Government operating in mid-1962 averaged approximately 3/100 of 1 per cent of loans outstanding and for no single program were they as high as 1 per cent.[11] For Federal credit programs of an earlier period, roughly 1932-1950, the loss-ratios were considerably higher but, with two exceptions, still under 4 per cent.[12] But this experience with domestic programs[13] offers little guidance in predicting the exposure

[11] Calculated from data in: U.S. Congress, House, Committee on Banking and Currency, Subcommittee on Domestic Finance, *A Study of Federal Credit Programs*, Washington, 1964, I, 107.

[12] *Ibid.*, p. 10 and sources therein cited. The two programs with loss ratios higher than 4 per cent were the Bank for Cooperatives and the disaster loans of the Reconstruction Finance Corporation.

[13] Of the 40-odd programs listed, only the Export-Import Bank involved foreign lending.

involved in lending for international economic development, with all the special risks such lending entails.

Because there seems to be no satisfactory basis for making a single estimate of the amount of public funds committed on a contingent basis to the various risk-sharing guaranty and insurance programs, we have instead made three alternative estimates for each such program: an upper limit, a lower limit, and a "best guess" lying somewhere in between. The upper limit is represented by the face value of guaranties issued in the case of the U.S. guaranty and insurance programs, and by the total callable portions of United States' capital subscriptions in the case of the World Bank and the Inter-American Development Bank. The figures in this group are limits rather than realistic estimates; they involve, for example, a great deal of double and even triple-counting in the case of the Investment Guaranty Program, and the figures for the two international organizations are larger in each case than the total gross amounts of bond and note issues for which they provide ultimate backing. The lower limit figures, on the other hand, are clearly much too low; they represent merely the net funds actually disbursed between 1945 and 1963 in payment of guaranty or insurance claims, and are zero for all programs except the DLF—AID comprehensive guaranty program, which paid a $650,000 claim in 1961.[14] The intermediate estimates were calculated for the U.S. programs on the basis of fractional reserve ratios which are either those currently in use by the organizations themselves or those which were used until the concept of fractional reserves was abolished altogether: 25 per cent in the case of the Investment Guaranty and Eximbank programs, 50 per cent in the case of the higher-risk DLF—AID extended-risk and housing

---

[14] Both the Investment Guaranty Program and the Eximbank guaranty program have paid a number of convertibility claims, but subsequent recovery of assets left them with no net losses.

guaranty programs.[15] For the two international banks, the intermediate figures were calculated as that fraction of gross bond and note issues represented by the United States' share of total callable capital: roughly one-third in the case of the World Bank, and 46 per cent in the case of the IDB.[16]

Because the use of the three alternative estimates of contingent commitments would yield three different rankings, it is not possible to rank the various risk-sharing programs according to the ratio between private capital and public funds when guarantied as well as unguarantied private capital and contingent as well as direct commitments of public funds are taken into account. In any case, the difficulties and ambiguities with which attempts to measure the relationship between private capital and public funds are fraught would make the use of such ratios to evaluate the relative effectiveness of the six risk-sharing organizations in mobilizing public funds very dangerous. But there is a more important reason for avoiding such inter-agency comparisons: the wide variation among them in the emphasis placed on the attraction of private capital vis-à-vis other goals; only two of the six have the mobilization of private funds as their sole or even primary objective. It is this variation, more than anything else, which accounts for the widely disparate

[15] The Eximbank guaranty and insurance programs currently operate under a 50 per cent reserve requirement; fractional reserves were abolished for all AID programs in 1963.

[16] The use of these percentages is based on the provision in the Articles of Agreement of both the IBRD and the IDB, that calls on the callable portions of the members' capital subscriptions, are required to be "uniform in percentage" (i.e. on a *pro rata* basis) on all shares. They do not, however, represent the maximum theoretical liability of the United States in both organizations, since members' obligations to make payments upon calls are also independent of each other, that is, in the event of default by some members, successive calls could be made on the other members to meet the Banks' obligations, up to the amount of the total unpaid (callable) balance of each member's capital subscription.

results of the two attempts to estimate the relative amounts of private and public funds entering into the lending operations of each agency: one which took into account only those transactions in which there was some participation by U.S. capital, another which considered all of the lending transactions engaged in by the various organizations. Which is the "proper" measure of effectiveness in mobilizing private funds? There is no clear-cut answer. The truth undoubtedly lies somewhere in between the two extremes; a number of the loans extended by the risk-sharing organizations were clearly designed for the public sector, without any intention of utilizing private money, while others which might have attracted private funds failed to do so.

No matter how it is calculated, the ratio of private to public funds from the United States involved in the activities of the six risk-sharing organizations reinforces our earlier conclusion: that the private funds which have moved from the United States into long-term investment abroad in conjunction with the activities of these organizations are only a fraction of the public monies which this country has committed to their operation. When unguarantied private flows are compared with direct commitments of public funds, the former turn out to be 24 per cent of the latter; when the comparison is between total U.S. private and public funds, the ratio varies from 29 to 44 per cent, depending on which concept of contingent commitment is used. In other words, whether one includes guarantied private funds and contingent government commitments or not, and however one defines contingent commitments, the broad conclusion remains the same: the United States Government has tied up between two and four dollars in the operations of the risk-sharing institutions for every dollar of American private capital which has gone abroad in direct association with their activities.

FUNDS FOR DEVELOPMENT: YESTERDAY AND TODAY

Clearly, a group of institutions which utilize several dollars of public funds for every dollar of private capital they draw into long-term investment abroad cannot be regarded as catalysts—and the inclusion of data for private and public funds from other countries than the United States could not change the figures enough to alter this basic conclusion. And yet it was the role of "catalysts" or "bridges" for private capital which the founders and early supporters of most of the risk-sharing institutions foresaw as their main function. In general, their expectations were based on the 19th century experience; the hope seemed to be that, with government stimulation, the export of private funds from the United States would come to play in the world economy of the mid-20th century a role akin to that filled by British private capital during the third of a century which ended with World War I. Between 1880 and 1913, the citizens of Great Britain annually invested abroad about one-twentieth of their total national income, which would amount to more than $30 billion per annum in the United States of the 1960's.[17] These funds, invested mainly in government or government-guarantied loans, were used for the construction of a variety of social overhead facilities, including transportation and communication facilities, particularly railroads, and other types of basic public utilities[18]—the same areas in which public loan and grant funds are being used so heavily for development today.

[17] Willard Thorp, *Trade, Aid or What?*, Baltimore, 1954, p. 183.
[18] British foreign investment was in 1913 divided as follows: 30 per cent in loans to governments (which in turn often used the funds for railroad or other public utility development); 40 per cent in railroads; 5 per cent in other public utilities; and 25 per cent in banking, insurance, manufacturing, and raw material extraction. Ragnar Nurkse, "International Investment Today in the Light of 19th Century Experience," *Economic Journal*, LXIV (Dec. 1954), 747.

This invocation of a situation which terminated more than half a century ago as the norm to be reached is based in part on a failure to take into account crucial differences in the conditions surrounding pre-World War I British and post-World War II American investment abroad, and in part on a basic misunderstanding of the British experience and what it achieved. There have been major changes in commercial and financial conditions since 1913: free trade has given way to an intricate network of tariffs and quantitative trade controls, and a world in which most currencies were anchored to a gold standard and stable exchange rates prevailed is today harassed by problems of currency fluctuation and inconvertibility. The political obstacles facing American foreign investors are also far greater than those met by their British predecessors. More than half of the British investment took place within the Empire and was thus foreign in a geographical but not in a political or psychological sense. And even outside the Empire, conditions were far more conducive to safe and profitable foreign investment than they are in many less-developed countries today, since no serious challenge to the capitalist system had yet arisen and hostile economic nationalism had not become a problem to contend with.

Finally, and most important, expectations concerning the possibilities of private foreign investment are often rooted in a misunderstanding of the British experience. Only about one-third of the private capital which moved abroad in the half-century preceding World War I went to the poor, densely populated areas which are today regarded as underdeveloped—and these were all within the British Empire. Nearly all the rest went to the sparsely settled, already high-income "regions of recent settlement" (i.e., Canada, Argentina, Australia, and New Zealand), and it was in these regions, with their vast areas, rich resources, temperate climates, and European populations that British capital built the infrastructure which made rapid industrialization possible.[19] And, along with each wave of capital exports went a wave of emigration of skilled, educated European labor, about 60 million people in all.[20] When British funds went to the poorer backward areas it was most often for colonial investments in the production of primary goods for world markets, investments which left the local economy and the local population relatively untouched. Even when substantial capital was invested in basic development projects in these areas it often failed, as did the Indian railroads, for instance, to bring about the expected acceleration of development. Only in regions where there was no problem of cultural adaptation, where the complementary prerequisites to rapid development along European lines were already present, did British capital become an instrument for rapid economic advancement. But British capital never really faced the challenge of investment in politically independent backward or underdeveloped areas—the challenge to which American private capital is expected to respond today.

For all these reasons, private foreign investment today, even assisted by the type of risk-sharing institutions here described, cannot be expected to perform the feats that British investors of the period 1870-1913 are popularly credited with, and thus to serve as a substitute for public lending and assistance for foreign economic development. This conclusion is borne out by the actual figures for postwar capital outflows from the United States—the major capital-exporting nation during this period—both public and private. True, as the annual rate of long-term U.S. private investment abroad increased over the immediate postwar era, the outflow of government economic grants and long-term credits was gradually reduced, from an average of $5.5 billion per annum in the 1946-1948 period

[19] *Ibid.*, p. 745.
[20] Raymond F. Mikesell, *Promoting United States Private Investment Abroad*, Washington, 1957, p. 5.

to a low of $1.9 billion in 1955-1957, rising slightly again to an average of $2.8 billion in 1961-1963. But, as the figures in Table 27 show, the fact that the public capital outflow fell as the private outflow rose does not reflect a smooth process of substitution of one for the other in the various geographical regions of the world.

In Western Europe there does seem to be such a pattern of substitution, with government assistance shrinking gradually as European economies recovered to the point where they became increasingly attractive to private investors. But in other parts of the world, where the job is not one of rebuilding what had existed before but the more difficult one of creating a totally new economic structure, and where increased private investment is just as likely to intensify the need for additional public aid, by making the shortage of social overhead facilities more urgent, as to reduce it, no such relationship is discernible. In Latin America the figures are very erratic, but the general pattern seems to be that substantial private investment preceded any sustained increase in government assistance, which came only in 1957, and in recent years government assistance has increased while private investment has dropped off markedly from its 1957 peak. In "other countries," a category which includes all the less-developed regions outside the Western Hemisphere as well as the advanced countries of Oceania and Japan, the movements have been roughly parallel, with government assistance increasing markedly after 1955 and private investment growing much more slowly over a longer period, but at an accelerated rate since 1959. In the less-developed areas of the world, public and private foreign capital appear today to be related, not as substitutes, but as complements, interacting on and stimulating each other.

BRIDGING THE GAP BETWEEN BORROWERS AND LENDERS

If the risk-sharing institutions have not fulfilled their founders' dreams by becoming "bridges" across which

U.S. Government Non-Military Grants and Long-Term
Capital Outflow (Net) and Net Long-Term Private Investment
Abroad,[a] by Areas, 1946-1963
(in millions of U.S. dollars)

Year	Total		Europe		Canada		Latin America		Other Countries		Internat'l. Insts.	
	Gov't.	Pvt.[b]	Gov't.	Pvt.	Gov't.	Pvt.	Gov't.	Pvt.	Gov't.	Pvt.	Gov't.	Pvt.
1946	5,531	406	2,917	70	—	134	73	26	695	176	1,846	—
1947	6,008	1,185	4,371	227	—	-24	99	519	634	230	904	243
1948	5,006	1,371	3,973	172	—	394	56	494	858	294	119	7
1949	5,476	1,176	4,341	201	1	277	69	461	941	253	124	4
1950	3,603	1,591	2,811	466	2	757	54	113	625	240	111	14
1951	3,188	1,696	2,296	280	1	648	110	360	725	225	56	184
1952[c]	2,378	1,989	1,563	258	6	699	87	533	656	334	66	165
1953	2,066	1,376	976	41	5	708	372	236	622	317	91	74
1954	1,446	1,689	795	206	-3	717	73	289	520	303	61	175
1955	1,868	2,026	627	397	-9	619	96	552	1,075	361	79	97
1956	1,799	3,729	291	853	-5	1,433	74	877	1,314	441	125	125
1957	1,950	4,664	482	651	-1	1,401	257	1,567	1,130	565	82	480
1958	2,248	3,570	338	604	—	1,188	562	493	1,290	662	58	624
1959	1,630	3,386	-233	900	—	1,228	337	564	1,443	534	83	160
1960	2,241	3,791	175	1,257	—	1,022	238	564	1,642	780	186	179
1961	2,519	3,678	-385	1,228	—	811	785	558	1,950	1,016	169	47
1962	2,768	4,079	-395	1,210	—	1,017	618	385	2,272	1,111	273	355
1963	3,108	5,071	-35	1,754	—	1,394	554	225	2,374	1,535	215	164

[a] Including reinvested earnings of subsidiaries

[b] These figures are equal to the data in Column 2 of Table 23 plus reinvested earnings of subsidiaries

[c] Finland, Spain, and Yugoslavia transferred to "Western Europe" from "Other" beginning 1952

Sources: Survey of Current Business (June 1964 and Aug. 1964), and Balance of Payments—Statistical Supplements (1952, 1958, 1963).

private capital can move to take over the task of aiding economic development, they have served and continue to serve as a bridge in another very important sense, by spanning the gap between the needs of borrowers and the demands of lenders in the international capital market. This problem of differing standards is the basis of the key difficulty faced by all the risk-sharing agencies, of finding their criteria either too strict to accommodate borrowers or too loose to suit the ultimate lenders, or both.[21] For these agencies can mobilize private funds for development lending only if the interest rates and terms they establish are such as will meet the standards of private lenders.

There are several reasons, some psychological and some economic, why such rates and terms may seem to borrowers so onerous as to be unacceptable. The psychological basis for such objections is due in part to the conditions under which funds have been made available to many developing countries through U.S. and international aid and "soft loan" programs of recent years, in part to a complex of convictions regarding the responsibility of high-income nations to contribute to the welfare of countries less fortunate economically. Governmental aid and loan programs have been criticized on the grounds that they "will create misunderstanding in the borrowing country about the rate of return on private loans or investments that is appropriate and commensurate with the risk."[22] While this statement is an insufficient and therefore a dangerous basis for the kind of sweeping criticisms of foreign aid with which it is generally associated, the confusion against which it warns has certainly been created at least in part by governmental aid activities, and public lending agencies which attempt to function on a "com-

[21] See: Jacob Viner, *International Trade and Economic Development*, Glencoe, Ill., 1952, pp. 139-140.

[22] American Enterprise Association, *American Private Enterprise . . .* , p. 53.

mercial" basis are particularly vulnerable to misunderstanding and criticism from borrowers whom past experience has led to expect a "better deal."

Developing countries are also likely to face very real problems in servicing external debts, and these difficulties are naturally greater the higher the interest rate and the shorter the repayment period. To make the repayment process smooth and automatic, the borrowed funds would have to be put to uses which, directly or indirectly, enabled the borrowing country to earn sufficient additional foreign exchange to cover interest and amortization costs. But many basic and essential projects in underdeveloped economies are not of this type: some are social overhead investments which do not lend themselves to the capture of direct monetary returns at all, others face long "infancy periods" before they start earning returns sufficient to cover costs, and still others may from the beginning earn adequate returns in local currency but still not provide directly the added exports or import-substitutes which would enable this return to be translated into increased foreign exchange earnings. In such cases, grace periods, long amortization periods, and low rates of interest would reduce and spread the debt burden and increase the time for economic adjustment to it. The result might well be to reduce the possibility of a default which might otherwise be inevitable, even if the borrowing country were well-intentioned and the uses to which the loans were put ultimately productive.

The risk-sharing agencies have sometimes shown considerable ingenuity in arrangements to bridge the gap between borrowers' and lenders' demands. One such arrangement is the World Bank participations set up in the form of serially-maturing securities, of which private lenders take the shorter maturities and the Bank itself the longer ones. The Eximbank, too, has often arranged loans with the maturities of its own portion extending well beyond those of the private lenders' share. In other cases, "bridging" efforts have been unsuccessful; the failure of the Eximbank to sell any of its loan portfolio at par to U.S. private lenders on an unguarantied basis is a clear indication that, on those terms, the returns are not high enough to be attractive. Until 1961, when it was authorized to invest in capital stock, the IFC's convertible debenture procedure proved in many cases more of a hindrance than a help in arranging financings, simply because in most of the world such a hybrid security is unknown and regarded with distrust. And, finally, in some cases an agency "solved" the problem simply by evading it: the DLF's acceptance of repayments in the borrower's currency obviously solved the latter's transfer problem, but it made the loans unacceptable to private lenders in the United States, except in cases where arrangements were made for the repayment of the private portion of the loan in dollars. This consideration was one of the factors underlying AID's shift to a policy requiring that dollar loans be repaid in dollars.

As an alternative solution to the conflict between borrowers' needs and private lenders' requirements, it has been suggested that the United States Treasury simply subsidize directly the difference between the interest rate the borrower will pay and the rate lenders will accept in cases where it is felt that the loan or investment under consideration would justify the cost in terms of the national interest.[23] This scheme has the paramount virtue of simplicity, with all that it entails: the potential for broad public appeal, the reduction of administrative expenses, and the possibility of estimating quantitatively the public costs of the subsidy. Such an arrangement would sacrifice, however, the peculiar advantage possessed by the risk-

[23] This suggestion was presented to me by Professor A. O. Hirschman. A similar idea is put forth by Robert E. Asher, who suggests the combination of grant aid with loan aid to lower the effective rate of interest on development assistance. See: *Grants, Loans and Local Currencies—Their Role in Foreign Aid*, Washington, 1961, p. 98.

sharing agencies in being able, because of their variety and flexibility, to divide up the capital-lending market into several separate markets and practice discriminatory pricing (or, in this case, discriminatory subsidizing), both among agencies—the IFC, for example appeals to a very different sort of investor than does the World Bank— and, to a lesser extent, on a case-by-case basis within a particular agency. Such discrimination should make the subsidy-cost required to stimulate a given amount of participation lower than in the single-price case; insofar as the lending market can be divided, one does not have to pay a subsidy of, say, 2 per cent to a lender who would be willing to accept only 1 per cent in order also to attract those lenders whose minimum demand is indeed 2 per cent. Although it has only rarely been exercised with full effectiveness, the potential for variety and flexibility inherent in the structure of the risk-sharing agencies suggests that intensified efforts within their general framework offer a more promising route to effective private capital mobilization than the substitution of a more rigid, uniform direct-subsidy arrangement.

SELECTIVITY AND ADAPTABILITY: THE SIX AGENCIES

The variety and adaptability of the arrangements offered by the risk-sharing agencies represent, in fact, their most valuable asset in the task of mobilizing private capital for foreign investment in the national interest. Another aspect of this adaptability is their ability to practice the geographical selectivity suggested by the differential effects of investment in advanced and in less-developed countries, in terms both of the United States' balance of payments difficulties and of its desire to encourage the process of economic development.

The activities of the six risk-sharing agencies have increasingly followed this pattern of geographical selectivity. Three of them, the International Finance Corporation, the Development Loan Fund—Agency for International Development, and the Inter-American Development Bank, were from their inception directed exclusively toward providing development capital to low-income countries. Of the older institutions, the Investment Guaranty Program was restricted by 1959 legislation to investments in such areas only, while the World Bank's loan authorizations have been increasingly, and by the end of the 1950's overwhelmingly, for the benefit of developing nations—in fiscal year 1963, more than 80 per cent of its authorizations were for projects in less-developed countries.[24] The Export-Import Bank, whose primary commitment is to aid United States exports, has moved more slowly in the same direction. Over its entire period of operations through 1963, the proportion of total credits directed toward less-developed areas was a little more than 50 per cent; in 1963 alone, it was more than 70 per cent.

Other methods of government stimulation of private foreign investment can, of course, also be exercised selectively. Investment and tax-sparing treaties can be negotiated bilaterally with selected countries, and there are a number of precedents for using unilateral tax relief to encourage private investment in particular areas—specifically in China and Latin America. But these methods suffer from an important disadvantage vis-à-vis the risk-sharing agencies: their criteria of selection must be laid down in advance, and they lack the flexibility which enables the agencies to adapt relatively quickly to changed situations or priorities. This flexibility also enables the agencies to exercise other forms of selectivity—by type of investment, for example—when they seem advisable. In the case of unilateral or bilateral tax relief, such adaptability could be achieved only through the ponderous procedures required to alter treaties or legislation.

Another facet of the risk-sharing institutions' adaptability is their potential for combining in a hybrid form

[24] If Yugoslavia is included among the less-developed countries, the proportion rises to 95 per cent.

those characteristics of direct and portfolio investment best suited to the requirements of developing countries.[25] Direct investment possesses such obvious advantages as the accompanying export of technical and managerial skills and a flexible remittance burden based on realized profits. But many borrowers regard foreign ownership and control, with all the attendant possibilities of friction, and the possibility of having to service very large returns on a small original equity base as factors weighing heavily on the debit side. Portfolio investment, in contrast, involves no foreign control and generally demands a much lower over-all return, but traditionally carries no "fringe benefits" with it and represents a fixed repayment burden which must be met whether earnings from which to pay it are realized or not. Such quasi-public institutions as the Eximbank, the World Bank, and the Inter-American Development Bank, on the other hand, offer the export of know-how without formal foreign control—although some of the paternalistic rules and procedures of the World Bank have at times been as irritating to the borrowing country as any foreign ownership. They also combine the relatively low returns characteristic of portfolio investments with the potential for repayment flexibility, in the form of grace periods and refundings, generally regarded as one of the unique advantages of direct investment.

SUBSIDY AND EFFECTIVENESS

The "ideal" form of government stimulation of private foreign investment should not only be capable of selectivity and adaptability in its operations, it should also be constituted so as to achieve maximum effectiveness for a given amount of subsidization or, to look at the same thing from the opposite side, to reach a given level of effectiveness at the lowest possible cost in subsidization.

[25] H. J. Dernburg, "Corporate International Investment—Discussion," *American Economic Review*, XLIV (May 1954), 628-633.

Role of Risk-Sharing Agencies

It is hard to say precisely, but there are a number of indications that the investment stimulus provided by risk-sharing agencies tends on the whole to involve less direct subsidization than, for example, tax concessions, which represent the other main form of investment encouragement offered or considered by the United States Government. In some cases, the risk-sharing agencies are simply providing, at some approximation of "commercial" rates, services which cannot be obtained commercially at any price: insurance against certain risks peculiar to foreign investment, for example, or long-term loan funds for foreign investment. This is almost certainly the case with the International Finance Corporation, and perhaps with the Investment Guaranty Program as well. In other cases, where debt capital is provided for private use at a cost clearly below that which the private capital market would charge even if there were no capital-rationing, as it is by the DLF—AID, an element of subsidy is of course involved. But even here, the subsidy is less direct than that offered by tax concessions, in that risk-sharing arrangements affect the range of possible outcomes of a given investment rather than the level of realized profit, and are also less likely to provide windfall gains to existing investments or investments which would have been made anyway.[26]

If the testimony of those most directly concerned is to be believed, however, the lower level of direct subsidization represented by risk-sharing arrangements results in a somewhat lower level of effectiveness as well. In each of a number of governmental studies of private investment abroad,[27] surveys of the business community re-

[26] See: Peggy Brewer Richman, *Taxation of Foreign Investment Income*, Baltimore, 1963, p. 59, for a discussion of the inefficiency of tax concessions as an instrument for stimulating private investment in underdeveloped countries.

[27] The most recent such study is: U.S. Department of Commerce, *Reportorial Review: Responses to Business Questionnaire Regarding Private Investment Abroad*, Washington, 1959.

vealed that, among present foreign investors and non-investors alike, the form of governmental encouragement most likely to stimulate direct investment abroad would be some type of tax reduction or related concessions. In every case, all other forms of stimulation, including risk-sharing, ranked lower in the eyes of the business community than did tax reduction.

This direct testimony must, of course, be weighed against the findings of Barlow and Wender, cited in Chapter III, that tax concessions would in actuality have far less effect on businessmen's foreign investment decisions than they themselves claim.[28] In addition, this testimony comes entirely from direct investors; it may well be that to portfolio investors, whose motives and decision-making processes seem to be quite different from those of business investors, the added protection afforded by the participation of risk-sharing agencies may be more important than the increased rate of return which would result from tax reductions. But it is certain that major tax reductions or concessions would have a simplicity and direct appeal which the lending and guarantying operations of the risk-sharing agencies lack, since their effect on prospects and profits are likely to be less familiar and more difficult to explain to large segments of the investing public. It is perhaps this very elementary fact which lay behind the view of a DLF official concerned with the stimulation of private enterprise that "nothing we can do can be as effective in stimulating American business investment in underdeveloped countries as some kind of U.S. tax-holiday for this class of investments would be."[29]

[28] Barlow and Wender, *U.S. Tax Incentives to Direct Private Foreign Investment*, Cambridge, Mass., 1954, pp. 2-5. This is particularly true because responses to any such questionnaire surveys tend to be dominated by those who are already foreign investors, and who are bound to have an interest in the "windfall" profits which general tax concessions would in part represent to them.

[29] Interview with officers of the Development Loan Fund, May 19, 1961.

The various instruments of investment stimulation differ not only in their direct effectiveness in moving American capital abroad, but also in the degree to which they are the source of indirect effects which may over the long run lead to substantial increases in the availability of capital for development even though one cannot observe any direct relationship between the increase and the original investment stimulus. The risk-sharing agencies possess considerable potential for exercising such indirect effects. They are in an ideal position, for example, to initiate contacts between business and institutional investors in the United States and potential borrowers or investment situations abroad which may lead to future transactions without the public agency as intermediary. They can also be instrumental, as the World Bank has shown, in opening or reopening the American securities market to foreign borrowers, both governmental and private. Japan, for example, did its first postwar borrowing in the United States in the form of a joint operation with the World Bank in 1959; two or three years later, the securities of its corporate borrowers were attracting considerable attention from U.S. investors on their own merits. It is through participation in the operations of the World Bank and the Eximbank, too, that U.S. commercial banks and their subsidiaries have been making a cautious entry into the field of medium and even long-term foreign lending. In general, where portfolio investment in less-developed areas is concerned, "the way has been led by public lending institutions such as the Export-Import Bank and the World Bank, both of which have had a nearly perfect repayment record during the postwar period."[30]

By creating and enlarging the contacts between would-be borrower and potential lenders, by giving the former opportunities to prove their creditworthiness and ability to administer borrowed funds on a businesslike basis and the latter increased familiarity and experience with for-

[30] Mikesell, *Promoting U.S. Private Investment Abroad*, p. 7.

eign investment, the risk-sharing institutions can exert powerful indirect influences on development investment in their role as borrowers or mobilizers of private capital. They can also exert such influences in their role as lenders by making infrastructure investments which may open up new opportunities for profitable private investment. An IDB loan to Corfo, the Chilean government investment corporation (to start a fishing industry) has led a number of U.S. and other foreign firms in the fishing, shipbuilding, and related industries to consider new investments in Chile. This is only one example among many, and probably one of the smaller ones, of the untraceable but important effects loans by the public lending agencies can have in attracting subsequent investments of private funds from abroad. Such investments, unlike participations and concurrent investments, do not and cannot show up in our figures, but their role in the development of borrowing economies may ultimately be far greater than is suggested by the magnitude of the figures for private investment which we are able to trace and record.

In addition to their effects on capital exports from the United States and other advanced countries, the risk-sharing agencies can, by spurring the creation and expansion of development banks and by creating contacts and disseminating information, uncover and enlarge local sources of development capital. This enormous potential for creating beneficial indirect effects in both the lending and the receiving countries suggests that, even if tax concessions might have a greater immediate impact on the export of American capital, in the long run the activities of the risk-sharing agencies, if planned wisely and imaginatively, may do far more to stimulate the worldwide availability of capital for economic development.

THE QUESTION OF FORM

A major advantage of the risk-sharing agency as an instrument for drawing American private capital into the task of economic development abroad is its potential for variety and adaptability to changing situations. At the same time, simplicity of operation and the elimination of confusion and wasteful duplication are essential both to make such institutions effective in attracting private funds and to hold the public costs of their activities to a minimum. But in what form can both flexibility and simplicity be best achieved? Do these criteria call for some consolidation of the various agencies acting, each in a somewhat different way, as mobilizers of private capital, or would such consolidation sacrifice some of the variety and adaptability which we have found to be such important assets?

One aspect of this consolidation question is whether the United States' long-term interests are best served by national or by international organizations, or by the existence of both together. There is little doubt of the advantage of "denationalized lending" through internationally controlled agencies in helping to overcome the hostility of many developing countries to foreign loan and investment capital, despite the fact that the weighted financial and voting structures of these institutions assure the United States a predominant role in the formulation of their policies. And, from the mid-1950's on, as "the efficacy of bilateral aid as a cementer of alliances is increasingly questioned" and "Western Europe and Japan have re-emerged as potential capital exporters," there has been "a resurgence of American support for multilateral efforts to promote development." This resurgence resulted in the creation of four new international aid agencies with United States backing between 1956 and 1960[31] and, as this is written, in the serious consideration of a variety of proposals for a multilateral investment in-

[31] The four agencies are: the International Finance Corporation (1956), the U.N. Special Fund (1959), the International Development Association (1960), and the Inter-American Development Bank (1959). These are discussed in: Robert E. Asher, *Grants, Loans, and Local Currencies* . . . , p. 53.

surance program.[32] The intensification of the United States' balance of payments difficulties will doubtless increase the pressure for expanded multilateral lending during the 1960's. But there remain situations in which the interests of the United States differ from those of the large group of countries represented by these international agencies and even from those of her fellow capital-exporting allies, and a national agency is necessary for the implementation of policies implied by these distinct interests. It is unlikely in the extreme, therefore, that the United States or, for that matter, any other advanced nation, should in the foreseeable future relinquish all direct sovereignty over the mobilization of funds for economic development by turning over these functions entirely to one or more international agencies.

Quite apart from political considerations, the consolidation of development lending and investment functions exclusively under international control would inevitably reduce the effectiveness of such agencies in mobilizing one important type of private capital. The experience of the World Bank indicates that an international agency can be quite effective in channeling private funds into foreign economic development in the form of portfolio investment, although even here the ultimate guaranty provided by the Bank's call on 90 per cent of the United States' capital subscription appears to be crucial to the success of these efforts. But the extreme difficulty encountered by the International Finance Corporation in finding suitable projects for the investment of its funds lends support to the view that an international institution is likely to be far less effective in stimulating increased direct investment abroad, at least where United States

[32] These proposals are described and the advantages and disadvantages of a multilateral program discussed in a 1962 Staff Report of the IBRD entitled *Multilateral Investment Insurance*. The appendix includes an analysis of replies by nearly 400 businessmen in 21 countries to a questionnaire concerning their views on investment insurance.

corporations and the directors who make their major decisions are involved. Such investors have repeatedly stated that, in view of the "political" risks of foreign investment today, a guaranty backed by their own government is the only kind which they regard as having any value. These same investors undoubtedly regard joint investment with a United States agency more confidently than a similar venture undertaken in connection with an internationally controlled institution. Insofar as the "fringe benefits" which naturally accompany direct investment are valuable to the receiving country, purely economic considerations lend support to the political preference for retaining a part of the risk-sharing function under national control.

FUNCTIONAL CONSOLIDATION: A SUGGESTION

This conclusion leaves room, however, for considerable streamlining of the guarantying and joint lending functions without any sacrifice of the flexibility which is perhaps their most important advantage. As far as the international institutions are concerned, there is probably some point in dividing the private capital-mobilization function, since the World Bank and the IFC are engaged in such very different types of lending and appeal to distinct, almost mutually exclusive groups of private lenders, and there are compelling political arguments for the existence of a separate bank for Latin America. But the organization of the United States agencies described here includes much unnecessary overlapping and duplication of functions.

In the area of investment guaranties, chaos was for a long time avoided only because neither the Eximbank nor the DLF exercised more than a fraction of its broad powers in this area and, even so, officers of the Investment Guaranty Program have frequently complained of the confusion and tension caused by overlapping authorities. The consolidation of the ICA and DLF guaranty authorities in AID in 1961 eliminated some of the confusion

and duplication, but even today the issuance of investment guaranties is divided within AID among the Investment Guaranty Program, the Office of Development Finance and Private Enterprise, and the Office of Capital
Development of the Bureau for Latin America, depending on the type of guaranty desired and the type and location of the investment it is desired for. And the somewhat
ambiguous role of the Eximbank in providing both export financing and development investment assistance
remains.

In the area of joint lending, the problem of duplication and overlapping jurisdictions was reflected as long
ago as 1957, in the fears of Eximbank officials that
the proposed DLF would inevitably encroach upon their
territory, despite legislative efforts to distinguish the types
of lending appropriate to each. More recently, the problem of "program competition" was a matter of serious
concern in the exhaustive 1963 *Study of Federal Credit
Programs*, which pointed out "that economic development
loans are available from the Export-Import Bank at an
interest rate of 5¾ percent, from the Agency for International Development at interest rates of ¾ to 5¾ percent, from the International Bank for Reconstruction
and Development at interest rates of 5½ percent, and,
in the case of loans to Latin America, from the Inter-
American Development Bank at rates of 5¾ percent for
ordinary operations and 1¼ to 2¾ percent for social
progress loans. Periodic consultations among the institutions lending to Latin America has disclosed that two of
them may be working on the same loan proposition, owing
to the fact that the applicant had filed with both institutions."[33]

Since, as has been pointed out, there are good reasons
why U.S. and international risk-sharing institutions
should continue to operate side by side, the only hope for
eliminating duplication and wasteful competition among

[33] *A Study of Federal Credit Programs*, I, 34.

these two groups lies in the development of improved techniques of consultation and coordination. But, within this limitation on consolidation, greater clarity and efficiency might be achieved if the U.S. institutions concerned with foreign lending were divided along strictly functional lines. This would suggest the creation of three agencies:

(1) An "Export Credit Bank" devoted exclusively to the stimulation of American exports, through the provision of limited-risk guaranties and perhaps also through the provision of public funds for the direct sharing of some portion of long-term credit financings. Here private participation would be in the form of credit-financings carried by the producers or exporters themselves and their commercial banks or of commercial insurance groups offering protection against the ordinary business risks attendant upon export operations.

(2) A government lending agency to provide "bankable" loans and investments repayable in dollars, with terms extended and flexible enough to meet the needs of developing countries but with interest rates high enough to attract private capital. The aim of this agency would be to attract a maximum amount of private participation in both direct and portfolio form, and it might invest both in projects begun on government initiative and in others originated by private lenders or investors. A program of limited political-risk guaranties for long-term investors might also be administered by this agency, perhaps in conjunction with private insurers who would offer protection against ordinary business risks in foreign investment.

(3) A true "foreign aid" agency, making funds available either on a grant or low-interest "soft loan" basis to countries and projects which could not afford to acquire the money on other terms, but where the objectives for which the money is intended seem to serve the long-run interests of the United States. Military and "special" aid

would fall under this agency, as would basic "social-overhead" assistance to countries whose economic structure could not bear the burden of commercial debt. Obviously, private participation in such transactions would be inappropriate.

THE REAL CONTRIBUTION OF THE RISK-SHARING AGENCIES

A survey of the first 18 years of the risk-sharing agencies in their role as mobilizers of private capital leaves no doubt that their function needs to be redefined. Clearly, they have not become "catalysts" drawing private funds directly into economic development; the term becomes meaningless when it is applied to a mechanism which requires two or three or four public dollars to move one private one. And, in any case, the magnitude of their capital-mobilizing operations is simply not great enough to cope with the problem of development assistance. During the period 1946-1963, more than $50 billion of U.S. Government money went to other countries in the form of economic grants or long-term loans; total long-term private foreign investment by Americans (including reinvested earnings) came to something less than $50 billion during the same period (see Table 27). These comparisons, particularly when joined with the earlier ones which suggested that the relationship between public and private foreign capital in less-developed areas tends to be that of complements rather than substitutes, indicate that unless the U.S. Government's contributions to economic development have been grossly excessive, the shifting of the burden to private hands would require an increase of several billions of dollars annually in private foreign lending and investment. And to a shift of this magnitude the six agencies, which mobilized in all some $6½ billion of American private capital during the years between 1946 and 1963, could make little contribution at their present scale of operation.

All this does not mean, however, that the risk-sharing agencies' role as mobilizers of private capital is a futile one, but only that the sort of "bridges" they represent are quite different from those most of their early supporters envisaged. For one thing, although procedures are now beginning to evolve whereby developing countries can obtain the "fringe benefits" of foreign investment, such as entrepreneurial experience and technological sophistication, without foreign ownership (through management contracts, for example), responsible direct investment remains probably the most efficient means of obtaining these skills, and the risk-sharing agencies are in an excellent position to steer some of this investment where it is needed and can best be utilized.

Because of their access to both public and private funds, the risk-sharing agencies are also in a unique position to help developing countries to make the most of the naturally complementary relationship between these two types of capital. It has often been pointed out that the investment of public funds in the provision of basic "social-overhead" facilities can pave the way for greatly increased private investment by creating in an underdeveloped economy some of the most important prerequisites for profitable enterprise. Less widely remarked, but equally important, is the stimulating effect which private investment can exert on public investment, by pinpointing the areas in which basic services are lacking and by creating a sense of pressure and urgency for their creation.[34] By consciously helping both to create and then to ease the pressures in both directions, the risk-sharing institutions can make an important contribution to the pace of development.

Finally, the joint public-private arrangements sponsored by such agencies may well give the business community

[34] A. O. Hirschman, in Chap. 5 of *The Strategy of Economic Development*, New Haven, 1958, introduces the concept of investment induced by a shortage of social overhead capital.

of the United States—as well as other capital-exporting countries—an increased knowledge, interest, and stake in economic development abroad and the role external financing plays in it. By thus breaking down in advanced countries some of the widespread hostility to foreign aid in its pure form, increased private participation in the activities of these agencies may even smooth the path for other development assistance transactions which do not and cannot involve such participation.

A realistic assessment of the achievements and the prospects of the risk-sharing institutions reinforces the conclusion that, if the United States is to make a significant contribution to foreign economic development, we must face the fact of a substantial foreign aid burden for some time to come. When viewed as a means of substituting private for public development financing on a large scale, the activities here discussed appear not only futile but actually dangerous to the national interest in their very inadequacy. It is when they are regarded as an instrument for creating a better complementary relationship between the two types of capital outflow that the risk-sharing agencies reveal their potential for aiding the process of economic development in a framework of political freedom, and thus their contribution to the most basic ultimate interests of the United States.

INDEX

Tables are indexed by page number with (t) following.